The Arab World

The Contributors

BAHA ABU-LABAN is Professor of Sociology at the University of Alberta.

SHARON ABU-LABAN is a member of the Department of Sociology at the University of Alberta.

MICHAEL ADAMS, formerly Middle East Correspondent for the *Manchester Guardian,* is Executive Secretary of the Council for the Advancement of Arab-British Understanding.

EQBAL AHMAD is a Fellow at the Adlai Stevenson Institute of International Affairs in Chicago.

FUAD BAALI is Professor of Sociology at Western Kentucky University.

AHMAD BAHA EL-DIN is Editor-in-Chief of *al-Musawwar,* Cairo.

ELMER BERGER is Director of American Jewish Alternatives to Zionism.

ANWAR CHEJNE is Professor and Chairman of the Department of Near Eastern Studies at the University of Minnesota.

NOAM CHOMSKY is Professor of Linguistics at Massachusetts Institute of Technology.

RICHARD COTTAM is Professor of Political Science at the University of Pittsburgh.

C. ERNEST DAWN is Professor of History at the University of Illinois.

SAMI G. HAJJAR is Associate Professor of Political Science at the University of Wyoming.

FAUZI M. NAJJAR is Professor of Social Science at Michigan State University.

EMILE A. NAKHLEH is Associate Professor of Political Science at St. Mary's College.

MAXIME RODINSON is Professor of Middle East History at the Sorbonne.

EDWARD W. SAID is Professor of English and Comparative Literature at Columbia University.

MAHMOUD EL-SHAZLY is an engineer.

RICHARD P. STEVENS is Professor of Political Science at Lincoln University.

JANICE TERRY is Assistant Professor of History at Eastern Michigan University.

AAUG MONOGRAPH SERIES: NO. 3

The Arab World
FROM NATIONALISM TO REVOLUTION

edited by Abdeen Jabara and Janice Terry

with a foreword by Ibrahim Abu-Lughod

The Medina University Press International
Wilmette, Illinois
1971

First published in the United States of America in 1971
by the Medina University Press International
908 Ashland Avenue
Wilmette, Ill.

Manufactured in the United States of America

Abdeen Jabara is an attorney at law in Detroit, Michigan.
Janice Terry is Assistant Professor of History at Eastern Michigan University.

Contents

THE ARABS AND THE WORLD

ZIONISM AND INTERNATIONAL POLITICS

THE FUTURE OF PALESTINE

Appendix: Text of Statement and Resolution Released at the End of the Third Annual Convention of the Association of Arab-American University Graduates, November, 1970, Evanston, Illinois.

Foreword

The essays in this volume were initially presented at the Third Annual Convention of the Association of Arab-American University Graduates, Inc., which was held in Evanston, Illinois, October 29–November 1, 1970. The theme of the convention was "The Arabs and the World: Perspectives on a Troubled Relationship"; approximately thirty-six papers were read on relevant aspects of this theme. The essays presented here were revised for publication on the assumption that a wider audience is interested in assessing the problems and achievements of the Arab world. Ever since its inception, the AAUG, in an effort to share with the public the findings of its scholars and the reflections of scholars on the Arab world, has published the proceedings of its annual conventions. The first convention resulted in publication of *The Arab-Americans: Studies in Assimilation,* the second in *The Palestinian Resistance to Israeli Occupation.*

Two events, linked in more ways than are readily apparent, cast their deep shadows over the Third Annual Convention: the eruption of civil war in Jordan and the premature death of President Gamal Abdel Nasser. The Jordanian civil war represents another in the series of unsuccessful attempts of imperialism and Zionism to liquidate the Palestinian people and to arrest the progressive drive of the Arab people for a dignified, free, and productive life, an effort that at this moment in history is symbolized by the Palestinian revolution. In some ways the civil war in Jordan can be viewed as the logical outcome of the Arab attempt to break away from the methods and techniques of social and economic transformation underlying the philosophy of President Nasser's era. In significant, though not explicit, ways, the papers presented at this convention were formulated and delivered in light of the changes that have occurred in the Arab world over the past century and a half, especially over the past two decades.

A number of essays in this work deal with structural changes, such as land reform, initially undertaken by the national reformist revolution of Egypt, and educational reform, calculated to enhance the technical competence of Arab society to cope with its social and economic problems and to spread the benefits of education to a much wider segment of the Arab community. These analyses and commentaries are concerned with a particular type of procedure of change closely associated with President Nasser's style, a style radical in tone but moderate in substance. Other essays, dealing with the Arabs' search for a viable self-definition, reflect the long-standing drive of the Arab people to break away from the universalistic bond of the Islamic community and from their acceptance of what has been characterized conventionally as a bourgeois secular nationalism, whether it is Arab or more parochially related to a specific portion of the Arab world. In both cases the external constraints on the Arabs are much in evidence.

The colonial system which imposed itself on the Arab people and retarded their drive for ultimate liberation has misrepresented the types of changes occurring in the Arab world and the aspirations of the Arab people, thereby contributing to greater tension in the relationships between the Arab people and the chief proponents of colonial occupation. The essays dealing with the mass media illuminate the degree to which the instrumentalities of colonialism are utilized to cast doubt on the integrity of the Arabs' aspirations and their struggle for ultimate liberation. The external constraints have operated much more directly and, however, effectively through their internal institutionalization, either by fragmenting the Arab world into seemingly independent territorial units that are, in fact, dependent on the colonial system or, more destructively, by implanting colonial settlements at the crossroads of the Arab world.

That a good deal of this book is concerned with the future of Palestine is an indication of the central relevance of the Palestine conflict to the future of the Arab world in general. The success of Israel is evidence of the continued triumph of colonialism in the Arab world and the corresponding tribulation of the anti-colonial drive of the Arab people. Although the participants in the conference noted the intimate connection between Israel and colonialism in general and the diversionary purpose that Israel seems to serve, this theme was much more explicitly elaborated in the keynote speech made by the Indian statesman Krishna Menon and in the remarks of Mrs. Shirley Graham DuBois, widow of the Black Pan-Africanist thinker W. E. B. DuBois. Drawing on Asian and African perspectives, both of these speakers pointed out the universal dimensions of colonialism, placed the Arab struggle in its world context, and emphasized the need for greater cohesion of anti-colonial forces the world over to combat colonialism successfully. Both speakers essentially represent the voices and reflections of a previous generation of Africans and Asians having a special type of relationship and experience with the colonial system. Many changes have taken place and new relationships among nations have been forged. The young Pakistani scholar Eqbal Ahmad, reflecting the thoughts and experiences of the new generation of Afro-Asians, alerted the participants to the new form of colonialism, its more subtle strategy, its strength, and its capacity to manipulate, and thereby provided new insights into and data on the nature of the current confrontation in the Middle East between the modern colonial system and the anti-colonial forces.

This book and the convention represent the cooperative endeavor of many people with whom I had the privilege of working as the program chairman. At all times the Board of Directors of the Association and its President for 1970, M. Cherif Bassiouni, provided wise counsel, support, and freedom, all of which account for the liveliness and diversity of the program and the participants. The willingness of many of the authors to prepare their papers for publication made it possible to share the proceedings with the public. Others contributed by delivering major addresses, chairing panels, or providing commentaries.

I should like to extend my personal appreciation and that of the Association to the Honorable Krishna Menon, Mrs. Shirley Graham DuBois, Clovis Maksud, Sadat Hassan, Charles J. Adams, Naseer Aruri, Tahseen Basheer, Rashid Bashshur, Rajaei Busailah, Haleem el Dabh, Rajaei El-Mallakh, Ceaser Farah, Ismail Faruqi, Elaine Hagopian, Tareq Ismael, Father Joseph Ryan, Elias Shoufani, and Michael Suleiman. The tremendous help I received from Vaughn Bishop, Jareer Dajani, and Ziyad Khateeb accounted for a well-organized and coordinated convention.

Professor of Political Science   IBRAHIM ABU-LUGHOD
Northwestern University

Introduction

Abdeen Jabara and Janice Terry

PRIOR TO WORLD WAR II, Britain and France had Balkanized the Middle East and had encouraged local elites, landowning and merchant classes, who sought to enhance their personal power through identification with the arbitrary borders created by the Western powers. Moreover Britain had secured an enclave of Zionist colonization in Palestine, the embryo of a developed Western society in an underdeveloped Arab hinterland. During this period the Arab nationalist movement, in close contact with the West, sought political independence in order to transform a society characterized by traditional loyalties to family, tribe, locality, and religion, the social inferiority of women and youth, and serious economic underdevelopment.

As the leading power in the post-World War II period, the United States sought to fill the vacuum created by British and French withdrawal from the Middle East. Among the factors contributing to direct United States involvement in the region were the developing cold-war rivalry with the Soviet Union, the importance of oil for its NATO allies in Europe, and the significance of oil profits for the United States balance of payments and the international monetary system. The United States intended to promote and safeguard its interests in the Arab states, but these policies were complicated by its commitment to Israel. The source of this commitment involved several factors including the influence of the Zionist lobby and the opinion of certain politicians and bureaucrats that an advanced capitalist Western society in the Middle East, with direct ties to the largest

Jewish community in the world, would be in the best interests of the United States.

United States involvement in the Middle East and in the Third World in general differed from the British and French imperialist dominance, characterized by direct physical occupation and control. The United States was content if states in Asia, Africa, Latin America, and the Middle East supported American policies internationally and engaged in "mutually beneficial" commercial relationships with the United States. In the Middle East, support of American policies meant joining military pacts which were allegedly to prevent Soviet expansion. "Mutually beneficial" commercial relationships meant supplying oil, a cheap, easily accessible source of energy, to Europe and Japan, providing investment markets for private U.S. capital, and buying U.S. goods.

In developing a global policy of containment of Communist expansion, the policy-formulators in the United States viewed the underdeveloped, newly independent states as useful strategic bases. During the 1950s the United States insisted that the Arab governments adhere to military alliances with the U.S. in return for American financial aid. Because some nationalist regimes in Asia and Africa viewed American assistance as infringing on their independence, the United States gradually developed a "third country" technique in which a small, developing "socialist" state, such as Israel, received American aid and military training as a conduit for U.S. influence in Asian and African states. When desired alignments were not secured, both overt and covert intervention occurred.

Colonialism in the Middle East went beyond what had occurred elsewhere in the Third World where military control had been maintained or where a settler minority had been established; in these cases the indigenous majority, although not assimilated, was permitted to remain on the land. In Palestine British imperialism and Zionism completely displaced one people in order to create a national state for another.

The creation of Israel at the expense of the Palestinian people at a time when several Arab states had achieved nationalist governments was seen not only as an affront to Arab independence but also as an attempt by the West to retain control of the region through a surrogate. The plight and demands of the Palestinians could not be ignored by nationalist Arab regimes since the Palestinian cause was integral to the Arab nationalist movement.

From 1949 to 1955 the policy of the nationalist Arab regimes toward Israel was one of nonrecognition and general avoidance of military confrontation. In 1955, after the Israeli attack on an Egyptian military installation in Gaza, Egypt became seriously concerned about its military weakness and Israeli military strength. Nasser sought military aid in order to counterbalance this inequality; after his requests were refused in the West, he turned to and received aid from the Soviet Union. This action challenged Israeli plans for political, military, and economic dominance of the area and initiated a steady escalation of armament buildups and hostilities.

Advanced nuclear technology, huge stockpiles of nuclear armaments capable of intercontinental delivery, and the Cuban missile crisis, which demonstrated the possibilities of nuclear war, caused the United States and the Soviet Union to shift from their cold-war confrontations. A tacit agreement between the U.S. and the U.S.S.R. permitted each of them to compete for political and military advantage while avoiding military interference with the vital interests of the other, particularly in Western and Eastern Europe. The necessity for U.S. military pacts with Third World nations, as a result of this development, greatly diminished.

Accompanying this move away from direct confrontation, the Kennedy administration initiated policies of arms control and nuclear nonproliferation and a new foreign policy toward the Third World—a policy of recognizing nonaligned, anti-imperialist, anticommunist, nationalist governments. Foreign-aid programs shifted to inducing social reform in states with the most reactionary regimes, particularly in Latin America, in order to prevent revolution. On the military level, the goal was to suppress antiimperialist liberation and revolutionary movements in the Third World. Emphasis was placed on counterinsurgency programs and on population control. To the extent that regimes were friendly, U.S. advisers were attached to various governmental departments to introduce and train personnel in the use of counterinsurgency techniques and equipment.

In the Middle East, nationalist, anti-imperialist governments wrested power from oligarchies in several states—for example, Egypt, Iraq, and Syria. The reformist military governments adopted programs of land reform, expropriated foreign enterprise, increased governmental responsibility for social welfare and education, and took quasi-socialist measures to aid the fledgling industrial base. In Egypt, for example, the nationalist government under Nasser emphasized rapid industrialization and agricultural development. These governments wished to transform their societies and create in each state a nationalist political party as the vehicle for involving the people in that transformation.

The army was frequently viewed as the only force in society capable of effectuating such changes. The seizure of power by the army, whose officers were largely from the middle class, destroyed the old oligarchic centers of power and redistributed the accumulated national wealth and services among a growing middle class. The middle class was absorbed into the bureaucratic structure of the state while the government searched for a viable economic ideology compatible with its reformist goals and resources. The Arab masses desired Arab unity, and this became a guiding principle of the nationalist regimes. Nasser emerged in 1956 as a symbol of the popular yearning for Arab unity, Arab development, and Arab independence. Such Arab states as Saudi Arabia and Jordan, in which traditional oligarchies continued to rule, were juxtaposed to nationalist, anti-imperialist regimes typified by Nasser's Egypt. In the Middle East, as elsewhere in the Third World, the United States primarily supported the conservative regimes, although during the Kennedy administration the strategy was somewhat altered to accommodate neutralist regimes like Nasser's.

The first active military intervention by the United States in the Middle East occurred in 1958, when United States troops landed in Lebanon and British troops in Jordan to forestall the tide of revolution created by the overthrow of the pro-Western Iraqi monarchy. The Eisenhower Doctrine notified nationalist Arabs that the United States considered its strategic and economic interests in the area so important that it would not allow friendly Middle Eastern regimes to be overthrown, even by the Arab citizenry of these states.

As the main supporter of Israel in the United Nations, the United States assisted in consolidating Israel's existence in the Middle East. In 1936 special tax benefits were accorded to Zionist fund-raising in the United States. Bonds for Israel sold in the U.S. were exempted from the Interest Equalization tax. A prototype treaty between the United States and a "most favored nation," the Treaty of Friendship, Commerce, and Navigation, was entered into with Israel in 1951 to facilitate private United States investment in Israel. On a per capita basis, Israel was receiving more official U.S. economic assistance than any other nation. Officially, however, the United States was neutral with regard to the Arab-Israeli conflict. Until 1967 direct United States military assistance to Israel was minimal, with Britain and France acting as the chief military suppliers. The view of a technologically advanced Israel as a center of control in the area had not fully developed. However, the deepening involvement of the United States in Southeast Asia, the growing success of the National Liberation Front in Viet Nam, as well as developments in the Middle East, occasioned a review of United States world strategy, more particularly, the role of Israel in the Middle East. Israel was increasingly viewed by United States policy-makers as a stable, reliable ally in an area where revolution appeared inevitable.

The 1967 June War, in which Israel successfully delivered a devastating blow to the military forces of the U.A.R., Syria, and Jordan and occupied the remainder of Palestine and portions of Syria and the U.A.R., promoted the growth and development of a revolutionary struggle against the Zionist settler state and the forces supporting it, both Arab and non-Arab. The war, more than any other event or series of events, revealed the failure of the nationalist, anti-imperialist Arab regimes to change Arab society and to provide necessary defense measures. This movement toward protracted popular warfare would receive its impetus from the disaffection of the Arab people. Out of a Palestinian Arab leadership developed a realistic ideology, revolutionary programs to realize ideological goals, and organizations pertinent to the needs of the Palestinians.

The strategy of the Palestinian Liberation Movement has been to destroy the fatalist attitude of the Arab masses through revolutionary armed struggle against the Zionist occupation. This struggle has given the revolution its physical, material, psychological, and geographic base. The nonbureaucratic, politically conscious leadership, recruiting members from local communities, has maintained continuous interaction with the masses. Fundamental to the movement is the principle that no revolutionary struggle can be successful without the support of the majority of the people. By drawing the people into the decision-making process, and establishing popular institutions the liberation movement has received the support of the masses and has been capable of meeting popular needs. The Palestinians, the people who had lost the most, formed the segment of Arab society most alienated from existing Arab regimes and were thus the most politically conscious. They became the axis upon which the revolutionary transformation of Arab society would turn. Charismatic leadership, exemplified by Nasser, was insufficient to make Arab society responsive to the needs of its people and the modern world. Leadership would now be a function of competence, achievement, and sacrifice for the welfare of the community.

For the movement it was crucial not only to win and maintain the support of the masses but to undermine the legitimacy of the forces of Zionism, imperialism, and Arab reaction. The legitimacy of authority can be maintained only when it is seen as providing a service to the community. When its legitimacy is undermined, the authority is forced to strike. As a result, the disaffection of the masses increasingly turns to desperation, which coupled with a revolutionary leadership, is the motivating force for action, demonstrating to the people that through concerted efforts they possess political power.

In the last analysis, the Palestinian revolution is directed against those Arab regimes and classes which maintain those institutions preventing radical change and development of Arab society. When threatened, these regimes and classes have brought their full force to bear against the effective existence of any popular armed struggle. Outbreaks of revolutionary war result from the failure of a ruling elite to respond to the challenge of modernization; the organization of a revolutionary struggle seeks to change this situation.

In the past, both the Soviet and United States models have emphasized the crucial role of technology and managers in the developmental process and have neglected the role of man and the human struggle in the radical transformation of peasant or tribal societies. In a popular war, the imperatives of defense and social change are effectively integrated by a revolutionary leadership and organization into a national movement. The experiences of China and Viet Nam have indicated to the Third World that mass involvement and commitment are the most importance resources for development. The lessons of June, 1967 will not be lost on the Arab people.

Structural Change
and Nationalist Ideology

Nationalism and Socialism

Fauzi M. Najjar

THE IDEOLOGICAL TRANSFORMATION of the Arab world, the merging of Western ideas, concepts, values, and institutions with those of Arab society, began to take place at the beginning of the nineteenth century. The fundamental cause of this transformation lay in the influx of ideas from the West and in the challenge Western civilization as a whole presented to Islamic civilization and its value system. The ideas of an advanced, technological, and dynamic civilization were introduced to a society that was traditional and stagnant. Reaction to this challenge took many forms, with attitudes ranging from extreme hostility to complete acceptance. While there existed among the intellectually and politically sophisticated a remarkable measure of agreement on the necessity for reform, there existed also considerable disagreement with regard to the nature of the envisioned society and the means of achieving it. While one school of thought advocated return to the ideal Islamic system, another called for unqualified acceptance of Western ideas of modernization regardless of their relevance to traditional values and concepts; and the views of many were between these two extremes.

Most modern political, social, and intellectual movements in the Arab world originated with the modernization generated by the impact of the West on traditional Arab-Muslim society. As the two dominant ideologies in the Arab world today, nationalism and socialism may best be understood as two stages in the same development, two phenomena of the same movement. Although both ideologies are conceptually and methodologically

3

Western in origin, much of their substance must emanate from, and their application take place in, the Arab-Islamic culture. Just as Arab nationalism in its search for cultural and intellectual content finds it impossible to dissociate itself from the Arab-Islamic heritage, so is socialism influenced by Arab nationalistic aspirations and by Islamic intellectual and ethical formulations.

It was the challenge from the West and all its ramifications that forced the Arabs to engage in ideological constructions in order to articulate their claims and aspirations and to strengthen their societies in the face of foreign imperialistic schemes and other threats to their cultural identity. The vision of a new life was inspired and conditioned as much by the Western model as by the glorious achievements of their history. The underlying impulse remains the quest for a better and secure life and a free and dignified existence, and a desire to play a leading role among nations.

The first decade of the twentieth century found the Arab world in a state of ideological bewilderment if not complete confusion. The traditional society that had existed more or less securely for a number of centuries had been shaken to its roots. The Islamic Ottoman polity, of which the Arab Fertile Crescent was an important part, was on the verge of final dissolution. Western imperialist powers were in control of most of the African parts of the Arab world and were scheming to dominate the rest. Traditional values and concepts were rapidly giving way to new ones. The need for change had been felt and advocated if for no other reason than to strengthen the society in the face of foreign intervention. The certainty of the need for reform was more than balanced by the uncertainty of how to go about it. Along with the apprehension that the basic structure was probably no longer capable of being reformed, there was concern over what new form would take its place.

Three main intellectual movements had by this time emerged to provide answers to the pressing questions. Ideologically and politically, the Arab individual in the first decade of the twentieth century could either accept the Western scientific concepts and values (secularism), adjust his values and beliefs to modern requirements (Islamic reformism), or find refuge in the values of pristine Islam (Islamic conservatism). The choice, however, was not as clear-cut as this description makes it sound. These same alternatives of thought and action still contend for primacy in the minds of the Arab peoples. Inevitably, time and historical conditions have altered the dimensions of these movements or their terms of reference, enhancing the practicability of the first (secularism) while narrowing the possibilities of the other two. For example, one of the tenets of both Islamic reformism and conservatism, the establishment of a caliphal form of government, has been rendered obsolete. Even the Muslim Brotherhood would hesitate to advocate the restoration of the caliphate. The postulates of Islamic reformism are eroding, and whatever is left of the movement is in a state of petrifaction.

With Islamic conservatism fighting a losing battle and Islamic reformism's intellectual energy largely spent, secularism as the means for modernization has become the dominant trend. The process has been slow, and the antisecularist forces have been successful in building roadblocks in the way of a radical secularist tranformation.

Whatever degree of articulation and consciousness nationalism and socialism may have achieved, their growth in the Arab world is rooted in the gradual secularization of that society and in its determination to modernize and transform its basic structure. Arabism is to provide the basis for a modern state system as well as the theory of a new national identity; socialism is to provide the theory or system for the economic and social restructuring of society. So far these are the two fundamental ideologies in terms of which the Arabs seem to be shaping their destiny.

The Emergence of Arab Nationalism

By the turn of the century the Arabs of the Fertile Crescent, who constituted the second-largest ethnic-cultural group in the Ottoman Empire, had become aware of their belonging to a particular community other than the larger one with which they identified. Their awakened sense of Arab consciousness, the full story of which has been told by a number of scholars,[1] assumed at first a cultural rather than a national character. Under the influence of Western ideas of nationalism and liberalism, certain Arab intellectuals advocated a separate Arab existence within the framework of the Islamic polity. Even the national program of action for the Arab lands, formulated at the Paris conference of June 18–23, 1913, did not advocate separation from the empire. In the proposals communicated to the Committee of Union and Progress, Christian as well as Muslim Arab leaders

1. See especially George Antonius, *The Arab Awakening* (New York, London: Hamish Hamilton, 1938); Z. N. Zeine, *Arab-Turkish Relations and the Emergence of Arab Nationalism* (Beirut: Khayats, 1958); Majid Khadduri, *Political Trends in the Arab World* (Baltimore: Johns Hopkins Univ. Press, 1970); Hisham Sharabi, *Arab Intellectuals and the West* (Baltimore: Johns Hopkins Univ. Press, 1970); Hassan Saab, *The Arab Federalists of the Ottoman Empire* (New York: Humanities, 1958).

demanded decentralization and stressed liberal reforms and special recognition of the cultural rights and personality of the Arab entity.[2] The Christian Arabs would probably have preferred the establishment of a separate secular territorial state in which nationality rather than religion would be the basis of citizenship. To the Muslims, who constituted the majority of the Arabs, the Islamic state represented their conception of a community *ummah,* and the sultan-caliph remained the symbol of their unity. As Arabs they were conscious of their unique position in the Islamic community. Their Arabness and their Islamness were not easily separated. In their attachment to both, there was no serious contradiction or crisis of conscience, for the glorious Arab achievements of the past were accomplished under the banner of Islam.

The historical and organic link between Arabism and Islam was, until 1916, largely responsible for the absence of a clear set of aims for the Arab nationalist movement. "Down to the First World War, even the Arab nationalists accommodated their political demands within the traditional and sheltering framework of the Ottoman Sultanate."[3] As Khadduri put it, "Arab nationalism scarcely aimed beyond the rehabilitation of the Arab race in a multinational empire."[4] Even those who called for a restoration of the Arab empire were merely interested in restoring the Arabs to their lost role in Islam.

As strong as the Islamic sentiment may have been, it did not withstand the ruthless policies of Jamal Pasha in Syria or the Turkification policy of the Young Turks. The metamorphosis of Arab consciousness into Arab nationalism was actually effected by the nationalist, exclusivist, and arrogant policies of the Young Turks. It is probably fanciful to speculate about the course of action the Arab movement might have followed had the Turks been more sincere and accommodating in their policy toward the Arabs. Although the Arab Revolt might have been delayed, it probably could not have been averted. The very principles upon which the Islamic state was based were no longer valid. The modern territorial nation-state, as an instrument for modernization and the realization of cultural and political self-determination and freedom, was almost universally accepted and championed. Islamic law could no longer cope with the problems of modern times; a more positive law had to be legislated and on a radically different basis.

2. Khadduri, *Political Trends,* pp. 17–18.
3. P. M. Holt, *Egypt and the Fertile Crescent 1516–1922: A Political History* (Ithaca, N.Y.: Cornell Univ. Press, 1966), p. 4.
4. Khadduri, *Political Trends,* p. 19.

It is important to note at this point that the Arab demand for separateness was motivated as much by a national consciousness as by a desire to modernize social and political institutions and shake off the legacy of centuries of stagnation. Western science furnished the vision of progress and a potential for power. *'Ilm'* ("science") became the magic word for an infinite number of possibilities and achievements. Fascination with science and scientific endeavor was bound to lead to the search for the framework within which science could properly flourish. A political regime governed by religious law does not supply fertile ground for cultivation of the scientific spirit. It was no accident that it was the Christian secularists who pressed for a form of nationalist existence in which citizenship was no longer contingent on religious affiliation. Science called for freedom of the mind, which in turn required the establishment of a political regime in which such freedom was possible. The political program for an independent liberal-democratic order had to go hand in hand with the striving for learning. At its inception, Arab nationalism was liberal, intellectual, humanistic, and positive.

Although it is easy to exaggerate the nationalist significance of the 1916 Arab Revolt against the Turks, it marked a turning point in the history of the Arab nation—the birth of a loyalty above that of religion. Except for a few intellectuals, the majority of the Arab people were moved by a vague sense of religious solidarity. Islamism was much stronger than secular Arab nationalism, and there is sufficient evidence that the latter was viewed merely as a vehicle for the former. The slogan "For the glory of the Arabs and Islam" remains to this day a source of considerable emotional appeal among the Arab masses.[5] Moreover, both the North Africans and the Egyptians resented the Arab Revolt against Ottoman unity and remained lukewarm toward Arab nationalism until after World War II.[6]

What Arab nationalism lacked in clarity and fervor was stimulated by the cynical betrayal of the Arab cause by Britain and France through the Sykes-Picot Agreement, the Balfour Declaration, and, finally, the peace settlement. Two broad consequences followed the division of the Arab

5. This remained true until the Kemalist revolution in Turkey finally abolished the caliphate, thus eliminating the last possible anchor for a pan-Islamic ideology. To a large degree, pan-Arabism was the beneficiary of the collapse of Islamic solidarity. Although the transition may not be complete, the nationalist ideology has been strengthened in reverse proportion to the weakening of the Islamic ideology.

6. Many Algerian intellectuals question their identity as Arabs; and in spite of a government-sponsored Arabization movement, "the main language of the press, of the educated public, and of the literary world is French" (Irene L. Gendzier, "Algeria 1970," *Christian Science Monitor,* September 19, 1970).

world into spheres of Western influence and control. First, the geographic fragmentation accentuated the fragmentation of the Arab nationalist movement by the creation of new sovereignties on the basis of religion or artificial nationalities. Second, while this fragmentation tended to strengthen local nationalisms, at the same time it promoted Arab nationalist ideology as the symbol of a pan-Arab liberation movement.

A common enemy created a common will to resist and helped bring to the surface a consciousness of common characteristics, a common history, and a sense of glory. Arabic has been the foundation of this national awareness, and the study of Arab literature remains the most consistent and engaging nationalist activity. Emphasis on language, literature, and history gradually secularized the Arab nationalist ideology and gave it a fundamentally cultural, rather than an ethnic, basis. Without a common language, literature, art, and folklore, no nationality is able to survive.

The situation in the post-World War I period may be summarized as follows: Britain and France artificially and arbitrarily partitioned the Arab world into political entities (kingdoms, sheikdoms, mandates, and protectorates) in fulfillment of their imperialistic designs. In addition there was the commitment, sanctioned by the Covenant of the League of Nations, to create in Palestine a non-Arab alien sovereignty—a national home for the Jews. It is understandable that during the interwar years Arab nationalism remained exclusively concerned with independence and national unity. These overriding negative aims diverted the attention of the Arab nationalist movement from relating the nationalist ideology to the desires and needs of the masses.

Negative as it may have been, the anti-imperialist nationalist struggle proved to be a seasoning experience, a kind of schooling for young nationalist intellectuals and leaders. At first, the leaders were recruited from the influential and wealthy elite, who possessed a conservative social and economic outlook. When they assumed power they behaved as if the newly independent states were their personal preserves. Their nationalism was "monarchic and hierarchic in political views, pro-Western in foreign policy, more cautious and traditional in social matters, more individualistic in economic policy."[7]

It soon became clear that an economically and socially conservative nationalist ideology could no longer depend on the hatred of foreigners or on religious zeal to command the loyalty of the awakened Arab masses.

7. Albert Hourani, "Near Eastern Nationalism Yesterday and Today," *Foreign Affairs*, XLII, no. 1 (October, 1963), 134.

The circumstances of World War II revealed to a new Arab elite that independence alone was not enough; the need for reform and social change was made evident. With a different outlook, they began to realize that "nationalism is not by itself a system of principles by which a state or a society can be organized; for that it must depend on the other ideas it can attract and absorb."[8]

Palestine and the Challenge to Arab Society

What is now paramount is not the question of independence but along what socioeconomic principles and within what forms of political organization Arab society is to be organized. To a large extent, the answer to this question is still being formulated. Nothing has revealed the urgency of this matter as did the Palestine tragedy, which exposed the inner contradictions and weaknesses of Arab society and glaringly betrayed the shallowness of the Arab nationalist consciousness.

The Arab League, formed with British support in 1945 to coordinate Arab policies and enforce bonds between all Arabs, did not survive the 1948 test. Not only did the Arab states fail to win a military victory, but—more importantly—it became obvious that they were working at cross-purposes. The defeat disclosed their unpreparedness, their lack of coordination, and, in certain cases, their collusion with the enemy. The inability of the ruling elite to represent the genuine needs and aspirations of the Arab peoples and to provide the leadership that would mobilize their energies for national construction was made clear. The myth that unity and progress in the Arab world had not been accomplished solely because of foreign domination was exploded. The causes lay much deeper in the structure of Arab society.

Ironically, the question asked two centuries earlier was reiterated with the same bewilderment: What are the secrets of the power and success of the West (Israel) and the causes of Arab weakness and failure? Such questions led to the radicalization of the Arab nationalist movement and to the advocacy of the total transformation of Arab society as a necessary condition for freedom, unity, and progress.

8. *Ibid.*, p. 133.

The Emergence of a Socialist Ideology

The emergence of a conscious socialist ideology in the Arab world in the second quarter of the twentieth century was a direct and necessary result of the Arabs' quest for modernization and unity. Except for a few doctrinaire Marxists, all Arab socialists are fundamentally nationalists. They have accepted socialism as the organizing economic and social principle of Arab national life.

The progress of nationalism from limited humanitarian beginnings (political autonomy and cultural self-determination) to social radicalism has been dictated as much by the nature and complexity of the social and economic conditions of Arab society as by the temper of the times. Viewed in terms of the deep-rooted differences within the Arab social structure and the pressure for rapid economic development as a means of satisfying rising expectations and integrating the Arab masses into the social whole, the radicalization of the Arab nationalist movement seems to have been inevitable. A number of factors, not the least of which is the West's own abandonment of the professed principles of Western civilization, have cooperated to discredit Western-type democratic-liberal economic and political institutions.

It is true that Western institutions were grafted on a society that was not yet ready for them; but it was the inner contradictions of these institutions that probably turned the rising Arab intelligentsia into doubters and cynics regarding their applicability under the existing conditions. Nationalism and democracy, which had dominated the minds of the upper-class ruling elite, proved unsatisfactory: democratic institutions established under Western influence tended to perpetuate the economic and social privileges of the elite. Consequently, the nationalist cry has been for freedom, not only from imperialism but also from feudalism, capitalism, exploitation, and privilege.

Prior to World War II, socialist ideology in the Arab world was largely utopian. Radical and socialist ideologies held little attraction for Arab intellectuals in the nineteenth century. Christian writers made only brief reference to leftist literature, specifically to the writings of French radicals. Socialist doctrines per se were presented as part of the historical exposition of Western political and philosophical thought.[9] Muslim writers were more cautious and defensive. For example, al-Afghani's treatise on socialism is to be seen as part of the literature defending Islamic reformism.[10]

9. Sharabi, *Arab Intellectuals*, p. 68.
10. Sami Hanna and George Gardner, *Arab Socialism* (Leiden: Brill, 1969), pp. 266–74.

In the first part of the twentieth century Arab intellectuals showed a more active interest in socialism. Traveling or studying in Europe, Arab writers were appalled by the sharp contrast between the living conditions there and those in their own societies. They saw in socialism the remedy for the glaring economic and social disparities between the ruling elite and the Arab masses. Their socialism reflected moral indignation and charity rather than ideological formulation. But it was one thing to speak of social injustice in a didactic or moral tone and quite another to outline and suggest concrete schemes of socialist thought and movement. Their writings were of the type called "protest literature." A few attempted to organize a socialist party, but their efforts were short-lived because of lack of a clear program.

Only the Communists managed during this period to establish party organizations and mobilize trade union support. However, in its first two decades of activity the Communist party in the Arab world was largely organized and controlled by non-Arabs. Consequently, its understanding of Arab problems and realities was influenced by the background of its personnel, and its activities were directed by Communist international bodies. It was more concerned with undermining Western imperialist rule in the Arab world than with providing specific approaches to the solution of problems.

Ba'ath Arab Socialism

The first organized ideological group in the Arab world to include in its platform revolutionary socialist reform tailored for Arab needs and formulated in Arab terms was the Ba'ath party. It was the first political party to blend successfully socialism with Arab nationalism. In the Ba'ath ideology socialism and nationalism become almost synonymous. As a principle of socioeconomic organization, socialism guarantees Arab society prosperity and social justice. As a spiritual bond, nationalism integrates the Arab world into a cultural whole. Both principles guide it along the road of progress and freedom.

The intellectual and theoretical synthesis of Arab nationalism and socialism is the work of Michel Aflaq, cofounder of the Ba'ath party. Aflaq's objective is the revival of the Arab nation and the reawakening of Arab thought. "Our great mission," he said, "is to lead the Arabs, individually and collectively, towards this healthy state of thought and mind," to enable them to see things "directly, freely, without artifice or imitation. Arab thought will then be in line with the laws of nature and of life; it will be able to understand problems in their true perspective and organize its work in a creative manner."[11]

This over-all objective is closely linked to Aflaq's view of nationalism. Nationalism is not something accidental and superficial, subject to changing political, social, or economic conditions. Although nourished by these conditions, nationalism is more permanent, rooted deeply in history. It is a spiritual bond uniting people who have shared one history and one culture. Thus understood, nationalism enhances rather than hinders the growth of a genuine sense of world community. *Insaniyya* ("humanism") is concomitant with nationalism. By contributing to understanding and cooperation as well as positive competition among nations, nationalism enriches human culture. Aflaq's nationalism is cultural, the culmination of centuries of interaction between members of human groups and physical and historical environments. Such interaction has created common spiritual bonds, the most important of which is that of culture.[12] Religion is regarded as a part of the national culture.

For Aflaq and the Ba'athists, Arab nationalism is an incontestable reality. The question confronting the Arabs is not one of identity. Their purpose is not to demonstrate the existence of the common bonds that unite them but rather to choose and determine the positive content of their Arabism. Will it be reactionary or progressive? Will it be fulfilled in an atmosphere of oppression or freedom? Will it survive in fragmentation or unity? Haunted by the prevailing decadence in Arab society, Ba'ath ideology calls for the transformation of a social system that chokes the Arabs' potentialities, destroys their capabilities, and dissipates their energies. The Arabs must free themselves from all the reactionary obstacles that confine the mind and bind society with the shackles of infirm customs and traditions.

Ba'ath ideology distinguishes between the idea of Arabism (that is, Arab nationalism) and the theory of nationalism. Whereas the idea of Arabism is self-evident and eternal, the nationalist ideology is the progressive manifestation of this idea in conformity with the circumstances and conditions of the time. Briefly, the ideology of Arab nationalism consists of freedom, socialism, and unity.[13]

Therefore, nationalism is not a social philosophy but an intellectual or spiritual framework within which different social philosophies may con-

---

11. Kamal Karpat, ed., *Political and Social Thought in the Contemporary Middle East* (New York: Praeger, 1968), pp. 189–90.

12. Michel Aflaq, Munif al-Razzaz, and Jamal al-Atassi, *On Nationalism, Unity, and Socialism* (Baghdad, 1958), pp. 3–5 (in Arabic).

13. *Ibid.*, p. 8.

tend. This position of the Ba'ath gives Arab nationalism a certain flexibility, enabling it to incorporate with the same ease and openness Arab-Islamic values as well as modern socioeconomic and scientific ones. It is precisely this characteristic that makes Ba'ath Arab socialism dynamic and progressive. "Arab nationalism," says Munif al-Razzaz, "is neither an end nor a means; it is rather a movement embodying a progressive and eternal mission. It is a framework and a content (a concept and a meaning); the framework is old, but the content derives from the circumstances of the period of struggle in which it finds itself." [14]

Does it follow that nationalism, as a concept, may also incorporate a communist social philosophy? The Ba'athists point to Tito and Mao, leaders who have "welded together communism with the spirit of nationalism. . . . Thus communism and nationalism in Yugoslavia were not contradictory, and both were realized at the same time. Tito was loyal both to his people and to his ideology." [15] Concerned about national solidarity and cultural unity, Ba'ath Arab socialism rejects the Marxian principle of class struggle and the atheism and materialism of communism. Moreover, it recognizes individual liberty and private property.

In almost mystical terms Aflaq and his colleagues assert the genuinely Arab character of their socialism. "There is a kind of synonymity (*taraduf*) and interblending (*tamazuj*) and interaction between our nationalism and our socialism. . . . We combine them in order to arrive at a new version of nationalism." [16]

The Ba'ath party also rejects capitalism and feudalism as bases of Arab nationalism; such systems, it is believed, institutionalize exploitation and alienate peasants, workers, and intellectuals from the state. Furthermore, capitalist and feudalist structures would provide fertile ground for international and populist movements seeking to smother the personality of the Arab nation.

Arab socialism is inseparable from Arab unity. Although in the realm of values unity assumes a higher priority than socialism, it remains a mere expression and a delusion unless it is built with the active participation of the Arab masses. The fusion of unity and socialism is like "giving a body to the concept of unity; socialism is the body and unity is the soul." [17]

With regard to ideology, there is little if any difference between the

14. *Ibid.,* p. 18.
15. Munif al-Razzaz, *The Evolution of the Meaning of Nationalism,* trans. Ibrahim Abu-Lughod (Garden City, N.Y.: Doubleday, 1963), p. 43.
16. Aflaq, al-Razzaz, and al-Atassi, *On Nationalism,* pp. 28–29.
17. *Ibid.,* pp. 34–35.

socialism of the Ba'ath and that of Nasserism. The only possible distinction is that Nasserite socialism is derived from an empirical reform experience in Egypt.

Conclusion

It is perhaps immature to speak of a coherent Arab socialist ideology. Arab socialism will for a long time be confronted with the conflict between some of its basic tenets and Islam's social morality. A strong shift toward secularism will run counter to fundamental Islamic principles; too much emphasis on Islamic principles of social justice may limit the flexibility of Arab socialism in coping with an increasing number of social and economic problems.

At the same time, Arab nationalism will have to face the ever-present crucial question of whether or not there exists the basis for a common loyalty to the idea of an Arab nation. It will have to overcome religious differences, social stratification, geographic distance, vested regional interests, and the lack of integration among the several cultural and ethnic groups constituting Arab society. Despite these difficulties, some broad outlines of a modernizing Arab-socialistic ideology have been established. Its nationalism will be cultural and progressive, and its principles of social justice will always take into account Islamic ethical and humanistic principles; for only such an ideology will be acceptable throughout the Arab world.

The Role of Language in The Growth of Arab Nationalism

Anwar Chejne

THE CONTRIBUTION OF ARABIC to the growth of Arab nationalism has been substantial. One might even say that Arab nationalism as embodied in the concept of Arabism *('urubah)* would be nonexistent without the Arabic language. During the time of Arab ascendancy, the Arab people had a great sense of pride in their language and in their cultural identity; but, as Arab power declined, this attitude began to disappear. Arabs came to be indifferent to—or even against—everything Arabic. Then came a time in which the Arabic-speaking individual began to ponder his identity and to ask himself, "Who am I?" This was the beginning of an awakening, the beginning of Arab nationalism.

This is an oversimplification of the long and complex history of the Arabs and of the changes in their attitudes toward their language and themselves. Reaching the modern age after a long period of lethargy, the Arabs awoke to the realization that they and their society were overwhelmed by forces beyond their ability to cope with, let alone control. Thus, torn between the old and the new, between pietism and secularism, they found themselves in a predicament. For a long time their loyalty and identity remained uncertain. They often referred to themselves as Ottoman citizens, Muslims, Christians, without a real conception of a nation-state and nationhood. At first they hoped that by living under an Ottoman umbrella they would receive some recognition of Arabness. Then, during World War I, they had dreams of establishing an Arab kingdom and thereby re-establishing their bygone glory. But the Arab kingdom was suf-

15

focated before birth; from that tragedy the Arabs were led to the present one in Palestine. In the process, they remained disconcerted and perplexed, even helpless. Their search for dignity and self-respect proved unproductive and frustrating; they became victims of their frightful experiences and indulged in quixotic pursuits, only to discover that each enterprise was followed by a more ridiculous one. Even their search for identity took different directions and often headed for collision and disaster. They would call themselves Lebanese of the Phoenician brand, Egyptians of the Pharaonic type, Iraqis of the Assyrian type, and so on. They would go to the extent of using a foreign language in preference to Arabic, denying the latter any usefulness and attributing to it all the elements of backwardness.

In the midst of this diversity and confusion, the question emerged as to whether Arabism and Islamism were one and the same or two quite different movements. To many, the distinction was difficult to make. Both movements often coincided in objectives and ideology, and both evoked a historical and cultural consciousness of great significance. In the end, however, there was a parting of the ways. This was due mainly to the influence of Christian Arabs and liberal Muslims, who were willing to accept local nationalism based on history and language rather than a religious nationalism that had been discredited.

Arab nationalists came to realize that Arabic was their most precious possession and could find ample justification in history for this belief. In medieval times Muslim scholars had distinguished people by what they believed to be a unique quality: the Greek was characterized by the superiority of his brain, the Chinese by the dexterity of his hands, and the Arab by the eloquence of his language. Throughout the centuries Arabs have held their language in great esteem and have appreciated its aesthetic, religious, and cultural values. Consequently, they have taken pride in possessing an eloquent and flowery Arabic. Even in modern times, and notwithstanding the great diversity of attitudes within the Arab world, it is not uncommon to hear Lebanese or Egyptians boasting that their Arabic surpasses all others in quality and purity. It would appear that their claim to the best and most correct Arabic rests on the level of education in their respective countries. On the other hand, Jordanians and Saudi Arabians would protest against these claims strongly, alleging that their Arabic is the purest because it exists closer to the desert. Also significant is the fact that writers have shown a propensity for obsolete expressions from medieval literature for no apparent reason except to display their linguistic dexterity.

In sum, the Arabs cherish their language. They take delight in its beauty, resonance, its rich images and similes, unusual metaphors, ornate expressions, elegant style, and sonority. Judging from the enormous amount of poetry produced over the centuries, we may be tempted to say that Arabs are poets at heart. They are prone to speak elegantly, eloquently, poetically, and at times rhetorically. There is also a tendency among Arabs to exaggerate: a simple act often is magnified until it becomes a great deed of an extraordinary man; a word of warning appears to be a threat of destruction. Moreover, Arabs often say the opposite of what they mean. In time of distress their seemingly belligerent talk camouflages their inner desires or their inability to act. This is shown in the relationship of Arab leaders who vilify each other on one occasion and profess their brotherhood on the next. Impulsiveness prevails over calm and considered judgment, and deeds frequently fall short of expressed intentions. This is perhaps part of Arab aesthetics and psychology, which are reflected in Arabic and which are an integral part of the Arab identity.

The Linguistic Cult

The Arabs' strong attachment to and admiration for their language led to the rise of a linguistic cult of great aesthetic, religious, cultural, and national significance. This cult was quite evident in pre-Islamic times. Its aesthetic dimension was echoed in the poet's words, which "flew across the desert faster than arrows," influencing the lives of the people, molding their minds, and giving immediacy to an ideal of Arab virtue. Eloquence *(fasahah),* the ability to express oneself correctly, was considered one of the basic attributes of the perfect man and a mark of wisdom. This linguistic cult gained a new dimension with the rise and spread of Islam. To the Arabs, the Arabic language became a God-given language and the mother of all languages. According to tradition, it was first taught to Adam, who was deprived of it when he disobeyed God and was forced to learn Syriac instead; it has remained ever since the language of the people of paradise. To the aesthetic and religious dimensions was added a third one with the dissemination of Arab culture. It should be emphasized that the role of Arabic as the instrument of culture had an enormous significance, as great as and perhaps greater than the interaction of Arabic and Islam. The great thinker and scientist al-Bīrunī (d. 1048), who saw Arabic as the container of all the sciences, preferred being reviled in Arabic to being praised in Persian. His admiration for the language was shared by many throughout the Muslim Empire, from Samarkand in the east to Spain in the west.

In this connection, Arabization went hand in hand with Islamization and in some instances transcended it, in that non-Muslims, mainly Jews and Christians, adopted Arabic for self-expression. This phenomenon no doubt began to give a secular character to the language. Its secular character has survived and is attested to by the role of Arabic with respect to the nationalist movement, which is based on Arabism and Arabness (al-ummah al-ʿarabiyyah) and not on the religious foundation of the Islamic community (al-ummah al-islāmiyyah).

Arabic and the Nationalist Movement

The inception of Arab nationalism based on language, culture, and history goes back to the nineteenth century, and the role of Arabic was quite conspicuous from the outset. The nationalist movement was based on and inspired by a strong historical consciousness, which was reinforced by the discovery of a great cultural reservoir in the Arabic language and by the Arabs' growing awareness of their rich and glorious past. During the Arab awakening (al-nahdah), which centered on language and history, Arabic was reactivated, its functions defined, and its virtues extolled. It became the symbol of revival and regeneration and was vehemently defended from the encroachment of a rampant vulgarism and the pressure of foreignism.

On the insistence of Christians and Westernized Muslims, the language took on another dimension and became a secular symbol of a national creed, embodied in the concept of ʿurubah. This national ideology has as its goal the union of all Arabic-speaking peoples into a single nation-state, in which the splendor of the past can be recaptured and, at the same time, Arab ascendancy, self-respect, and dignity can be attained.

The Arab intelligentsia agree, for the most part, that intellectual revival and national consciousness have linguistic and historical traditions as their indispensable foundations, and that Arabic is the faithful register of Arab cultural achievement and the basis for politico-cultural resurgence throughout the Arab world. In other words, the language has become the driving force behind Arab aspirations for national and cultural ascendancy, and Arabic and the national movement have complemented each other to such a degree that they can hardly be separated. Arabic has become the *raison d'être* of nationalism, and nationalism the driving force behind linguistic regeneration.

In its new role as a pillar of Arab nationalism, Arabic has become the object of adulation—a role similar if not identical to the one that it enjoyed in medieval times. Its distinctive qualities, together with its important role in the life of society, have been extolled in glowing terms. In the context of nationalism, which has become the secular creed, Arabic has played a role like the one it had played earlier with regard to Islam. Nowhere is the Arab awakening more evident than in the wide interest in Arabic—in its role, its superior qualities, and the potentialities it offers the Arabic-speaking people. Its significance has transcended national and religious boundaries. Farhat (d. 1732), the Bustanis, Yaziji, Bishop Yusuf Dibs (d. 1907), Bishop Yusuf Dawud (d. 1890), Father Kirmili, and many other Christian and Muslim laymen made enormous contributions to the revival of Arabic. They took pride in and had great attachment to the language. They, and others like them, were responsible for giving Arabic a new meaning and dimension of tremendous significance. Henceforth, Arabic was conceived to be the Arabs' most important tradition, the spirit and vitality of the community, and the sustenance of nationalism. It is inseparable from the life of the community and reflects its actual condition. To al-Husri, the best representative theoretician on Arab nationalism, language is the lifeblood and soul of a nation, the strongest bond of unity, and the principal pillar of nationalism, providing a link between the past and the present, Arabic has been the faithful guardian of the cultural heritage of the Arabs, the register of their past glory as well as their downfalls. His views have found echoes among a good number of Arab nationalists. George Hanna of Lebanon maintains that any person who abandons his language is an outsider to his social group. He adds that, if language were not the faithful guardian of the Arab cultural heritage, the colonialists would not have taken the trouble to obstruct its progress and undermine its structure. Similarly, 'Uthmān of Syria says that the colonialists have repeatedly misled the followers of Egyptian, Lebanese, Syrian, Sudanese, and Berber nationalisms by reviving a nationalism which died a long time ago and whose languages have "melted in the Great Arab Ocean."

In conclusion, the intimate interaction between a people and their language cannot be underestimated. Viewed in this light, the state of Arabic in the present Arab world has a far-reaching significance, inasmuch as it reflects the state of Arab society and the level of its emotional, political, social, and intellectual development. Moreover, it can be safely said that the Arab countries have a common denominator in their language. Although the Arabs find themselves politically divided, their language betrays a unity more basic than any single institution. So far no Arab country has undertaken a linguistic revolt, and it does not appear at the moment that any such revolt is in the making. Thus there is assurance that the Arab world will remain united in language and will eventually fulfill the hopes and ideals of *'urubah*.

The Impact of Land Reform

Fuad Baali

IN RECENT YEARS agrarian reform has received great attention in many parts of the world, especially in Asia, Africa, and Latin America. Contemporary agrarian-reform laws deal with economic, political, and social objectives. Such legislation usually endeavors to improve the abilities, capacities, and performances of those who cultivate the land and to increase agricultural output. Often the removal of inequalities in landownership, the promotion of greater security of tenure for tenants, the improvement of the status of the agricultural laborers, and the development of democratic institutions are included in agrarian-reform programs. This paper will analyze and evaluate the nature, scope, and implications of agrarian reform in the Arab countries.

With the exception of Saudi Arabia and Yemen, all Arab countries were once under foreign occupation. Most rural people were dominated by feudal landlords, and as a result rural development received very little attention. In Iraq, for example, British authorities perpetuated the land system of the Ottoman Empire and encouraged the absentee landlords and tribal chiefs of rural areas to strengthen their power. During the occupation (1917–20) and the years of the mandate (1920–32) the British made no serious efforts to effect development. A high degree of concentration in landownership also characterized Egypt. A few agricultural cooperatives were established, but the majority of the peasants remained in abject poverty.

In Algeria, Morocco, and Tunisia, credit institutions and fertile lands were owned by French colonists. Such conditions were also true of the Italian farm settlements in Libya. In Syria, the Ghab Valley scheme and the Jezireh scheme, designed to increase the area of cultivable land and improve irrigation facilities, did not elevate the standard of living of the peasants, who were subject to the large landowners. The Gezira scheme in the Sudan was a successful endeavor. Although there was great emphasis on irrigation projects, the Gezira region served as a settlement place for several migrant tribes.

The newly independent Arab countries inherited the problems of highly concentrated landownership, a complicated system of share tenancy, an extreme degree of social stratification, and a large peasant population with a low standard of living. It has been difficult for these countries to overcome the hopelessness of the peasants and to improve rural conditions.

Iraq

When Iraq gained its independence (1921), it inherited a confused system of landownership and discovered that many records of land titles had been either destroyed or lost. When legislation was passed in 1932 stipulating that all people must register the title or deed to the land they possessed, the sheiks—not the tribesmen who exercised the customary rights of collective ownership—benefited. Because the tribesmen were not fully informed of the provisions of this law, the sheiks were able to register the tribal lands as their personal property. Consequently, the relationship between the sheik and his fellow tribesmen became one of landlord to share tenants. The government was aware of this illegal action but took no serious action against it.[1]

Inequality in landownership and land tenure relationships, which had caused such rural problems as deplorably low incomes, wide illiteracy, and poor health, also created new ones such as a lack of cooperation between the landowners and the peasants and a continuous migration to urban areas. As a result of the peasants' growing discontent, the government acted to improve their economic condition by allowing them to own land distrib-

---

1. See Fuad Baali, "Relationships of Man to the Land in Iraq," *Rural Sociology*, XXXI, no. 2 (June, 1966), 171–82; and *idem*, "Agrarian Reform in Iraq: Some Socioeconomic Aspects," *American Journal of Economics and Sociology*, XXVIII, no. 1 (January, 1969), 61–76.

uted by the government in the Dujailah area (south-central Iraq) and by providing them with many services, especially schools, health care, and technical assistance. One of the most significant features of this project was that the settlers were selected from different tribes. It was hoped that this would lessen tribal prejudice and at the same time foster a spirit of nationalism among the settlers.

In spite of the fact that the project encountered such difficulties as salinity of the soil, inadequate drainage facilities, an inadequate system of agricultural credit, and failure of the cooperative society (which was established in 1947 and failed in 1952), it is considered to be a successful experiment in rural development. Significantly, the settlers were content. The project was applauded by peasants and others as a move against the power of the big landlords. The government, encouraged by this success, in 1951 passed legislation paving the way for six more settlement projects.[2] However, these projects were beneficial to only a small number of farmers in a few localities, and most peasants remained under the influence of the big landlords.

Only after the revolution of July 14, 1958, did the landlords' influence begin to decline. The purpose of the Agrarian Reform Act of 1958 was to raise the peasants' standard of living as well as the level of agricultural production. Farmers continue to establish agricultural cooperative associations, which are encouraged by the government. Loans from the Agricultural Bank are granted to the cooperative associations and also to farmers who are not members of cooperatives. However, adult education in rural areas has received very little attention, and the government's attempts to improve health conditions have been limited almost entirely to urban areas.

Syria

A concentration of large farms, absentee ownership, and a low living standard among the peasants have also characterized independent Syria. Until 1958, reform programs emphasized the expansion of irrigation and land reclamation. Legislation passed in 1952, which was intended to distribute lands among the citizens and which accorded landless peasants preference in the distribution of land, was largely ineffective.

The Agrarian Reform Law of 1958 not only dealt with the expropriation and redistribution of land but also encouraged the establishment of agricul-

---

2. For detailed information of these projects, see Hassan Ali, *Land Reclamation and Settlement in Iraq* (Baghdad: Baghdad Printing Press, 1955), pp. 70–190.

tural cooperatives through government loans and grants. The law was amended in 1962, but emphasis on the cooperative movement has continued. In addition, both the First Five-Year Plan (1960–65) and the Second Five-Year Plan (1965–70) gave priority to agricultural development. As in Iraq, little attention has been given to fundamental education and other major institutional services.

Jordan

Most farms in Jordan are small and are operated by the owner. The small number of large landowners does not constitute a problem for rural development. The Jordan Development Board and the Agricultural Credit Corporation were established, the main function of the latter being to provide credit to cooperatives. This service is complemented by the Agricultural Bank, which has been able to provide long-term loans to farmers.

To stimulate economic development, a five-year plan (1962–67) was adopted. Later, the plan was considered unrealistic and was replaced by a seven-year plan (1964–70). Approximately 27 per cent of the plan's total investment was allocated to agriculture—for example, to modernizing farming techniques and making use of the country's irrigation potential. The East Ghor Canal project, designed to increase agricultural productivity, was one of the irrigation schemes which received great attention.

The 1967 June War adversely affected Jordan's planning efforts, especially in the West Bank territory, now under Israeli occupation. The East Ghor project area has more than once been a target of Israeli shelling, which has kept many farmers from their fields.

Lebanon

Although there is some absentee landlordism in Lebanon, most of the farms in this country are small and fragmented, and in some areas the income of the farmers is meager. Because mortgages on farms are usually unavailable, farmers are forced to borrow from moneylenders at exorbitant interest rates. This has discouraged many rural dwellers from self-improvement and has brought about their migration to Beirut and other urban areas.

The major development programs have been land-reclamation and irrigation schemes such as the Green Plan, a ten-year program of land reclamation, and the Five-Year Development Program (1965–69), which devoted 18 per cent of its expenditures to increasing the irrigated area in the

Biq'a region. The United Nations Food and Agriculture Organization has contributed to land-reclamation projects.

Saudi Arabia

Although development planning in Saudi Arabia can be traced back to al-Kharj experimental farm (1937), serious efforts have taken place only in the 1960s. In 1960 a mission from the International Bank for Reconstruction and Development (IBRD), after studying Saudi Arabia's potential for development, recommended that the government, preferably through a planning board, undertake projects beneficial to the population in general. As a result the Supreme Planning Council, established in 1961 and reorganized and renamed the Central Planning Organization in 1965, has emphasized land reclamation, improvement of agricultural techniques, establishment of farm cooperatives, and provision of agricultural credits and technical advice to farmers. These services have been extended as well to the recently established agricultural centers in Jizan, al-Madina, Qasim, and Hofuf. Al-Hasa, considered the largest agricultural project in Saudi Arabia, is designed to provide water resources to an estimated 190,000 people residing in 40 villages. One of the latest government efforts is the construction of a $3.5 million agricultural training center in Riyadh, designed to improve agricultural production by training officials, technicians, and farmers.

Kuwait

A harsh climate and lack of water are obstacles to agricultural development in Kuwait, but interest in agriculture, evidenced by the establishment of an experimental farm, is increasing.

The United Arab Republic (Egypt)

Before the 1952 revolution, Egypt attempted to improve the peasants' living conditions through the establishment of rural social centers, which were to provide such necessary services as vocational guidance and maternity care. However, their success was limited by a shortage of experienced personnel and the objections of large landowners to some planned reforms.

The objectives of the Agrarian Reform Law of 1952 were similar to those in Iraq and Syria: to distribute landownership among the peasants, to eliminate the political dominance of the large landowners, to improve the living standard of the peasants, and to raise agricultural productivity. The law and its amendments have been generally effective in raising the income of the agricultural population. Agricultural cooperatives have been formed and have been encouraged to obtain "all types of agricultural loans"; and the peasants have been provided with other "necessary requisites for the exploitation of their land."[3]

Owing to scattered holdings in some areas, the government initiated a program at Nawag to encourage collective farming; villages were divided into several large farms, each of which was to cultivate one crop. Although the farmers were told that the pattern of ownership would not be altered, they were nevertheless cautious. The first experiment was such a success, however, that the next year the farmers agreed to extend the program.

Another illustration of the planning for development in the U. A. R. is the Ten-Year Plan (1960–70), implemented in two five-year phases. Some of the plan's major objectives were to double the national income, to improve the peasants' standard of living, and to reclaim uncultivable areas. The proposed increase in the national income was an ambitious goal for a country with limited resources and with a considerably high rate of population growth (close to 3 per cent annually). The U.A.R., determined to make fuller use of the vast desert which covers about 95 per cent of its total area, has made efforts to reclaim uncultivable areas (for example, Wadi el Natrun, east of the Suez Canal, and Sinai). Moreover, the faulty planning for land reclamation in the Liberation Province is being corrected.

Sudan

The flooding caused by construction of the Aswan Dam has necessitated the resettlement of the people who lived in the Wadi Halfa district in Sudan. Khashm el-Girba, an area about eight hundred miles southeast of Wadi Halfa on the Atbara River, was chosen as the resettlement site. Compensation by the U.A.R. has made possible the establishment of

---

3. Egypt, Agrarian Reform Law of 1952, Article 19. In the U.A.R., as in Iraq, membership in agricultural cooperative associations is obligatory. Peasants who receive land from the government must join cooperative associations supervised by the government. In September, 1959, the U.A.R. extended membership in cooperatives to independent owners or tenants who own or operate small holdings. Independent farm operators often refuse to join for fear of losing freedom of action. See Gabriel S. Saab, *The Egyptian Agrarian Reform: 1952–1962* (London: Oxford Univ. Press, 1967), p. 51.

twenty-two villages, which are provided with such services as mosques, police posts, clubs, dispensaries, schools, and post and telegraph offices. The establishment of cooperative associations has also been facilitated. The most important aspect of this project has been the settlers' ability to overcome the shock of being displaced from their homes and their success in settling in an alien environment.[4]

The resettlement scheme at Khashm el-Girba is one major project of the Ten-Year Plan (1961-71), which is concerned also with the construction of storage dams and irrigation facilities and places some emphasis on education, health, and housing.

Libya

In Libya, where approximately only 1 per cent of the total area is suitable for agriculture, rural development faces tremendous obstacles. A mission organized by the IBRD in 1960 to study economic development in Libya found the condition of most farmers poor, the facilities for agricultural credit inadequate, and the rural cooperative movement still in its infancy. The mission also found that, while foreign aid was contributing to agricultural development, the small farmer was unable to sell his produce on a competitive basis with imported goods. These factors and also the growth of the petroleum industry have brought about migration from rural to urban areas. It is estimated that migrant workers constitute two-thirds of the total labor force.[5] The mission recommended that, in order to develop small-scale farming, first priority should be given to the former Italian farm settlements and that an agricultural-development board should be created to undertake this task.

The IBRD mission drew up a development program to be carried out during the five-year period from April 1, 1960, to March 31, 1965. The plan recommended that (1) the shortage of trained men should not preclude efforts in development, (2) a larger proportion of the country's resources should be devoted to long-term schemes to provide a better way of life for those engaged in agriculture, (3) attention should be paid to the management and supervision of the cooperative movements and of agricultural credit facilities, (4) more public wells should be built in the desert

4. See D. J. Shaw, "Resettlement from the Nile in Sudan," *Middle East Journal,* XXI, no. 4 (Autumn, 1967), 463, 473, 482, 487.
5. U.S., Department of Agriculture, Economic Research Service, "Libya's Agricultural Economy in Brief" (March, 1966), p. 3.

oases to provide the small cultivators with access to water for irrigation, and (5) low-cost housing should be constructed for the agricultural workers. Accordingly, the government of Libya instituted the First Five-Year Economic and Social Development Plan (1963–68). This plan concentrated on improving the condition of the village inhabitants. In addition to resettlement projects, it emphasized improvement of agricultural marketing, irrigation, agricultural machinery, and agricultural credit. It seems, however, that in spite of these efforts the level of agricultural production remains low.

Algeria

In Algeria the government completed nationalization of the French estates in September, 1963, and in October, 1964, seized the large estates of some Algerian citizens who had collaborated with the French during the war for independence. The government sought to reintegrate these lands into the national rural economy. Since most of the holdings of Algerian farmers were small and inferior in quality, the government introduced the Cuban system of collective farming through the amalgamation of small farms. The key organizations in carrying out this task have been the Cooperative Committees for Agrarian Reform, which have played an important role in the attempt to provide farmers with available mechanical aids and other necessary facilities. The workers' attitudes to collective management have been disturbing to the officials. "Many of them continued to look on their work as just a job in which they engaged for the sake of the income it provided, without any real identification with their collective." The officials not only denounced this attitude but frequently dismissed committee members.

> The consequent situation has sometimes proved unsatisfactory in two senses: the new officials have less experience and skill, while the old ones burn with resentment at being subject to the direction—sometimes the mistaken direction—of people less experienced than themselves.[6]

The major problem for a short- or long-term plan for the Algerian agricultural population is how to deal with approximately 8 million people who

6. United Nations, Department of Economic and Social Affairs, *Progress in Land Reform: Fourth Report* (1966), pp. 76–77.

depend for their livelihood on only 2.7 million hectares (6.75 million acres) of fertile land. The Algerian government is trying to find the best solution to this problem. Since December 31, 1963, when a plan was initiated to give greater attention to rural-improvement schemes, Algeria has been committed to serious planning for rural reform.

Morocco

Immediately after independence, the government of Morocco began planning to modernize the countryside, increase agricultural productivity, and improve the living standard of the rural population. The major step was the distribution to the landless peasants of lands that had been seized from those Europeans and Moroccans who had collaborated with the French. In order to modernize the traditional methods of agriculture and increase agricultural productivity, the government initiated a cooperative cultivation program in 1957. The program called for the consolidation of small fragmented plots of land into farms large enough to make effective use of agricultural machinery. Although the program was successful in its first year of operation, its importance continuously decreased, mainly because of the suspicion of the farmers and the decline in agricultural production in 1959.

Another endeavor was the Five-Year Plan (1960–65), which covered such areas as agriculture, education, technical training, and social services. Continual changes in the cabinet, lack of coordination among governmental departments, and shortage of skilled personnel are some of the factors that contributed to the ineffectiveness of this plan. The disappointment of many farmers with the performance of their government has caused them to migrate to the cities, which already are suffering from a high rate of unemployment.

Tunisia

In Tunisia the majority of peasants own small, fragmented plots of land and enjoy few agricultural facilities. Because of the low living standard and the high rate of unemployment, many peasants have migrated to urban areas, a problem which the Tunisian government is attempting to solve. A major objective of planning in Tunisia is to improve rural conditions. An example of the government's efforts in this regard is the Medjerda Valley Development, an important agricultural project which has provided some rural areas with irrigation. Although a variety of problems have obstructed this project—for example, salinity of soil and administrative difficulties—it has encouraged some peasants to join agricultural cooperatives. The establishment of cooperative associations (especially Productive Unit Cooperative) was emphasized in the Three-Year Plan (1962–65). In addition, the Ten-Year Plan (1962–72) sought to increase the national income.[7]

Evaluation

In evaluating the present state of agrarian-reform programs in the Arab world, certain factors must be considered. First of all, an essential element for sound agrarian reform is accurate basic data (including statistical data) on the natural and human resources of rural life. The dearth of such data for the Arab countries makes long-term planning and projections difficult.

Second, though the financial resources in most Arab countries are sufficient for agents of change to carry out their plans, at times these resources are not efficiently utilized. Moreover, most of the resources are spent lavishly on urban and industrial development and, following the 1967 June War, on defense.

Third, there is not a sufficient number of skilled personnel to deal with agrarian reform. Qualified social scientists are practically absent from participation in rural-development planning. Furthermore, many experienced individuals are appointed to positions which do not correspond to their orientation and experience. This is even true in advanced Lebanon, where

> the lack of coordination between education and need has been carried to such an extreme that even government employees who are given scholarships for advanced training abroad often find, upon their return home, that no one—including the government—requires their newly acquired skill.[8]

7. Discussion of development planning in Yemen and South Yemen is not dealt with in this paper because of the lack of data. For a detailed description and analysis of Abu Dhabi's new Five-Year Development Plan (1968–72), see Ragaei El-Mallakh, "The Challenge of Affluence: Abu Dhabi," *Middle East Journal*, XXIV, no. 2 (Spring, 1970), 135–46.

8. Paul J. Klat, "Economics and Manpower Planning," *Middle East Economic Papers*, 1960 (Beirut: American Univ. of Beirut, Economic Research Institute, 1960), pp. 60–61.

Fourth, the instability of the governments in most of the Arab countries is an obstacle to effective coordination of reform programs among various departments. Because of the frequent cabinet changes, few competent personnel remain long in their positions. Dismissal of experienced individuals because of their political beliefs is another repercussion. Thus, agrarian reform is shaped by political development but suffers from political instability.

Fifth, an understanding of the impact that planned change will have on people and their mode of life is essential to effective development. In the Arab world, people are generally bound by kinship ties and/or strong traditional patterns, and development programs must take this factor into account. In the case of governmental efforts to settle nomadic people on agricultural lands, cultural and psychological factors were seldom taken into account. "Thorough research in tribal organization and comprehensive understanding of the tribal way of life should precede any attempt at drawing up plans or the application of projects for settlement."[9] The process should be one of transitional rather than radical change from nomadism to agrarianism, and such change should be undertaken only with the cooperation of the nomadic people. These are important and necessary conditions for planning; Bedóuins despise professions and look down on men who depend for their livelihood on jobs and occupations, including farming.[10]

Sixth, rural areas respond favorably to planned change if they understand the benefits such change is to bring about.

Seventh, rural people do not participate in planning for the improvement of their communities. In the Arab world, agrarian reform is usually carried out by the state.

Eighth, agrarian-reform programs have been successful in lessening inequalities of wealth and narrowing "traditional" differences between the landlord (ranked very high on the socioeconomic scale) and the peasant (ranked at the very bottom). It must be noted that when an agrarian reform brings about radical change in the social structure, the reform is likely to encounter some obstacles. The resistance of large landowners—for example, in Iraq, the U.A.R., and Syria—to change in the rural power structure and to governmental efforts to eliminate the abuses of the feudal social order has contributed to social tension and conflict in the early stages of reform.

9. Afif I. Tannous, "The Arab Tribal Community in a Nationalistic State," *Middle East Journal,* I, no. 1 (January, 1947), 12.

10. See, for example, Ali Wardi, *Dirasat fi Tabi'at al-Mujtamaa al-Iraqi* (Baghdad: Ani Press, 1966). For the English-speaking reader, see my review of this book in the *American Sociological Review,* December, 1966, p. 883.

Ninth, one of the goals of agrarian reform is to improve the economic condition of the peasants, who constitute nearly two-thirds of the population of the Arab world. To accomplish this goal land has been distributed to them, and agricultural equipment has been made available. In some areas, however, where such equipment is considered inadequate or has not been introduced, a feeling of frustration has resulted in little incentive on the part of some peasants to farm efficiently. Because of this and other related reasons, peasants in Iraq, Lebanon, Libya, Morocco, and Tunisia have migrated to urban centers. This migration has had many repercussions, among the most significant of which is the cultural gap or conflict between the values and norms of the rural migrants and those of the established urban dwellers. The migrants are concentrated in a few localities, where they maintain their traditions, customs, and ethnocentric behavior and attitudes, a condition which sets them apart and delays the process of adjustment.[11]

Although the general well-being of the agricultural population is a basic objective of any agrarian-reform program, neither in economically advanced countries nor elsewhere is there a model that suits the needs and desires of all people. Therefore, agrarian-reform programs are likely to face a number of difficulties. In some Arab countries, such as Iraq and Syria, such programs were introduced hastily and were carried out under political pressure. Moreover, in recent years some development schemes have been deferred due to the continuous tension between the Arab world and Israel. This has been especially true in Jordan. As Bertrand Russell put it, "Israel condemns the Arab nations, only recently emerging from colonial status, to continuing impoverishment as military demands take precedence over national development."

The programs of agrarian reform in the Arab world have made a positive contribution toward breaking the yoke of feudalism and overcoming much of the insecurity characterizing the conditions of tenancy. Though the Arab peasant is poor and his socioeconomic status is low, he now feels a sense of dignity after decades of injustice.

11. For detailed information on the adjustment of rural migrants to city life, see Janet Abu-Lughod, "Migrant Adjustment to City Life: The Egyptian Case," *American Journal of Sociology,* LXVII, no. 1 (July, 1961), 22–32; Doris Phillips, "Rural-to-Urban Migration in Iraq," *Economic Development and Cultural Change,* VII (July, 1959), 405–21; and Fuad Baali, "Social Factors in Iraqi Rural-Urban Migration," *American Journal of Economics and Sociology,* XXV, no. 4 (October, 1966), 359–64.

Educational Development

Baha and Sharon Abu-Laban

PRIOR TO WORLD WAR I, education of Arab youth was left largely to local communities and individuals. The dominant educational institution was the Islamic *kuttab,* which stressed religious instruction and tradition. Manned by local religious leaders, the *kuttab* followed a relatively simple form of instruction and extended the benefits of literacy to only a fraction of the young. High schools, except in certain limited regions, were practically unknown.

Following World War II, the newly independent Arab states brought about the demise of the *kuttab.* The acquisition of independence marked the first opportunity in many centuries for these countries to engage in deliberate national efforts toward social and economic development. The most feasible first steps toward modernization were in the area of education. As C. Arnold Anderson has stated, "Western-type schooling is one of the institutions most easily grafted onto a non-Western society."[1] Hence, in recent decades most Arab states have widened their educational bases and have moved toward formalization, universalization, and secularization of their educational systems. The social and economic circumstances of different Arab states have varied, as have their rates of educational growth, but the trend toward increasing emphasis on education has been a dominant force.

This paper first will examine various conditions of the institutional struc-

1. C. Arnold Anderson, "Education and Political Development: Reactions to a Conference," in *Education and Political Development,* ed. James S. Coleman (Princeton: Princeton Univ. Press, 1962), p. 5.

ture of Arab society which have been responsible for educational development and growth. This will be followed by a detailed statistical and evaluative exposition regarding expansion of educational opportunities at the primary, secondary, and university levels in the Arab states. In the next section the discussion will focus on the education of women. The paper will conclude with a discussion of structural consequences of educational development, with special emphasis on the class structure of Arab society.

Factors in Educational Development

There is little doubt that Western ideology was influential in the development of Arab aspirations for education. Increased emphasis on education in the Arab world was enhanced by at least three conditions. First, nineteenth-century Arab intellectuals and social reformers, many of whom had studied or traveled in Europe, agitated for the development of a modern educational system similar to the one which they had observed in Europe. Second, nineteenth- and twentieth-century French, British, and American missionaries were instrumental in developing, in various parts of the Arab world, modern private schools based on Western techniques and forms of organization. Third, following World War I the mandatory powers, in response to Arab agitation, assisted in developing modern public schools. The relative importance of each of these conditions varied from one country to another, and in certain Arab countries formal education was not an integral part of the culture until very recently.

A second main factor in educational growth in the Arab world has been social and economic development. Prior to World War I agricultural productivity in the region was very low, and industry was largely of the handicraft variety with distribution limited to local markets. Various attempts at social and economic development were started during the interwar period, but the process did not accelerate until after World War II. Arab governments in the past twenty-five years not only have encouraged but also have participated directly in industrial development projects. This has led to bureaucratic growth, both in the public and the private sectors of the economy. It is commonly known that social and economic development and bureaucratic expansion, resulting in a more complex occupational structure with increased rank differentiation, create a greater demand for trained personnel. The agency that can cope with these demands most effectively is a modern system of education. Hence, education has come to be associated with economic development.

Economic development appears to have stimulated educational growth in yet another way. There is little doubt that economic development has been an important factor in stimulating the process of urbanization and rural-urban migration. For example, in a recent study of industrialization in Alexandria, about one-third of the workers interviewed came from rural areas.[2] Similarly, Cairo has attracted a large number of rural migrants. Janet Abu-Lughod notes that throughout this century over one-third of Cairo's population has been of rural origin.[3] The growth in urbanization was accompanied by an increased popular demand for a host of public services including education. The response of many Arab governments was favorable for many reasons, among them the fact that educational costs are relatively lower in urban (heavily populated) areas than in rural ones. Educational facilities in urban areas continue to be better and more numerous than those in rural areas.

Fifty years ago the Arab world was struggling for political liberation and nurturing a nationalistic ideology which emphasized, among other things, progress and development. When independence was achieved, many governments attempted to focus national efforts on social and economic development. Special attention was paid to education, partly because it was perceived to be connected with national welfare and partly because of a developing, albeit nebulous, egalitarian ideology which sought to equalize opportunities through education.

The task of social and economic development proved to be an onerous one, not only because of the prevalence of strong traditional orientations, which in many ways were inimical to the requirements of industrialization, but also because of the absence of a regional master plan and the lack of technical competence. Other factors impeding economic transformation in the Arab world included rapid population growth, heavy rural-urban migration, and increasing demands, especially in urban centers, for governmental services and public welfare. An added emphasis on education appeared to be both a feasible and a politically desirable step toward solving these problems.

2. See Hassan Saati and G. K. Hirabayashi, *Industrialization in Alexandria: Some Social and Ecological Aspects* (Cairo: American Univ. Press, 1959).

3. Janet Abu-Lughod, "Cairo: Perspective and Prospectus," a paper presented at the Twenty-First Annual Near East Conference on Urban Planning and Urban Prospects in the Near East and North Africa, 1970.

The Problems of Educational Growth

Currently, the Arab countries are attempting to expand educational opportunities at a faster rate than that which was achieved by Western societies. While it may be said that the Arab countries can learn from the experiences of the West, the speed with which such goals are being sought creates special problems. The experience of the Arab states suggests that present emphasis on educational development can act as both a help and a hindrance, as both an integrative and a disintegrative force in society. This section will consider the magnitude of expansion of educational opportunities at the three main educational levels. The discussion is confined to the post–World War II period—specifically, from 1950 to 1965—for which comparable statistical information is available for all of the Arab states.

Primary Education

Government leaders who wish to reduce the illiteracy rate in their primary country usually make an effort to expand primary school enrollment. They are well aware that a high rate of illiteracy is a political embarrassment at both local and international levels. Table 1 shows school enrollment ratios for the first (primary) and second (secondary) levels of education for thirteen Arab states. The unadjusted ratios are percentage ratios based on school enrollment at a particular level related to the estimated population of the appropriate age-group for that level; the adjusted ratios are calculated in such a way as to minimize the effect of differences between national school systems. The substantial expansion in the educational systems of these states during the post–World War II period is evident. The school enrollment ratios increased regularly, both at the first and second levels, between 1950 and 1964. This fact notwithstanding, the systems of these countries by no means provide universal public education, even at the first level, though certain countries (Jordan, Kuwait, and Lebanon) come closer to achieving this goal than do others.

In 1964, at the first level of education, (five- to fourteen-year-olds), Lebanon had the highest school enrollment ratio (74), followed by Kuwait (72), Jordan (65), Tunisia (62), Libya (53), Syria (49), Iraq (48), the U.A.R. (46), Algeria (41), Morocco (34), Sudan (15), Saudi Arabia (12) and Yemen (9). Fifteen years earlier all of these countries had very low school enrollment ratios, ranging from 2 for Saudi Arabia to 35 for Syria, the majority of the others being between 15 and 30. Between 1950 and

TABLE 1.
UNADJUSTED SCHOOL ENROLLMENT RATIOS FOR SELECTED
ARAB STATES*

State	Year	1st Level	2nd Level	1st and 2nd Levels	Adjusted Ratios for 1st and 2nd Levels*
Algeria	1950	15	5	12	14
	1955	18	6	14	17
	1960	28	8	22	26
	1964	41	9	32	37
Iraq	1950	16	6	13	18
	1955	23	10	19	26
	1960	43	21	37	50
	1964	48	29	43	58
Jordan	1950	26	5	21	27
	1955	49	27	43	54
	1960	51	35	46	58
	1964	65	46	59	73
Kuwait	1952	23	2	17	21
	1955	35	5	26	33
	1960	52	55	53	66
	1964	72	102	81	101
Lebanon	1950	--	--	--	--
	1954	45	20	38	47
	1960	64	28	53	66
	1964	74	43	65	81
Libya	1950	12	0.6	9	11
	1955	23	5	18	22
	1960	41	14	33	42
	1964	53	21	44	55
Morocco	1950	11	2	9	12
	1956	17	4	13	17
	1960	27	7	21	29
	1964	34	13	28	38
Saudi Arabia	1949	2	0.3	2	2
	1955	4	0.4	3	4
	1960	6	2	5	6
	1964	12	4	10	12
Sudan	1950	6	0.5	4	5
	1955	6	1	5	6
	1960	11	6	9	12
	1964	15	7	13	16

TABLE 1. (Cont'd)
UNADJUSTED SCHOOL ENROLLMENT RATIOS FOR SELECTED
ARAB STATES*

State	Year	1st Level	2nd Level	1st and 2nd Levels	Adjusted Ratios for 1st and 2nd Levels*
Syria	1950	35	11	28	35
	1955	33	17	29	36
	1960	43	20	36	45
	1964	49	34	45	46
Tunisia	1950	18	9	15	19
	1955	26	11	21	27
	1960	44	15	36	45
	1964	62	20	50	63
U.A.R.	1950	26	7	20	25
(Egypt)	1955	32	21	29	36
	1960	40	21	35	43
	1964	46	29	41	51
Yemen	1950	--	--	--	--
	1956	13	0.1	9	11
	1962	8	0.4	6	8
	1964	9	0.6	7	9

*"The unadjusted school enrollment ratio for the first level of education
is a percentage ratio based on the enrollment at this level related to the
estimated population 5-14 years old; the corresponding ratio for the second
level of education is based on the enrollment in all types of schools (general,
vocational, and teacher training) at this level related to the estimated
population 15-19 years old; the combined ratio for the first and second levels
is based on the total enrollment at the first and second levels related to the
estimated population 5-19 years old. The adjusted school enrollment ratio for
the first and second levels has been computed according to the same principles,
but on the basis of a population figure adjusted to correspond to the actual
duration of schooling. It should be borne in mind, in interpreting these
ratios, that the actual age ranges of the pupils enrolled in primary and
secondary schools do not exactly correspond to the arbitrary age groups 5-14,
15-19, 5-19. Furthermore, the length of schooling at each level of education
and in each type of school varies widely from one country to the other. It
follows that the maximum value for any particular enrollment ratio may be
either above or below 100. For the same reasons, certain countries show a
higher ratio for the second than for the first level. Very high ratios often
result when very low enrollment and population data are involved in the
calculation . . . The adjusted ratio . . . is an attempt to minimize the effect
in the calculation of differences in the national school systems.
" (Statistical Yearbook, 1966, p.59.)

Source: UNESCO, Statistical Yearbook, 1966 (Paris: UNESCO, 1968), Table 2.5,
pp. 59-78. (A few qualifying footnotes which appear in the original
source are omitted here.)

1964, six Arab states (Iraq, Kuwait, Libya, Morocco, Saudi Arabia, and Tunisia) more than tripled their first-level school enrollment ratios; three states (Algeria, Jordan, and Sudan) more than doubled these ratios. Though Syria began with the highest enrollment ratio in 1950, it had, during the fifteen-year period, the lowest rate of increase of all the countries with the exception of Yemen, whose ratio actually declined.

Though we have no precise figures, Fahim Qubain estimates that in Arab countries the drop-out rate at the first level is high.[4] The rate is probably highest in rural areas. Even if a village is populous enough to have its own school, it is likely that the school comprises only a few grades. After completing these grades, the student is required to transfer to a larger school away from the local village in order to continue his education. Such a transfer can be achieved only at some expense to the family, and it is sometimes easier just to withdraw the child from school. Assuming that children must have at least four years of schooling to attain and retain literacy, it is easy to understand why literacy rates may remain low, even if educational facilities are expanded.

The drop-out rate at the primary level raises a problem with regard to unemployment. A few years of primary education in underdeveloped areas may be just enough to raise the job aspirations of the student yet not enough to provide him with any marketable skills. While he may look with disdain on manual work, he lacks the specific skills that would enable him to compete successfully in the labor market. The presence of many such people tends to create pockets of dissatisfaction within the country.

At both the primary and secondary levels there unfortunately is a lack of well-trained teachers. The attraction of qualified people is handicapped by the relatively low status accorded primary schoolteachers. Table 2 shows the number of teachers and pupils and the proportion of females in each category for two selected years. This table is limited to the first level of education and thus complements the second column in Table 1. The phenomenal growth in teaching staff and student enrollments at the first level during the ten- to fifteen-year period under consideration far exceeds the growth in population. The data in Table 2 indicate the magnitude of the task confronting the Arab countries with regard to education.

Most Arab governments do not provide preschool programs, the exception being affluent Kuwait. At a time when Western countries are emphasizing preschool training in the form of government-sponsored programs for

4. Fahim Qubain, *Education and Science in the Arab World* (Baltimore: Johns Hopkins Univ. Press, 1966).

TABLE 2.
EDUCATION AT THE FIRST LEVEL: TEACHERS AND PUPILS

State	Year	Teaching Staff	F %	Pupils	F %
Algeria	1950	9,693	57	337,330	33
	1960	20,568	57	--	--
Iraq	1950	7,116	33	203,106	24
	1964	36,144	--	957,841	28
Jordan	1950	2,363	30	100,354	25
	1964	7,260	45	275,177	41
Kuwait	1952	505	34	10,183	35
	1965	1,284	81	49,562	49
Lebanon	1954	8,924	47	154,753	40
	1965	14,786	--	354,270	--
Libya	1950	1,028	--	32,115	11
	1964	5,937	22	175,591	24
Morocco	1950	9,864	26	257,764	27
	1965	27,621	--	1,124,078	30
Saudi Arabia	1949	875	--	27,712	--
	1964	--	--	218,990	20
Sudan	1955	3,229	22	161,144	20
	1965	10,895	--	492,085	27
Syria	1950	7,374	31	279,193	26
	1965	19,040	36	688,165	32
Tunisia	1950	4,579	--	156,821	27
	1965	12,868	--	734,316	33
U.A.R. (Egypt)	1950	44,753	20	1,310,169	36
	1965	87,390	42	3,450,338	39
Yemen	1956	2,701	--	93,099	--
	1963	1,294	12	57,894	5

Source: UNESCO, Statistical Yearbook, 1966 (Paris: UNESCO, 1968), Table 2.7, pp. 90-108. (A few qualifying footnotes which appear in the original source are omitted here.)

underprivileged children, educational television programs aimed at the disadvantaged, and free breakfast and lunch programs for children whose learning may suffer due to malnutrition, most Arab countries, in which so many children could benefit from such programs, have not begun to make efforts in this direction. Such private preschool programs as do exist are for the financially comfortable in urban areas.

Secondary Education

Secondary education is the level most likely to be slighted by the governments, which are often pressured to expand elementary education and to gain prestige by developing a local university. In most Arab countries, educational opportunities at the secondary level (fifteen- to nineteen-year-olds) are more limited than at the primary level. Table 1 shows that in 1964 the school enrollment ratios at the second level were highest in Kuwait (102), Jordan (46), and Lebanon (43); lower in Syria (34), Iraq (29), and the U.A.R. (29); and still lower in the other countries (ranging from 0.6 for Yemen to 21 for Libya). As with the first level, educational opportunities at the second level throughout the Arab world increased substantially from 1950. Nevertheless it is clear that many Arab youth are deprived of the possibility of a high school education. In this connection, it is relevant to note that selectivity in the recruitment of high school students tends to operate in favor of the economically advantaged urban male youth. The system is far from providing an equal opportunity for education to all.

The last column in Table 1 shows the adjusted school enrollment ratios for the combined first and second educational levels. This column reflects the over-all educational opportunities, including high school. The adjusted enrollment ratios for Kuwait, Lebanon, and, to a lesser degree, Jordan compare favorably with the enrollment ratios of such modern industrial societies as Canada and the United States. The wealth of Kuwait, the traditional emphasis on education in Lebanon (starting over a century ago with the introduction of foreign missionary schools), and UNESCO-UNRWA's educational role in Jordan appear to be important factors in the educational development of these countries. Comparable ratios for educational development in Tunisia, Iraq, Libya, and the U.A.R. range from 50 to 63, but the ratios in the remainder of the Arab states are below 50. The youth of Saudi Arabia, Sudan, and Yemen are among the most educationally disadvantaged not only in the Arab world but in the world at large.

Education at the secondary level includes general education, vocational education, and teacher training. Table 3 gives the number of students enrolled in each category for two selected years.

There has been a great increase in the number of students enrolled in general education programs at the secondary level. The only countries in which this has not occurred are Algeria and the U.A.R. Neither of these two countries was able to double the number of students in this category during the twelve- to fifteen-year period in question. Algeria's slower growth rate can be attributed, in part, to the special problems arising from the war for independence. In Egypt, though the increase in this category has not been very large, emphasis has been placed on vocational training, with enrollments more than quintupling in a twelve-year period.

The number of students enrolled in vocational training includes only those enrolled in strictly vocational schools and not those who are attending vocational training programs in general high schools. Additionally, the data on vocational schools do not differentiate between the number of part-time and the number of full-time teachers and pupils. Both of these factors should be taken into account in any interpretation of the data for this category.

There has been an increasing emphasis on teacher training at the secondary level. Although there has been a trend in Western countries to require teachers to have a university education, this has not been occurring in the Arab world.

University Education

Developing countries tend to view a local university as a source of prestige. A local university not only brings some measure of respect in the eyes of the West but also is a form of insurance against the loss or "contamination" of the indigenous elite.

Any country that finds it necessary to depend on other countries to educate its youth should take cognizance of several potential problems. (1) Education abroad is not likely to be geared toward the special problems of the native country. (2) The educated person may decide to settle in the host country. (3) Education abroad is almost certain to lack appreciation of native history and customs. (4) Even if the educated person does return home, he may be critical of his own country; he may remain there for only a short time and his attitude may be less than enthusiastic. Though education abroad has been viewed as a means of welding together the best of two worlds, the native country has on occasion found that education abroad has

TABLE 3.
EDUCATION AT THE SECOND LEVEL: TEACHERS AND PUPILS

State	Year	General Education				Vocational				Teacher Training			
		Teachers Total	%F	Pupils Total	%F	Teachers Total	%F	Pupils Total	%F	Teachers Total	%F	Pupils Total	%F
Algeria	1950	---	--	46,287	43	---	--	13,764	--	52	50	654	42
	1965	---	--	94,745	31	---	--	34,685	28	---	--	2,518	33
Iraq	1950	1,796	24	32,443	19	333	61	1,071	--	53	21	1,489	31
	1964	5,447	--	221,834	30	643	--	7,328	47	---	--	6,742	38
Jordan	1950	352	23	5,476	18	13	--	201	--	---	--	---	--
	1965	4,297	28	98,896	28	---	--	2,909	10	---	--	254	100
Kuwait	1952	31	--	320	13	---	--	50	--	---	--	---	--
	1965	1,783	40	29,494	39	155	--	1,033	--	163	37	1,144	37
Lebanon	1954	---	--	25,883	35	---	--	---	--	47	19	205	29
	1965	4,878	--	82,073	--	317	--	1,394	--	267	--	1,714	--
Libya	1950	49	--	300	5	19	--	237	--	8	--	89	--
	1964	1,647	8	23,212	12	218	9	2,197	20	195	19	2,401	31
Morocco	1950	600	19	14,391	30	150	--	3,500	33	6	50	72	38
	1965	8,100	--	170,890	21	---	--	12,981	22	---	--	1,057	19
Saudi Arabia	1949	121	--	1,116	--	4	--	21	--	31	--	200	--
	1963	1,002	--	18,082	6	445	--	4,200	--	465	--	7,842	6
Sudan	1950	---	--	3.682	10	---	--	309	--	---	--	548	30
	1965	4,453	--	92,407	--	479	--	6,391	44	174	--	1,680	--
Syria	1950	1,340	37	34,874	24	79	14	1,875	18	55	18	955	33
	1965	7,326	--	177,174	21	945	10	8,030	13	572	--	7,038	33
Tunisia	1950	1,268	34	21,230	20	857	38	11,057	49	44	36	345	43
	1965	---	--	104,339	28	---	--	6,394	8	---	--	4,745	--
U.A.R. (Egypt)	1953	17,181	14	440,636	19	3,103	2	21,615	3	1,721	--	23,908	47
	1965	34,819	21	819,373	28	9,975	--	127,734	20	4,531	32	49,448	42
Yemen	1956	69	--	296	--	---	--	---	--	16	--	50	--
	1965	126	--	1,949	--	---	--	45	--	5	--	125	--

Source: UNESCO, *Statistical Yearbook, 1966* (Paris: UNESCO, 1968). (A few qualifying footnotes which appear in the original source are omitted here.)

contributed to the production of a misfit—a man who finds he can call no place home.

Daniel da Cruz estimates that 25,000 Arab students are studying outside the Arab world, principally in the United States and Western Europe.[5] In 1961–62, of the Near and Middle Eastern students on U.S. campuses, 32 per cent were postgraduate students and 62 per cent were undergraduates.[6] This is a large proportion of undergraduates, and it is probably these very students who are the most vunerable to influence from the new culture.

Figures on the loss, whether physical or psychological, of Arab students to outside countries are not readily available. It is estimated that approximately 10 per cent of the foreign students in the United States eventually remain there, but the proportions are not uniform across nationality groupings.[7]

To avoid the problems mentioned above, a developing country may establish its own institutions of higher learning. This alternative, however, makes heavy demands on the national budget and is often faced with such problems as a dearth of textbook and other instructional materials and—in most Arab countries, with the possible exception of the U.A.R.—the unavailability of qualified nationals to serve as professors. The latter problem may lead to the employment of foreign professors who are unfamiliar with the local culture or, worse yet, somewhat condescending toward those aspects of the culture which they do know. Moreover, since foreign professors are likely to receive a substantially higher salary than their Arab colleagues, their employment may create a number of organizational problems.

National universities are faced with yet another difficulty. It is understandable that such universities would be under pressure to hire Arab professors. However, because of an unfortunate tendency toward localization, the universities are urged to hire professors from the state in which the university is located. This practice tends to further provincialism in the Arab world at a time when a flow of personnel between Arab states could serve the cause of Arab unity.

Disparities among Arab countries in educational growth and development, while apparent at the primary and secondary levels, are much more

5. Daniel da Cruz, "The New Breed," *ARAMCO World Magazine,* November–December, 1969.

6. M. Brewster-Smith, "Foreign vs. Indigenous Education," in *Post-Primary Education and Political and Economic Development,* ed. Don C. Piper and Taylor Cole (Durham, N.C.: Duke Univ. Press, 1964), pp. 48–74.

7. *Ibid.,* p. 74.

TABLE 4.
EDUCATION AT THE THIRD LEVEL: TEACHERS AND PUPILS

State	Year	Teaching Staff	F %	Pupils	F %	No. of Students per 100,000 Inhabitants
Algeria	1960	416	--	7,248	32	67
	1964	501	--	5,926	20	54
Iraq	1960	1,122	20	12,260	23	185
	1964	--	--	24,662	26	352
Jordan	1960	80	38	891	27	53
	1964	88	19	1,267	23	67
Kuwait	--	--	--	--	--	--
	--	--	--	--	--	--
Lebanon	1962	1,361	--	11,265	--	517
	1964	1,336	--	17,352	20	761
Libya	1960	--	--	742	--	55
	1965	198	--	1,936	--	120
Morocco	1960	140	11	4,665	14	40
	1964	451	9	10,136	14	78
Saudi Arabia	1960	56	--	343	--	5
	1964	175	--	1,568	--	24
Sudan	1960	513	--	3,974	5	34
	1965	737	--	7,701	--	57
Syria	1960	--	--	14,370	17	315
	1965	839	--	31,993	--	604
Tunisia	1960	--	--	2,782	--	66
	1964	156	--	4,629	19	101
U.A.R. (Egypt)	1960	4,251	14	106,780	17	413
	1964	10,406	--	144,496	20	500
Yemen	--	--	--	--	--	--
	--	--	--	--	--	--

Source: UNESCO, Statistical Yearbook, 1966 (Paris: UNESCO, 1968), Table 2.10, pp. 155-69 (A few qualifying footnotes which appear in the original source are omitted here.)

pronounced at the college and university level. Table 4 gives the number of teachers and students at this level in eleven Arab states and also the number of college students per 100,000 inhabitants. As the data show, the Arab world has witnessed a considerable expansion of education at this level in the recent past. Although the increase in the college student population over the five-year period 1960–65 is not as phenomenal as the increase in student enrollment at the primary level for this period, it is nevertheless proportionately greater than the increase in the general population. This is confirmed by the figures pertaining to the number of students per 100,000 inhabitants. This number increased in all of the Arab states except Algeria, where the college student enrollment declined from 7,248 in 1960 to 5,926 in 1964. This was mainly due to the withdrawal of many French nationals from the University of Algiers, following Algerian independence in 1962. Correspondingly, the number of students per 100,000 inhabitants declined from 67 shortly before independence to 54 shortly after independence. Following this critical period, however, college enrollment in Algeria grew to 9,700 in 1967–68.

As the data in Table 4 suggest, there seems to be an acute shortage of qualified professors. The expansion of this element in the college community has not paralleled the increase in the number of students. Indeed, many educators in the Arab world consider the shortage of professors to be one of the most serious problems facing higher education.

There are at least two aspects to the regional disparities in higher education in the Arab world. First, there are wide variations in the number of college students per capita in the different Arab countries (see Table 4). Higher education is most readily available in Lebanon, where there were 761 students for every 100,000 inhabitants in 1964, and to a lesser degree in Syria (604 per 100,000), the U.A.R. (500 per 100,000), and Iraq (352 per 100,000). The remainder of the Arab states had a student ratio ranging from 24 per 100,000 inhabitants in Saudi Arabia to 120 per 100,000 in Libya. Although the above ratios do not take into account Arabs studying abroad or foreigners studying in the Arab world, they seem to be a fair reflection of the availability of higher education in the area. Assuming their validity, these ratios strongly indicate the elitist nature of higher education in the Arab world. By contrast, in North America the number of students per 100,000 inhabitants is several times greater than that in Lebanon—the most advantaged country in the Arab world.

The second aspect of disparity in the educational systems of Arab states relates to the quality of higher education. It is probably safe to assume that financial resources affect the quality of higher education with respect to staff hiring, physical facilities, and equipment. Also, professors are less likely to moonlight when they are receiving good pay and fringe benefits and therefore are likely to direct more of their time and energy to university tasks.

Table 5 lists the twenty-seven principal four-year colleges and universities in the Arab world and the total annual expenditures of each of these institutions. It should be noted that the figures in Table 4 include non-degree-granting institutions of higher learning, while Table 5 is limited to principal degree-granting institutions. Further, Table 4 is based on data gathered in 1964 or, at the latest, 1965, whereas Table 5 is based on data gathered during the 1967–68 academic year. During the short period between 1964 and 1968, four institutions of higher learning were established. In combination, these factors largely account for discrepancies between the two tables.

Considering only those institutions established prior to 1960 (to avoid the complex budgetary factors in newly founded institutions), the annual expenditures per student ranged from a low of $145 at Damascus University to a high of $3,582 at the American University of Beirut. Most of the other institutions expended between $300 and $500 per student annually. The total expenditures per student show that there is a great difference between American institutions and others in the area. The high quality of education at the American University of Beirut is frequently noted.

Differences in the quality of education among the national universities are difficult to determine for several reasons. First, lacking an itemized budget for each institution, it may be risky to rank them according to quality of education on the basis of slight differences in annual expenditures per student. Second, by American standards all of the institutions under consideration appear to be financially rather poor; accordingly, evaluation becomes more difficult without proper measurement and quantification of relevant variables. Third, there are money-saving policies which must be taken into account in order to interpret differences in institutional budgets more adequately. For example, Damascus University accepts "external" students, that is, students who may register without having to attend classes regularly. At the end of the year, such students may take final examinations and eventually may receive degrees. This system is not as taxing on the institutional budget as one in which students are expected to attend classes regularly. For this reason, it may be unwise to prejudge the quality of education at Damascus University relative to other national institutions on the basis of its low annual expenditure per student.

Some of the recently founded institutions, such as the University of

TABLE 5.
PRINCIPAL FOUR-YEAR COLLEGES AND UNIVERSITIES IN THE ARAB WORLD, 1967-68

National Universities	Year of Founding	Student Enrollment Male	Female	Total	Budget
U.A.R. (Egypt)					
1. Cairo University	1908			57,450	$17,800,000
2. Alexandria University	1942			37,700	11,000,000
3. Ain Shams University	1950			31,250	9,100,000
4. Assiut University	1957			7,350	4,600,000
LEBANON					
5. Lebanese University	1953	6,850	1,160	8,010	2,000,000
SYRIA					
6. Aleppo University	1937			4,350	1,000,000
7. Damascus University	1924			27,400	4,000,000
JORDAN					
8. University of Jordan	1962	1,660	540	2,200	3,400,000
IRAQ					
9. Baghdad University	1958	17,950	6,100	24,050	15,600,000
10. Mosul University	1967	1,000	250	1,250	3,100,000
11. Basra University	1967	650	150	800	2,000,000
KUWAIT					
12. University of Kuwait	1966	470	420	890	5,800,000
SAUDI ARABIA					
13. Riyadh University	1957	1,470	110	1,580	850,000
SUDAN					
14. University of Khartoum	1956	3,000	300	3,300	--
LIBYA					
15. University of Libya	1956	1,800	200	2,000	--

TABLE 5. (Cont'd)
PRINCIPAL FOUR-YEAR COLLEGES AND UNIVERSITIES IN THE ARAB WORLD, 1967-68

National Universities	Year of Founding	STUDENT ENROLLMENT Male	Female	Total	Budget
TUNISIA					
16. University of Tunis	1960	--	--	8,500	--
ALGERIA					
17. University of Algiers	1909	--	--	9,700	--
MOROCCO					
18. Mohammed V. University	1959	5,640	980	6,620	--
Private or Foreign Institutions					
U.A.R.					
19. Al-Azhar University	970	16,000	1,400	17,400	$5,400,000
20. American University of Cairo	1919	--	--	750	--
SUDAN					
21. University of Cairo (Khartoum Branch)	1955	3,000	300	3,300	--
SAUDI ARABIA					
22. King Abd al-Aziz University	1967	70	30	100	950,000
LEBANON					
23. American University of Beirut	1866	2,450	900	3,350	12,000,000
24. St. Joseph University	1881	--	--	2,800	--
25. Arab University of Beirut	1960	--	--	1,600	--
26. Beirut College for Women	1924	--	610	610	650,000
27. Haigazian College	1955	--	--	350	165,000

Source: Daniel da Cruz, "The New Breed," ARAMCO World Magazine, XX (November-December, 1969), 32.

Kuwait and to a lesser degree the University of Jordan, may be able to maintain superior budgets and thus distinguish themselves as high quality institutions. However, it is still too early to make sound predictions.

The low budgets of Arab universities and the high regard for traditional European education have combined to create a situation in which the needs of technological development are not being met. An overabundance of students are enrolled in law, humanities, and the arts with relatively few students in engineering and the physical sciences. This is due in part to the fact that, faced with increasing numbers of students, it is more economically feasible to expand a college of law than to expand and equip an institution specializing in the physical sciences.

One of the consequences of this heavy emphasis on law, humanities, and the arts is that university graduates have difficulty finding employment. If they do find work, it is likely to be in the overcrowded government bureaucracy. The lack of long-range planning to direct students into fields where there will be jobs available undermines the national welfare. In addition, these university graduates with "unmarketable" skills can compare themselves with the older generation of university graduates, whose education took them far. The sharp contrast between the fortunes of the two groups can only contribute to the number of restless and unhappy citizens.

Education of Women

In the Arab world the proportion of students who are female, even at the primary level, is far below their proportion in the general population. In the mid-1960s Kuwait and Lebanon and, to a lesser degree, Jordan and the U.A.R. came close to having an egalitarian system of education. In the remaining Arab countries the number of females at the primary level ranged from about one-third of the total enrollment at that level (in Syria and Tunisia) to a low of one-twentieth (in Yemen). In virtually all of the Arab countries the number of females at the primary level has been increasing, but, as the data in Table 2 show, this number is not yet proportionate to the number of females in the population.

Where the education of females has existed, it has traditionally been separate from that of males. Such separation increases the cost of education. By moving toward coeducation, Arab countries not only should reduce the per unit cost of education but at the same time may improve schooling in rural areas. As was mentioned earlier, the inability of some areas to support their own schools tends to restrict the educational opportunities of rural children. With increased emphasis on coeducational facilities, many areas will be able to boast a large enough number of children to warrant local schools with several grades. This should help to lower the drop-out rate among rural youth.

Table 4 indicates that the number of females enrolled in universities is much smaller than the number of males. Female student enrollment at the university level is approximately one-fifth of the total. Again, this is clear evidence of the restrictions on the educational development of Arab women. A comparison of the data in Tables 4 and 5 indicates that, while the number of Arab women in colleges and universities increased between 1964 and 1967, particularly in Kuwait, Jordan, and Iraq, this increase did not substantially improve their limited chances for higher education. Only the University of Kuwait had close to a 50-50 sex ratio, and this may be less an indication of equality than of pressure on Kuwaiti women to receive their education close to home and the tendency for males to go abroad for further training.

Those countries seeking modernization at least pay lip-service to the goal of equal educational opportunities for women. Using Western experience as a guide, equality in education together with smaller family size and lengthened life expectancy may give rise to the kinds of issues regarding role definition which are facing women in the West today. Considering the slow expansion of the economic base in most of the Arab countries and the current problems in absorbing all of the potential workers, a large-scale increase in the number of women seeking employment could result in further discontent in the Arab world.

Structural Consequences of Educational Development

Educational development represents a major structural change in society. While it is a product of a multiplicity of internal and external conditions, it, too, acts as an independent variable and a prime mover in furthering change and development. In this connection, it is important to note that educational development tends to influence some of the very conditions which stimulated it in the first place, though it is extremely difficult to single out its structural effects in precise terms. This section will focus on selected aspects of structural and institutional change for which educational development appears to be a major prerequisite.

Perhaps the most important consequence of the Arab educational renaissance is the change that has occurred in the structure of society. Empirical evidence of this change in the social structure is surprisingly limited, a fact that places corresponding limits on the present discussion.

Although economic development has not kept up with Arab aspirations, recent changes appear to have effected changes in the occupational structure. There is increasing demand at the present time for professional and technical personnel, as well as for skilled labor. Relevant to this, the educational institution serves two important functions. First, by responding to the demands of industrial development it contributes to the development of native talent. Second, it equips students with the resources necessary for upward social mobility. In combination, these two functions influence the structure of society by contributing to the expansion of the middle classes and upgrading the labor force.

In an essay on the Arab middle class, Morroe Berger indicates that, on the basis of the 1947 census, the Egyptian middle class constituted about 6 per cent (definitely no more than 10 per cent) of the entire labor force.[8] The middle class, which was the most literate group in the population, clearly was numerically weak in 1947. Unfortunately, we do not have comparable information on the size of this class in more recent years.

A 1960 survey made in Amman, Jordan, shows that the middle class (including professional, administrative, clerical, and sales workers) accounted for 29 per cent of the labor force in that city.[9] Fuad Khuri, in his study of the class structure in "Cedarstown," a Lebanese community of growing economic differentiation, identifies four social classes: a class at each extreme of the social spectrum and two in the middle. The two middle classes—the affluent middle class and the honorable poor—accounted for 70 per cent of the families in "Cedarstown," the size of the former social class (48 per cent) being considerably larger than that of the latter (22 per cent). Members of the affluent class included "wealthy landowners and merchants, university graduates and the professional class of medical doctors, engineers and lawyers."[10] Members of the lower middle class, on the other hand, included "small landowners and shopkeepers, teachers, technicians, tradesmen and those who earn their living independently by owning and managing their own capital resources. They also include minor clerks,

8. Morroe Berger, "The Middle Class in the Arab World," in *The Middle East in Transition,* ed. Walter Z. Laquer (New York: Praeger, 1958), pp. 61–71.

9. Faud I. Khuri, "The Changing Class Structure in Lebanon," *Middle East Journal,* XXIII, no. 1 (January, 1969), 29–44.

10. *Ibid.,* p. 37.

secretaries, and ordinary soldiers."[11] Significantly, most of the men who belong to the affluent class achieved their status through education; and "their emphasis on achievement makes them receptive to modernization more than any other class."[12]

The above evidence is cited for illustrative purposes rather than for making broad generalizations about the urban middle class in Arab cities. While there may be some controversy over the size, nature, and economic role of the Arab middle class,[13] we may tentatively conclude that there is a large urban middle class in certain parts of the Arab world. This class could not have reached its present size without appropriate educational advantages.

Educational development, coupled with an expanding middle class, tends to stimulate social and geographical mobility. A survey in Lebanon in 1968 revealed fairly high mobility aspirations among Arab youth, about two-thirds of whom planned to go to college.[14] This has added importance in view of the fact that some particularistic criteria are still used in occupational placement and promotion in Lebanon, as elsewhere in the Arab world. However, there is strong evidence to suggest that emphasis is being placed increasingly on educational qualifications and other universalistic criteria as a basis for occupational placement and advancement. If such were not the case, there would be no purpose in having a modern educational system. The same survey shows that a substantial number of youth (about four out of ten) were prepared to change residence and disengage themselves from the local setting. Although the referent to geographical mobility in the survey involved a choice between going away to college and attending college in one's home town, the results nevertheless suggest a modernistic orientation on the part of Arab youth.

High social and geographic mobility rates can have a disintegrative effect on the extended family. William Goode, for example, notes that rural-urban migrants feel somewhat alienated from the village family, and individual concerns tend to overshadow feelings of obligation to kin. Recent

11. *Ibid.*
12. *Ibid.*
13. See Amos Perlmutter, "Egypt and the Myth of the New Middle Class: A Comparative Analysis," *Comparative Studies in Society and History,* 1967, pp. 46–65; Manfred Halpern, *The Politics of Social Change in the Middle East and North Africa* (Princeton: Princeton Univ. Press, 1963); and *idem,* "Egypt and the New Middle Class: Reaffirmation and New Explorations," *Comparative Studies in Society and History,* 1969, pp. 97–108.
14. William J. Goode, *World Revolution and Family Patterns* (New York: Free Press, 1963).

community research evidence shows that the combined effect of educational and occupational opportunity has been to weaken the traditional hold of the Arab family on its members.[14] Manifestations of this decline in traditional orientation toward the family have appeared in many forms and contexts. Judging from the leading part the Arab middle class has played in the emancipation of women, the expansion of this class may have implications for the role of women in the family. The middle classes were the first to send their daughters on for higher education and out into the labor force.[15]

In the economic sphere there has been a noticeable increase in independence from the family. This has been facilitated by expansion of economic opportunities as well as by an institutional trend toward contractual-and-specific economic relationships. The political implications of this state of affairs are summarized in the comments of three leaders from Sidon, Lebanon:

> 1. About fifteen years ago, the family (including the extended kinship group) provided the basis for political orientations and action. Following World War II, however, new elements have emerged, and political leadership today is based on people's support rather than family or traditional considerations.
> 2. Increasing economic independence from the family makes it possible to take a different or opposite stand from that held by family "notables."
> 3. Political orientations used to be based on acceptance of a traditional leader or family notable. At present political orientations are based on an ideological commitment to socialism.[16]

The above observations concerning heightened political independence from the extended family represent only one dimension of political change. Available evidence indicates that formal education is a decisive factor in political socialization and mobilization.[17] Almost invariably educational development and its usual concomitants, namely, urbanization and industrialization, tend to cast a new political role for the urban workers and middle-class segments of the population. Grass roots participation becomes more of a reality, and traditional bonds of political integration tend to give way to "modern" orientations and attitudes. Enhanced political involvement tends, on the one hand, to cause the political elite to respond to the

15. Morroe Berger, *The Arab World Today* (Garden City, N.Y.: Doubleday, 1962).
16. Baha Abu-Laban, "Social Change and Local Politics in Sidon, Lebanon." *Journal of Developing Areas,* 1970, pp. 27–42.
17. Coleman, *Education and Political Development,* pp. 18–25.

demands of the growing mass of enfranchised citizens and, on the other hand, to divide political orientations along class lines.[18]

To summarize, educational development is apparently an important factor in the expansion of the middle class and in the development of "middle-class values." There is general agreement that members of the middle class, particularly the educated, are important agents of modernization in the Arab world.[19] One important aspect of modernization involves a shift from traditional relationships to modern, or segmented, relationships. Influenced by educational development and other factors, this shift, which is far from being complete, characterizes many institutional areas including family, economy, and polity.

Conclusion

The progress of education in the Arab world is characterized by unevenness. There are disparities among countries in educational development, and there are rural-urban, male-female, and class differences in access to education. Such disparities are not uncommon in other parts of the world, but they are not as pronounced in Western societies. For the Arab world the challenge is to use and extend a developed system of education—primarily a Western system—and, at the same time, to integrate it into a non-Western culture. Without such integration, advancement may be misdirected.

Obviously the road to modernity will be different for the Arab world than it was for Western countries. There are cultural and historical differences, and there exists the opportunity to analyze and learn from the errors of others. A sound, well-developed educational program in the Arab world, *for* the Arab world, may be distinctly different from programs existing in the West today.

18. See Bert F. Hoselitz, *Sociological Aspects of Economic Growth* (New York: Free Press, 1960); and Max F. Millikan and L. M. Blackmer, eds., *The Emerging Nations: Their Growth and United States Policy* (Boston: M.I.T. Univ. Press, 1961).

19. See Berger, "Middle Class"; Halpern, *Politics of Social Change;* and Leonard Binder, ed., *Politics in Lebanon* (New York: Wiley, 1966).

The Development of Nationalism in Syria

C. Ernest Dawn

PERHAPS THE MOST ENDURING LEGACY of the French Revolution is the belief that political and ideological changes are the results of changes in the structure of society. This favorite tool of nineteenth-century European political polemicists, taken up by Western scholars by the beginning of the twentieth century, has become a commonplace of modern world thought. Thus, the earliest Western writers on Arab nationalism explained the phenomenon as the political movement of the emergent Arab middle class. This conception still dominates the literature on this subject, but each generation of observers dates the emergence of the new middle class somewhat later than its predecessor did. More recently, however, Western and Arab analysts are beginning to postulate the emergence of the masses—the working class and the peasants—as the effective instrument of the contemporary political process in the Arab world. What follows is a dissent from the prevailing view, and I offer it with caution. To analyze the structural or class qualities of a political movement or group requires knowledge of the individuals who are its components. Such biographical data is difficult to find. The dreadful state of existing biographical dictionaries is well known, and even personal observation is unreliable.

The Conversion to Arab Nationalism

The first great political change in the modern history of the Arab world was the replacement of Ottomanism by Arabism. The Arab movement began at the turn of the century, had visible and vocal adherents by 1914, and dominated Arab political life after 1918. In Syria, the Arab nationalists were a small minority before 1914. Their social characteristics were not substantially different from those of their opponents, who were loyal Otto-manists. Arabists and Ottomanists both were members of the upper class. But by 1918, men who had been loyal Ottomanists before and during World War I had become Arab nationalists. The converts—for example, Hashim al-Atasi—gained control of the Syrian Constituent Assembly and the Arab political societies and dominated Syrian politics and government to the end of the 1940s, even to the beginning of the 1960s. The prewar nationalists took a back seat. Although this was partly due to their losses at the hands of Turkish executioners, the main reason was their former oppo-nents' ability to form an all-powerful coalition. Arabism thus did not become dominant in Syria through the political victory of the original Arab nationalists but when the dominant party of Syrian Ottomanists adopted it as their ideology in 1918. The reason for the conversion seems clear. The Arab Revolt, the alliance between Arabism and the Entente powers, and the Ottoman military defeat left the Syrian Ottomanists with no alternative to Arabism except regional patriotism.[1]

This was a case in which people who were essentially the same were fighting over ideology or social identification, that is, over the relative mer-its of Arabism and Ottomanism. Some of the early Arabists appear to have been poor relations of eminent men, members of the lesser branches of great families. Other early Arabists belonged to families that had seen better days. One need not be a cynic to believe that 'Abd al-Rahman al-Kawaki-bi's career was strongly influenced by the declining fortunes of the Kawaki-bis in their long struggle with the Jabiris and Qudsis for pre-eminence among the *ashraf* of Aleppo. Another factor sometimes at work was a cul-tural-occupational one. Graduates of *madrasahs* were slightly more likely to be Arab nationalists than were those with degrees in law or engineering from the Ottoman state schools or from foreign universities. But even these sociocultural distinctions cannot be discerned in most cases. Arabists and Ottomanists alike possessed influence and income as well as high social status. In most cases, ideological division seems to have been a concomitant of the quest for office, as, for example, in the case of the Ottomanist Atasis and the Arabist Jundis in Homs.

---

1. C. Ernest Dawn, "The Rise of Arabism in Syria," *Middle East Journal,* XVI (1962), 145–68. This study compares the social characteristics of the various Syrian parties and organizations up to 1920.

The newly converted Arab nationalists dominated political life in Syria until 1949. They all agreed on expulsion of the French and also on excluding the pre-1914 Arab nationalists, who, with a few important exceptions, remained in the political wilderness. But endemic factionalism kept political life highly fluid, with only brief spells of collaboration brought about by such gifted leaders as Hashim al-Atasi, Jamil Mardam, Faris al-Khuri, Sa 'dullah al-Jabiri, and Shukri al-Quwatli. Political contests had little ideological content. The antagonists vied only in attempting to paint each other as more closely tied to the French and as more skilled in the practice of corruption.

New terms and concepts were infused into Syrian political culture by the mid-1930s. In the early 1930s a young lawyer, Sabri al-'Asali, returned from his studies in Paris to enter political life. 'Asali was from a prominent Damascene family which had attained high position under the Ottomans. The 'Asalis had converted to Arabism well before 1914, and like most early Arabists had been excluded from power after 1918. 'Asali founded the League of National Action in 1933, which, following the most ancient and persistent tradition, was designed to mobilize the educated youth in the *jihad* to save a decadent and corrupt society from itself. 'Asali was up-to-date; twentieth-century ideology was especially evident in the league's concentration of its fire on "imperialism."[2]

The mid-1930s also saw the growth of the Syrian National Party (subsequently the Syrian Social Nationalist Party), one of the first important ideological parties in the Arab world, and the beginnings of a local Syrian Communist party. This movement continued into the early 1940s with the Arab Renaissance, or Ba'ath party. By 1945 almost all politicians, except some of the tribal deputies, were talking about social reform and revival and imperialism. But the pioneers in introducing twentieth-century sociopolitical concepts were men like 'Asali.

Political Development in Hama

Members of the upper echelon of the political classes had begun to use the new political vocabulary in provincial politics well before the League of

2. Syria, al-'Asabah al-'Amal al-Qawmi [The League of National Action], *Bayan al-mu'tamar al-ta'sisi . . . a-mun'aqid fi Qarnayil fi 24 Āb 1933 [Declaration of the constituent convention . . . held at Qarnayil, August 24, 1933];* al-Nahar (Beirut), December 17, 1936; and *Man huwa fi-Suriyah [Who's Who in Syria],* (Damascus: Maktab al-Dirasah al-Suriyah wa al-'Arabiyah, 1951), s.v. "Sabri al-'Asali."

National Action employed it on a national scale. This was notable in the province of Hama. In 1918 the three dominant leaders in the province were Najib al-Barazi, Husni al-Barazi, and 'Abd al-Qadir al-Kilani, representing two of the three most important families in the district. All three spent the 1920s engaged in anti-French activity. Nawras al-Kilani, a mufti who had advanced under the French to become governor, was forced to retire after the Syrian rebellion of 1925–26. Najib and Husni al-Barazi and 'Abd al-Qadir al-Kilani represented the province in the national government after 1928. Nawras al-Kilani did not withdraw permanently, however. In 1926 he became active in organizing the artisans and craftsmen of Hama into syndicates. He was assisted by Tawfiq and Ibrahim al-Shishakli, members of a landowning family of second rank, and various members of the Barudi and Barazi clans. Also among his associates were 'Abd al-Hamid Qunbaz, a pharmacist, Ra'if al-Mulqi, a lawyer, and Mustafa al-Hawrani, a civil servant. The Hawranis, although not a landowning family, were almost as important in the area as the Shishakli family. Using the support of such lesser notables, and relying upon the votes of the workers' syndicates, Nawras al-Kilani re-entered the lists against Husni al-Barazi. Kilani and his associates presented themselves as the representatives of the educated nationalist youth and attacked their opponents as uneducated and reactionary landowners.[3]

Nawras al-Kilani gained no political advantage from his activities. His principal protégé, Tawfiq al-Shishakli, accepted a place on the National Bloc list with Najib al-Barazi, and both were elected to the parliament in 1931. From then on, Tawfiq al-Shishakli and Najib and Husni al-Barazi dominated the politics of Hama. Ra'if al-Mulqi and Mustafa al-Hawrani also deserted Kilani and attempted to displace 'Abd al-Hamid Qunbaz as head of the federation of workers' syndicates. By the elections of 1943, Tawfiq al-Shishakli had been replaced by Ra'if al-Mulqi and Akram al-Hawrani, who joined the National Bloc list with Najib al-Barazi. Another member of the list was Ghalib al-'Azm, who had cooperated with 'Asali in forming the League of National Action in 1933. Perhaps 'Azm was friendly with Mulqi and Hawrani on ideological grounds; in any event, the Shara-

---

3. Jean Gaulmier, "Notes sur le mouvement syndicaliste à Hama," *Revue des Études Islamiques,* 1932, pp. 99–105, 118; *Man huwa,* s.v. "Husni al-Barazi," "Najib al-Barazi," "Fakhri al-Kilani," "Khadr al-Shishakli," "Fawzi al-Barazi," "Mahmud al-Barazi," "'Uthman al-Hawrani," "Mustafa al-Hawrani"; *Oriente Moderno,* IV (1924), 36, 311, VI (1926), 283, 327, VII (1927), 221, 568, VIII (1928), 105, 106, 194, 196–97, XVI (1936), 128, XIX (1939), 588; and *Alif-Ba'* (Damascus), July 1, 3, 11, 1947, November 13, 1949, April 3, 1949.

batis of Hama, who had also been part of the League of National Action, were close to Mulqi and Hawrani. All four candidates won election to the parliament.[4] During its term (1943-47), Mulqi and Hawrani distinguished themselves as critics of the cabinets formed by the dominant coalition.

In the elections of 1947, competition among the notables of Hama was intense. Farid al-'Azm and Najib al-Barazi essentially followed an independent course. Mulqi and Hawrani quarreled over tactics. Khadr al-Shishakli, brother of Tawfiq, entered the lists on his own. The beneficiary of this competition was Muhammad al-Sarraj, a lawyer whose social position was remarkably similar to Akram al-Hawrani's. Sarraj, like Tawfiq al-Shishakli, had maintained a long and profitable association with the National Bloc while he distinguished himself in the radical tradition. He published, in French, a book on the necessity of land reform in Syria. He also became the leader of the workers' organization in Hama, where he cooperated with 'Abd al-Hamid Qunbaz, Nawras al-Kilani's protégé, whom Mulqi had displaced in the mid-1930s. When the elections were finally over, Mulqi and Barazi had been defeated; Sarraj and Hawrani had been elected.[5]

The great families of Hama did not repeat the mistakes of 1947 during the elections of 1949. Hawrani by this time had established friendly contacts with the Ba'ath. In Hama, Hawrani's Youth party entered a slate of four candidates, including Muhammad al-Sarraj. Hawrani's campaign speeches were filled with fierce attacks on "feudalism, tribalism, and familyism" and with peremptory demands for land reform. But the 'Azms and the Barazis put together a list which had the support of Khadr al-Shishakli and the *'ulama,* who in 1947 had won a seat with their own candidate. Of the Youth party candidates, only Hawrani was able to win. The other three seats went to the "feudalists."[6]

By the elections of 1949, the national army had become the arbiter of politics in Syria. Here the dissidents had another opportunity to achieve

4. Gaulmier, "Notes," pp. 118-19; *Oriente Moderno,* XI (1931), 229, XII (1932), 51, 54, 241, XIII (1933), 244, 623, 627, XIV (1934), 25, 378, XV (1935), 378, 451, XVI (1936), 60, 127-28, 218, 318, 610, 681, XVII (1937), 31, 179, 232, 295, 614, XVIII (1938), 15, 294, 427, 591, 604, XX (1940), 540; *Man huwa,* s.v. "Ghalib al-'Azm," "'Adnan al-Atasi," "Fikri al-Atasi," "Makram al-Atasi"; and *Alif-Ba';* June 12, 1947.

5. On the election campaign, see *Alif-Ba',* May 15, 27, 29, June 3, 4, 5, 6, 10, 12, 13, 18, 20, 22, July 1, 3, 9, 11, 12, 13, 19, 1947. On Sarraj, see *Alif-Ba',* July 3, 1947, April 3, 1949; and *Man huwa,* s.v. "Muhammad al-Sarraj."

6. *Alif-Ba',* September 24, October 7, 22, November 13, 16, 22, December 2, 1949.

what they had failed to do in the parliament. But, in fact, the entrance of the army made no essential difference. The social characteristics of the army officers who have dominated Syrian politics since 1949 do not differ in any major way from those of the parliamentarians who ruled before 1949. Adib al-Shishakli, the officer who was most outstanding in planning and leading the coups of 1949, was a native of Hama and a nephew of Husni al-Barazi. Furthermore, Shishakli was a cousin of a nephew of Akram al-Hawrani, who played a very important part in the army's political activities. From 1949 into the early 1960s, the officers who played the most important political roles had names such as Atasi, 'Azm, Husayni, Kilani, Qudsi, Nizam al-Din, Sarraj, and Maliki. At the same time, until the early 1960s, the army governments always included civilians who were in no important respect sociologically different from the parliamentarians of the old regime.

The Ba'athist Governments

Common opinion today is that the Ba'athist governments since 1963 are of a radically different order. However, among the founding fathers of the Ba'ath were an Atasi and a Bitar of Damascus; and one of the first two Ba'athists to win election in Syria (two deputies from Dayr al-Zawr in 1949) was Qasim al-Hunaydi, who had been elected twice before as deputy. Close analysis suggests that even the Ba'athists of 1963–67 have intimate connections with the men who ran the old Syria.

But there is a major difference. Except for Nur al-Din, Atasis have not been prominent since 1963, and the famous names from Damascus, Homs, Hama, and Aleppo are rarely borne by ministers, members of the party command apparatus, or the higher commanders in the armed forces. (One should point out, however, that a Kawakibi has reappeared in the cabinet.) At the same time, in the provinces the continuity is readily apparent. Miqdad, Mahamid, and Zu'bi still represent Hawran in both the army and the civilian authority as they did in the old days. In Lattakia the situation is mixed: Shuman, formerly connected with the National Bloc as a candidate for the parliament, appears among the Ba'athist ministers, but Harun and the other leading names from the parliamentary period are absent. On the other hand, the families of Al-Mir Mahmud, Ibrahim al-'Ali, and Tawil, who were active in politics with the National Bloc in the old days, have reached the highest level in the Ba'athist army. Among the Ismailis of Salamiyah, the Jundis are to be found at the top in both army and civilian apparatus, and the 'Ali family is represented in the upper civilian echelon. Both families were prominent in the parliamentary period, and their connections were with the National Bloc. From the Druzes, Shufi, Atrash, and 'Aysami are represented in the highest civilian echelon under the Ba'athists, while Hatum, 'Ubayd, and Abu-'Asali are among the top commanders in the army. All were politically powerful in the parliamentary period. Aleppo is represented in the top army command by Talas, whose connections were with the National Bloc.[7] People like those just described constitute two-thirds of the twenty or thirty people who dominated the Ba'ath in Syria in the years 1963–67. The actual percentage is probably greater still, for the Ba'athists comprise still others with familiar names; but this analysis includes only those individuals whose connections with the old regime can be established with a high degree of likelihood.

To summarize, the top national leadership of the parliamentary period, the famous Sunni names from the great cities, have disappeared from public life in the Ba'athist period. At the same time, families that were important on the local level in these cities in the old days and allied politically with the National Bloc have become very important, especially in the army. In the provinces, the Ba'athist period exhibits a great deal of continuity with the parliamentary era in both the military and the civilian elements of the regime. The Ba'ath revolution, then, may be another case of the rise of the provinces against the big towns, of "Middle Syria," so to speak, against the bourgeois elements of the metropolis.

7. The Ba'athist higher leadership during 1963–67 was officially secret, and little information is to be found in the Ba'athist press of the period, whether published in Syria or Lebanon, dissident or pro-regime. The information on the Ba'athist upper echelon comes from the established press of Beirut; see especially *al-Nahar,* May 12, August 6, 1963, December 11, 1964, December 23, 1965, September 7, 24, 1966; *al-Hayat,* October 31, 1963, December 10, 18, 1964, August 17, September 24, October 13, 1965, September 8, 1966; and *al-Jaridah,* February 24, 1966. For indications of Ba'athist connections with the parliamentary period, see *al-Nida'* (Beirut), November 26, December 29, 1931, July 7, September 9, December 17, 1932; *al-Nahar,* April 1, September 4, December 4, 1936; *Alif Ba',* April 10, 1947; and *al-Qabas* (Damascus), March 24, August 30, 1944, March 11, May 9, June 5, 8, 11, 17, 25, July 1, 3, 1947.

The Syrian
Social Nationalist Party

Sami G. Hajjar

THE ARAB AWAKENING and the rise of Arab nationalism can be traced back to World War I. The aim of Arab nationalism has been to reject a long history of foreign domination, first by the Turks and later by Western nations exercising mandatory powers over much of the Arab world. More recently, in an effort to confront Israel effectively, Arab nationalism has tended toward secularism and modernization. The emphasis on science and technology has become the dominant theme of all Arab intellectuals, particularly since the 1967 June War.

The major secular movements in the Arab world that have commanded wide popular support are the Arab nationalist movement, known also as Nasserism, and the Arab Ba'ath socialist party. An examination of both of these movements will show that both have leftist orientations and that ideologically there is very little difference between them. The Syrian Social Nationalist Party (SSNP), although not a major political force in the Arab world, is the only secular party with distinctly rightist leanings.

This paper will examine the SSNP's major ideological premises and its most recent tactics in an effort to determine whether the recent events have caused a transformation of the party's ideology and tactics. It is my contention that the ideology of the party has not changed since its inception in 1934, despite political events in the area since that time. It seems that these political events, particularly the 1967 June War, have enforced the party's ideology. The tactics of the SSNP, on the other hand, are experiencing a major but gradual transformation, notably since December, 1969, when the party's first general convention was held in Lebanon.[1] The newly emerging tactical postures of the party are aimed at giving it a leftist-democratic image, although the ideology remains rightist. For a rightist ideological party to be fundamentally maneuvering its tactics, adapting them to changing political circumstances, is a curious development; this phenomenon is usually associated with leftist ideological parties.

The Ideological Premises of the SSNP

The ideology of the SSNP was set forth by Antun K. Sa'adeh, a Lebanese who was, in the early 1930s, a professor of German at the American University in Beirut. Sa'adeh founded the party and served as its chief until his death in 1949. Sa'adeh and his followers consider the ideology of Syrian Social Nationalism to be an original one, following no particular school of thought nor patterned after the ideas of one political thinker. The arguments in support of the basic ideological points are not, they claim, based on one philosophy or another. Syrian nationalists insist that their ideology has evolved from the long history and culture of the Syrian nation and is dedicated to that nation's service. Sa'adeh's originality lies in his ability to adapt certain philosophies to his Syrian ideology. The political program which he proposed was the first systematic secular program to appear in the Arab world.

The ideology of the SSNP is composed of eight fundamental principles and five reformatory ones. The fundamental principles are:

1. Syria is for Syrians, who constitute a complete nation. Syrians have a right to sovereignty and the establishment of an independent state.
2. The Syrian national cause is an integral cause, distinct from and independent of any other cause. Non-Syrians have no right to interfere with the Syrians' realization of their ideals: freedom, duty, discipline, and power.
3. The Syrian cause is the cause of the Syrian nation and the Syrian homeland. Having lived in the same environment for such a long time, Syrians have common interests and aims.
4. The Syrian nation is the product of the ethnic unity of the Syrian

1. The SSNP was outlawed in Lebanon as in all other Arab countries. An official Lebanese relaxation trend toward the party was evident, beginning with the general amnesty granted its jailed leaders in 1968. Jumblat, the Lebanese minister of interior and socialist leader, granted legal recognition to the SSNP in August, 1970, along with the Ba'ath and Communist parties.

people, which has developed throughout history, going back to prehistoric times. The principle of Syrian nationhood is not based on race or blood but rather on the natural social unity of people who live together on the same land.

5. The Syrian homeland is the geographic environment in which the Syrian nation evolved. Its natural boundaries, which separate it from other nations, extend from the Taurus Range in the northwest and the Zagros Mountains in the northeast to the Suez Canal and the Red Sea in the south, including the Sinai Peninsula and the Gulf of Aqaba; from the Syrian Sea (Mediterranean) in the west, including the island of Cyprus, to the arch of the Arabian Desert and the Persian Gulf in the east. (This region is also called the Syrian Fertile Crescent, the island of Cyprus being its star.)

6. The Syrian nation is one indivisible society.

7. The Syrian Social Nationalist movement derives its inspiration from the genius of the Syrian nation and its national, cultural, and political history.

8. Syria's interest supersedes and is prior to every other interest.

The five reform principles, which are the immediate political goals of the party, are:

1. Religion and state must be separate. A politico-religious bond constitutes a serious threat to the existence of nations and their interests.

2. The clergy must be prevented from interfering in national political and judicial matters.

3. All barriers between religious sects must be removed.

4. Feudalism must be abolished, and the national economy organized on the basis of the principle of production, the protection of the right to work, and the interests of the nation and the state.

5. A strong army must be prepared and organized in order to determine the destiny of the country and the nation effectively.[2]

These principles are based on Sa'adeh's view that a true social being is not the individual but society, which is the most complete living entity. A society acquires its distinctive characteristics and peculiar identity from the geographic environment in which it exists. This view is the social truth from which Sa'adeh derives all his argumentations. Two concepts that he deduced from this truth, the concept of the new being and the concept of the new system or order, are the ideological themes which dominate his political thinking.

2. These principles are listed and explained in Antun Sa'adeh, *al-Muhadarat al-Ashr [The Ten Lectures]* (Beirut: Nassar, 1956).

The Concept of the New Being

Sa'adeh argues that the rise of national consciousness has directly affected the development of the concept of the new being. National consciousness, the most important phenomenon of modern times, came about through an evolutionary process. A major turn in the history of civilization occurred when the Sophists gave philosophy a new subject, man, as opposed to traditional concern with the universe. Protagoras led the way in focusing philosophical discussion on man and his nature. This new philosophical topic was discussed in the ancient Syrian civilization; questions pertaining to man's nature, his origin, and his destiny were raised, for example, in the laws of Hammurabi and the Gilgamesh Epic. Such questions were prerequisites to understanding the concept of society as a nation.[3] The idea of society as a being is as ancient as civilization itself; however, the determination of its identity is an intellectual problem that can be formulated only in advanced civilizations. The identity of a society is an organic unity comprising social, economic, and philosophical factors. Furthermore, a society exists within the triad of environment, body, and spirit, which are the characteristics of life.

The most general interpretation of the environment of man in the triad of life includes the entire planet Earth. A society exists in a specific geographic area where social interaction is possible. Society and land affect each other, and this relationship is what gives each society its distinctive characteristics. This is why, according to Sa'adeh, the inhabitants of Earth are grouped into several societies (nations), resulting from a long evolutionary process of history. As to whether the world will continue to be composed of several distinct societies or whether it will become one society, Sa'adeh's remark is "Who knows?"[4] For now, he argues, the existence of several distinct societies is a fact, and Syria is such a fact. Therefore, Syrian society is a distinguishable one existing within clearly defined geographic boundaries.

The second aspect of the triad of life—the body or matter in the composition of society—refers to the individuals who make up society and who are to be treated as one people with a distinct identity. According to Sa'adeh, "The individual does not choose the society of which he is a member, just

3. Sa'adeh refers to the Cananite Curse to illustrate that the ancient Syrian people were aware of their identity as a separate society. See Antun Sa'adeh, *Nushu' al-Uman [Growth of Nations]* (Damascus: Fatah al-Arab, 1951), pp. 178, 145–46. Syrian national consciousness, however, is a recent phenomenon.

4. See Sa'adeh, *Nushu' al-Uman,* p. 79.

as he does not choose his parents."[5] The members of a society are one people by virtue of the social interaction which the geographic environment
facilitates. Therefore Saʿadeh's notions of society and nation require a certain homogeneous area in which individuals interact, but his ideas do not
require a racially or ethnically homogeneous population.

Finally, the reference to spirit is to the product of the interaction between
people and land which gives a society its distinctive characteristics. These
characteristics are manifested in the pattern of social interaction, the economic system, and the psychological make-up of the people. Spirit, furthermore, becomes the object of national consciousness, the aim of which is to
resurrect the identity of a people as a natural social unity.

This view of life produces a concept of society as being highly integrated
and unified. Society is prior to the individual; the individual lacks a separate identity from the society of which he is a member. In other words,
society is the living person, and the individual is a cell in that person.[6] Society is the only complete and distinct being; the individual, although a vital
part in the continuing existence of that being, is not in himself the cause of
that being's existence. A society can continue to function without a particular individual or group of individuals, but the reverse is not true. The new
being is therefore the rebirth of the Syrian nation, which is the product of
the ethnic unity of the Syrian people as it has developed throughout history, the result of the interaction between the Syrian people living together
on the same land. For this new being Saʿadeh advocates a new system or
order based on a material-spiritual premise.[7]

The Concept of the New System

The material-spiritual premise of the new system, although borrowed
from the Greeks, particularly from Aristotle, is used by Saʿadeh in an original manner. In addition to the argument of the Greeks that a society
founded on the material-spiritual premise is destined to self-fulfillment and
ultimate happiness, Saʿadeh uses this premise to attack both capitalist and
Marxist economic doctrines as well as such movements as Arab and

5. *Ibid.*, p. 143. Society according to this description is not the product of a social
contract, that is, it is not willed, but is a natural phenomenon over which individuals
have no control.

6. See Saʿadeh, *al-Muhadarat al-Ashr*, pp. 142–46.

7. See Saʿadeh, *Nushuʾ al-Umam*, pp. 150–53.

Lebanese nationalism, which he considered to be based on purely religious premises.[8]

With respect to the material premise Sa'adeh argues that the present system in Syria appears to satisfy the material needs of only a few. The economic system is an archaic one, best described as feudal although feudalism has been abolished in all of the Syrian states.[9] The vast disparity between rich and poor is an obvious effect of the present economic system. The alternative, according to Sa'adeh, is to reorganize the national economy on the basis of production, which is "the only method by which a proper balance between the distribution of work and the distribution of wealth can be secured. Each member of the state ought to be productive in one way or another."[10]

The objective of this economic policy is to provide material and social security to each member of society. In elaborating the meaning of this policy, Sa'adeh begins with an attack on both capitalism and communism and proposes instead that capital be treated as the property of the nation. This does not mean that private ownership of capital is to be abolished, as the Communists advocate; individuals are to continue to own the capital but are to treat it as a trust. They do not have complete freedom to dispose of it as they see fit, as in capitalism. The state plays a major role in the control and direction of private capital, fostering as much as possible the creation of industrial executives who are primarily agents of the state. The state will also control labor. Sa'adeh is highly critical of labor unions, regarding them as a source of cleavage in society. Unions, he argues, often make unreasonable demands, not unlike the demands of a child. The total effect is competition among competing unions, acting intuitively for selfish interests, for a larger share in the national wealth. Unions are divisive, threaten the organic cohesiveness of society, and therefore must be abolished. Sa'adeh proposes instead a system of technical classification of production as the

---

8. In *Nushu' al-Uman,* Sa'adeh argues that the needs or interests of a society are three: (1) basic needs which are either biological (sex) or nonbiological (shelter and clothing); (2) moral (rational) needs which are either intellectual (science, philosophy, religion, and civics) or artistic; and (3) private needs which are material and financial honor and power. The highest form of private need is the political need, and the state is the institution of that need. However, in a letter addressed to party members dated January 15, 1947, Sa'adeh uses the term *madrahi,* or "material-spiritual interests," which each society seeks. This term presumably includes the three different needs mentioned above. See *Nushu' al-Umam,* pp. 152-53.

9. Sa'adeh, *al-Muhadarat al-Ashr,* p. 102.

10. *Ibid.,* p. 103.

proper basis for the distribution of wealth.[11] This proposition is ambiguous, to say the least, and neither Sa'adeh nor his followers have stated exactly what it means.

The spiritual premise is concerned with religion. Sa'adeh argues that religion is a manifestation of civilization and, in a sense, a measure of it.[12] Religion develops from witchcraft and ritualistic beliefs to a belief in one god, creator of man and all visible and invisible things. This notion of one omnipotent god "is an ancient Syrian notion, as are the notions of retribution and of life after death and the commandment to do good and shun evil."[13] The spread of Christianity and Islam in Syria resulted in the attempt to develop a theory of nationalism based on religious premises. To Sa'adeh such an attempt is based on a misinterpretation of the meaning of Christian and Islamic doctrines. After comparing numerous verses from the Bible with those from the Koran, he concludes that the essence of Christianity and the essence of Islam are fundamentally the same. Both religions (1) seek to create a belief in one god, (2) require good deeds and avoidance of evil, and (3) establish a belief in life after death and in divine retribution. They differ from each other in rituals and interpretation rather than in basic doctrine. Their differences can be attributed to the fact that the divine messages were delivered at different times to peoples with differing social and economic compositions. Since the purposes of both religions are the same, and since religion does not view life from a social-economic-civic point of view, Sa'adeh concludes that religion and politics must be separate.

The SSNP, Sa'adeh states, does not restrict the individual's freedom in his metaphysical beliefs; it is incapable of doing so. The new religion for the new system is the total ideology of the party. In Sa'adeh's words, "The world has witnessed in these lands of ours religions descending from Heaven to earth; but today it witnesses the rise of a new religion from earth, lifting spirits with a red thunderbolt to Heaven."[14] In other words, the sciences of sociology and politics cannot address themselves to metaphysical questions and should therefore be concerned only with social-economic-civic problems.

---

11. See *Ibid.*, pp. 101–15.
12. See Sa'adeh's discussion of religion and its relationship to civilization in *Nushu' al-Umam,* p. 90 ff.
13. Antun Sa'adeh, *al-Islam Fi Risalateih al-Massihieh wal-Muhammadieh [Islam in Its Two Messages, Christianity and Muhammadism]* (Beirut, 1958), pp. 168, 112.
14. Sa'adeh, *al-Muhadarat al-Ashr,* p. 100. The red thunderbolt is the party's symbol; its four edges symbolize duty, discipline, power, and freedom.

Judaism is excluded from Sa'adeh's notion of religion, and the Jews are likewise excluded from his concept of the Syrian nation. He writes:

> Every Syrian is a Muslim. . . . Islam has united us; some of us submit to God through the Bible, some through the Koran, and some through the Hikmat. . . . We have no enemy that fights us in our religion, in our rights, and in our homeland except the Jews.[15]

His argument against the Jews is twofold. First, Judaism is totemistic, or a theologically nondeveloped religious doctrine. Judaism teaches that Yahweh is the god, not of all people, but exclusively of the Jews, and that he will eventually assure their domination of the world. Central to the Jewish doctrine is the idea of a chosen people who have special preference in the eyes of God. Second, according to Sa'adeh the concept of the chosen people, which gave rise to the notion of a Jewish nation, has contributed to the Jews' clannishness. Throughout history they have never developed a sense of loyalty to any nation other than the Jewish nation. Consequently, Jews have persistently refused to interact with other peoples. Therefore, the exclusive nature of their religious doctrine and their clannishness, together with their demand for a national homeland in Syria, make the Jews the archenemy of Sa'adeh's ideology. In believing that they are a chosen people, they foster sectarian cleavages and threaten the integrative nature of the Syrian people; by demanding a homeland in Syria, they threaten the geographical unity of the Syrian nation. It should be noted that Sa'adeh makes no distinction between Judaism and Zionism. He merely states that Jews and Judaism are the main enemies of the Syrian nation and the Syrian people.[16]

Ideological Transformation

The ideology of the SSNP, unmistakably neofascist in character, is, furthermore, a manifestation of conditions peculiar to Syrian culture and development. As I stated earlier, this ideology has not changed since 1934. In 1970 the president of the party, Abdullah Sa'adeh (no relation to Antun

15. Antun Sa'adeh, *Marahel al-Mas'alat al-Filistinieh [Stages of the Palestinian Question]* (Beirut: Jihad, n.d.), p. 58. Hikmat is the book of the Druze, a Muslim sect.

16. See Sa'adeh's speech of March 1, 1949, in *Saadeh Fi Awal Athar [Saadeh in the First of March]* (Beirut: Lebanon Printings, 1956), pp. 97–103.

Sa'adeh), made a number of public statements regarding the ideological premises of the party. He maintained that the official party line remains faithful to the ideas of Antun Sa'adeh and that the view of man and of society continues to be exactly the same. He pointed out that, in principle, an ideological transformation is possible, for the founder taught that "principles are founded for life, not life for principles"; but he indicated that at present there is no need for any such change. The party's first convention, which had been held in 1969, recommended that the members seek to elaborate and explain the founder's theories, primarily the material-spiritual concept. The party appears to recognize a need for further study and elaboration of its ideology but not a need for change.

It is interesting to speculate why further study and explanation are called for rather than fundamental transformation. In my opinion, there are two possible reasons for this. First, the ideological premises are considered by the party leaders to be rational laws, the products of logic and science. The average Syrian individual has been unable to comprehend these laws, for traditional political institutions, systems, and ideologies have swayed him intellectually. The outcome of the 1967 June War resulted in widespread disenchantment with these traditional institutions and ideas, thus creating an intellectual vacuum. It is reasonable to assume that the SSNP leadership seeks to fill this vacuum by generating discussion and debate of its ideology and political program, presenting it as an alternative to traditional ideas and institutions.

Second, since the current Middle East crisis is one of national identity and competing demands for national rights, the ideology of the SSNP can be assumed to be more appealing than leftist ideologies, some of which tend to view the crisis in political terms. It can be further assumed that a discussion of the party's ideology would attract many of those on the left of the political spectrum by appealing to their national aspirations, which ruling leftist parties such as the Ba'ath have failed to satisfy. Indeed, the political atmosphere in the Arab world today is causing leftist parties to move to the right rather than causing rightist parties to move to the left. The events of October–November, 1970, in which a moderate faction of the Ba'ath party took control of the Syrian government from the leftist wing of the party, illustrate this point.

If both hypotheses are correct, then the SSNP leadership has been wise in resisting ideological transformation despite the temptation to do so. Recently the party's rhetoric has been used as a tactic to give the SSNP a new image.

The Party's Tactics

From its inception until 1969, the tactics of the SSNP could best be described as flamboyant and inflexible. The party continued to be highly critical of communism and communist countries, of all Arab leftist movements and regimes, and of Arab leaders such as the late President Nasser. In general its tactical attitude was negative. The organization of the party also remained bureaucratic, rigid, hierarchical, and highly centralized. Beginning in December, 1969, however, basic tactical transformations have become evident.

A careful examination of the statements of the party's president reveals a calculated attempt to accentuate the positive, and the following tactical points are especially emphasized.

1. *The Arabian character of the Syrian Social Nationalist movement.* Addressing the American University in Beirut in 1970, Abdullah Sa'adeh used the words of the party's founder: "Those who say the SSNP has advocated that Syria abandon the Arabian cause have committed a grave error." In the view of the SSNP, the Arab world is composed of four nations, each with distinct social, economic, and psychological characteristics. These four nations are the Maghreb (Arabic-speaking North Africa); the Nile Valley nation; the Arabian Peninsula nation; and, finally, the Syrian nation. The party now, more than ever before, seems to be emphasizing that the Syrian nation is an integral part of the Arab world rather than emphasizing the differences among these four Arab nations.

This point is carried a step further. In a press conference early in 1970 Abdullah Sa'adeh was asked what, in his opinion, was the proper means to insure Arab unity. He replied that the party is seeking to insure the unity of the Syrian states by removing the causes and conditions that continue to separate them into distinct political entities. This is not to be done through military conquest or through diplomatic and political arrangements. Syrian unity will emerge naturally and will be spontaneously demanded by the Syrian masses when old beliefs and old allegiances are abandoned in favor of the new ones offered by the party. Similarly, he argued, Arab unity will be possible only when the social-economic-psychological characteristics that distinguish the various Arab nations fade away. Only then will conditions be conducive to the creation of a meaningful Arab unity. The implication of this argument is that the SSNP is not struggling against Arab unity, but is proposing it on different grounds than the ones commonly held and the ones used to create the United Arab Republic. The SSNP grounds are scientific and rational rather than emotional.

2. *The revolutionary character of the SSNP.* The party is attempting to change its old image as a rightist party, aligned with the West and the agent of imperialism in the Arab world. By emphasizing that the SSNP is revolutionary, Abdullah Sa'adeh means that the party totally rejects the present political and economic systems of the various Syrian states and seeks to replace them with a new system by revolutionizing the concept of man and society. The party must therefore be characterized as leftist, he argues, insofar as it seeks to bring about drastic changes in man and society. He emphasizes, however, that the party is not to be considered leftist in the Marxist-Leninist sense; Marxist-Leninist ideology continues to be attacked by the SSNP.

The SSNP distinguishes between the Marxist ideology and the Communist states. Abdullah Sa'adeh praises these states, especially the Soviet Union, for having supported the Arab cause in its struggle against the Zionist state and calls for greater ties with socialist countries and all revolutionary movements in the world. In a speech delivered in a Beirut suburb on the occasion of May Day, 1970, he even advocated that the Lebanese government recognize the Lebanese Communist party. On the other hand, the SSNP, has taken an extreme position, more extreme than the official position of such Arab states as the United Arab Republic, regarding the Western nations, notably the United States and Great Britain, and has advocated severing all relations with these imperialist forces.

3. *Cooperation with other revolutionary parties and movements in the Arab world.* Abdullah Sa'adeh argues that, since the Israeli issue is the foremost concern of the Arab world—and especially of the Syrian nation—today, revolutionary parties and movements must put aside their differences and coordinate their efforts in combating the Israeli enemy. Special reference is made to the possibility of cooperation and positive exchange with the Ba'ath party. This tactic, it might be suggested, is calculated to gain permission from the ruling Ba'ath party to operate in Syria, where the party has some followers and where a number of its leaders, such as Isam Mahairi, are in jail.

4. *Total and unconditional support of the Palestinian Liberation Organization.* The SSNP has placed support of the PLO high on its list of priorities, calling on all members to actively support the organization in any way possible. It is interesting to note that the SSNP is critical of separate resistance movements and calls instead for a unified effort. Therefore, unlike the Communist and the Ba'ath parties, the SSNP has not sponsored a splinter resistance organization. This tactical measure is designed to win the favor of the PLO—especially Al-Fatah, which the party favors.

5. *The reorganization of the party.* The organizational principles of the party, which were formulated by Antun Sa'adeh, are highly centralized and hierarchial. During the lifetime of the founder, all legislative and executive powers were retained by him. At the top of the hierarchical pyramid is the supreme council, with final legislative and judicial authority. Membership in the council was, until 1970, restricted to the members of the board of trustees. The title of trustee was conferred by Sa'adeh to between seventy and seventy-five individuals who, he believed, were especially dedicated to the party and its ideology. The supreme council selects a man from the board of trustees to serve as party president for a period of two years. He, in turn, selects his aides—commissaries of interior, information, justice, military, and so on. The rank and file of the membership are then grouped according to professional occupation and/or place of residence. The largest such group is called *Munafizieh;* each *Munafizieh* is composed of a number of cells called either *Mudirieh* or *Mufawwadieh* depending on size, the *Mufawwadieh* being the smallest. All major party decisions come from the top, and the members are expected to carry them out first and question them later through the hierarchy. In short, the SSNP has been a paramilitary organization.

On the recommendation of the 1969 party convention, the supreme council amended the party's constitution on April 23, 1970, making the organization more democratic. Two major changes can be noted. First, the oath of allegiance to the chief, which was part of the official party oath, was replaced by an oath of allegiance to the constitutional authorities of the party. This change is to emphasize that party leadership is collective and is restricted by constitutional provisions. Second, a national council was created, to be composed of representatives of the party cells and the regional units, who will elect the supreme council. Any party member over twenty-five years of age who has been an active member for at least five years can become a candidate for the supreme council. This is a fundamental change from the old regulation, whereby only members of the board of trustees could become members of the supreme council. Obviously the change is an effort to give the general membership an effective role in choosing party leaders.

Conclusion

The SSNP's history and its failure to come to power in any of the Syrian states, its popular image as a rightist and conservative party, and recent political events in the area are some factors that have caused the leadership of the SSNP to undergo self-examination. The leadership continues to be faithful to the fundamental principles of Antun Sa'adeh but has embarked on a program designed to change the party's image.

Throughout its history, the SSNP has had only limited success in cooperating with other political parties in Syria and Lebanon. Its rightist ideology has isolated it from leftist groups; and its demand for a Greater Syria has likewise isolated it from rightist groups who resist the concept of Syrian or Arab unity. The tactical transformation, the purpose of which has been, in part, to bestow a leftist image on the party, will most likely bring the party closer to the large segment of the population with leftist leanings. It will also enable the SSNP to cooperate more meaningfully with leftist parties. The reorganization of the party's hierarchy along more democratic lines will avoid such experiences as those following the attempted *coup d'etat* in Lebanon on December 31, 1961, in which the leadership of the SSNP was severely criticized by the general membership and the very existence of the party was threatened. Both of these tactical transformations, according to the opinion of the leadership, will increase the party's popularity among the masses and, more importantly, will strengthen it internally.

It is difficult at this time to make any long-term predictions as to the future of the SSNP. One thing appears certain: the party has revived itself. It is safe to say that, in the short run, the SSNP is likely to increase its membership. Beyond this simple speculation, it is impossible to predict exactly how the tactical changes will affect the party unless future political events and circumstances can also be predicted.

The Arabs and the World

World Media and the Arabs: An Arab Perspective

Ahmad Baha el-Din

THE PHRASE "WORLD MEDIA" generally refers to the media of the Western world—specifically those of the United States and Western Europe. French and English are still the most widespread languages, and, if we except the U.S.S.R. and Japan, the United States and Europe represent the world's most industrially advanced areas. Therefore, American and European media have enormous impact on the media of underdeveloped countries. The intellectual hold that they exercise is similar to the political, economic, and military influence wielded by the United States and Western Europe on the rest of the world. And of course the superior quality of this media is part of the technical and material superiority of these countries.

Even those who most obstinately reject the political influence of the Western world cannot free themselves completely from the powerful grip of its media. The educated classes in the developing countries, who usually can read either French or English or who have graduated from Western universities, feel the need to keep in touch with the "advanced world," perhaps through *Newsweek* or the *Economist;* even those who only read the local papers—serviced by Western news agencies such as UP, AP, or AFP—also listen in to the programs of the BBC or the Voice of America or at least go to Western films.

According to Marshall McLuhan, Vance Packard, and others, media are very much liable to the danger that threatens all sciences—namely, the imbalance between technological advancement as a goal in itself and the content of this science and its use in the service of man.

Although the media that influences the intellects of men, their instincts, and their working life should have been impervious to the dangers of technical manipulation, which would make the content come second to the technological form, this is exactly what happened. "The hidden persuaders," in the selling of cigarettes and washing machines and the selling of presidents, too—with their "motivation analysts," their "depth probers," and their "symbol manipulators"—were applied to the sale of social, political, and religious beliefs.

When the Arabs were defeated in the 1967 June War, they were told by Western politicians and political commentators alike, both scoldingly and apologetically, "You see, Israel knows how to manipulate world opinion, and you don't." On the morning of June 5, when Israel announced that the Egyptian Army was attacking Israel, the Israeli Air Force had already destroyed the Egyptian Air Force on the ground, and not a single army unit had moved an inch. Yet for several days world public opinion held that Egypt had started the war. And, after the war was over, when Moshe Dayan declared that the question of who started it was merely a theoretical one, he was quite right. For the Western press and news agencies found nothing sensational in reversing what they had published earlier. The game was over; the first round had been won through the clever manipulation of world media, and only admiration was felt for the cunning player who had outwitted his opponent.

Again, when King Hussein's army surrounded the refugee camps in Amman, fired on the defenseless people inside, and killed and wounded thousands, the British *Daily Express* and *Daily Telegraph,* for example, published not a photograph of the massacre but one of Princess Muna and her children in London, closely guarded by an English policeman. The caption spoke of the English girl's anxiety—her worry about the young king living amid danger in Amman and her fear that the Palestinians would take revenge on her children. The magazine *Paris-Match* published two pages on the massacre in Amman, and further on, four pages of colored pictures of the young king and his pretty wife and children sitting in a well-kept beautiful garden with danger of chaos threatening to engulf them.

The "motivation analysts" decree that a touching story of the love of an English girl for an Arab king who marries her and makes her a princess sells more and is more appealing to the ordinary person than the story of a massacre, especially if the victims are unknown or are trouble-makers. One of the basic rules in the press is that stories about individuals sell much better than stories about groups of people and are a great success with readers of the popular dailies. One of the rooted beliefs of the popular press is "to make the important seem trifling and the trifling important."

There is undoubtedly a deep bias in the attitude of the Western media toward the Arab question, and it is important for us to understand its roots and what keeps it alive and flourishing. The easiest explanation is that Zionists control world media. This may in a sense be true, but it is one truth among many. Zionist propaganda was so devastatingly effective just because it had carefully and methodically studied its field of activity and addressed itself to beliefs deeply embedded in Western culture. These inherent beliefs are the ones that we must analyze and take into consideration.

Sources of Bias

The causes for the bias against Arabs which is prevalent in the Western media can generally be described under four headings: (1) bias which the Arab countries as underdeveloped countries share with others of the Third World; (2) bias which had its origins in the political clashes during the era of decolonization; (3) bias which stems from ideological differences; and (4) bias against the Arabs as such.

Bias toward underdeveloped countries is easy to understand. The underdeveloped nations are on the whole nothing but a headache to the ordinary citizen in an advanced society. His feelings may be likened to those of the owner of a beautiful house in an exclusive suburb who becomes threatened with the proximity of slum dwellers. His feelings may range from mere dislike—slum dwellers are "different," are obviously not a success, don't care to keep up appearances, are not very clean or even healthy, and are therefore responsible for their own plight—to more complicated feelings of resentment and guilt, combined with an uneasy sense of responsibility. All of this makes the suburban dweller unhappy and worried. This is especially true if he feels that their poverty is a reflection on his wealth; for then he feels that something must be done about it, as it is not possible to ignore their presence forever since they may affect his own life in the long run.

These feelings are, I believe, almost identical to those felt by people in advanced countries toward the people of underdeveloped countries. These underdeveloped countries are a constant source of trouble and worry. They fill the pages of Western papers with news of famine, disease, and civil war. They people the television screens with the hungry faces of Nigerian children or refugees in Jordan. Their ugly reality intrudes on Western man's gracious way of living and his television advertisements. They are also a constant source of amazement and puzzlement when they insist on bringing more and more children into the world or when they fight each other, as the Arabs have done, under the gleeful eyes of their common enemy.

These feelings become accentuated and turn into prejudice in the mind of Western man when he feels that he cannot ignore the existence of these people, for he is inextricably bound to them. He has to go to them for raw materials, he has to sell them his finished products, and he even invests his money in their lands. This leads his government to send fleets and aircraft to tour the Third World. Sometimes, to his horror, he even has to send his sons to fight in one or the other of these impossible places.

He will willingly concede, on the other hand, that there may be some aspects of beauty in the Third World. The tourist agencies do their best to promote them. The tombs of the Pharaohs in the Valley of the Kings, the ruins of Angkor in Cambodia, the African safaris, and the glittering shores of the Mediterranean are really "quite an experience"; but this romantic image of the Golden East, so quaintly described in the diaries of nineteenth-century travelers and so prettily depicted in the folders of tourist agencies, crumbles to dust under the pressure of the present-day problems of these countries. These backward nations are noisily awakening from their sleep and are quickly rejecting their romantic image. They want to become modern. Tourists in chartered planes—if they are not hijacked on the way—may find themselves trapped in a civil war. Instead of being met by a procession of elephants covered with gold braid and rubies, they are met by hordes of ragged people clamoring for bread. Lawrence's Arabia has disappeared and so has Hemingway's Kilimanjaro. Even Katmandu has expelled the hippies from its borders; in their place fighting, strife, and danger reign.

This image then is at the root of Western man's bias toward the Third World, which includes the Arab world. The image is not completely false, but it does make him receptive to his media when they want to tell him that these people are usually on the wrong side.

The ordinary man in the Western world finds it easy to understand and condone the long religious wars that devastated Europe for decades and to accept the European political and economic strife that plunged the world into two great wars; but he finds himself incapable of understanding a border fight between two Indian states, the survival of tribalism in Africa, or a disagreement between two Arab countries. He can believe that Nazism and gas chambers were just a passing blot in European history and civilization, but he is firmly convinced that any act of cruelty committed in an underdeveloped country is due to the nature of the people of that country, that they are "born with a cruel streak."

Political clashes during the era of decolonization—those between the West as a whole, particularly the developed countries, and the Third World—have been a second source of bias against the Arabs. For twenty-five years, since the end of World War II, the struggle for independence has been fiercely waged. Although the fight against colonization started centuries ago, the most dramatic changes have occurred in the years after World War II. The developed countries found that they had to give up—on political, economic, and military levels—India, China, and most of Asia and Africa. They found their armies being pushed out of Indochina, Indonesia, Algeria, and South Yemen. Even military expeditions sent to enforce the laws of the Western world either met with failure, like the Suez invasion, or were bogged down in an endless war, like the Americans in Viet Nam.

Some Western leaders went along with and accepted this process of decolonization as an essential part of history, and a section of Western media sympathized with the struggles for independence; but decolonization inevitably led to a profound split between the developed and the underdeveloped countries. Certain groups in the West could not resign themselves to the situation; full of anger, rage, and frustration, they yearned for their glorious colonial past. Even to the ordinary Western man the change was too quick and too violent. The spectacle of white soldiers dying at the hands of black people and brown people while representatives of these same people stood in the United Nations accusing the West of all sorts of crimes was sometimes difficult to swallow. The resulting bias of course included Arabs, for the Arabs played a prominent role in the process of decolonization.

It was easy then for Western man to believe the world media when they attributed a lack of wheat in India, for example, to that country's having sent away the British. "These Indians do not know how to run their own country." Even if this were true, it is the result of many reasons, among them definitely the three centuries of British rule.

But the political clash between developed and underdeveloped countries did not stop here. These newly independent countries, on their emergence, found themselves in the middle of a cold war between East and West. Their attempts to hang onto their newly won independence and their refusal to join one side or the other only led to further alienation of the Western mind.

What can be called an *ideological bias* is in a sense a development of the second source of bias. The world today is divided between two basic forms of society, each of which represents a certain set of values. The West stands for the multiparty system, individual freedom, and free enterprise. The East, whether it be the Soviet Union or China, stands for another set of values. But the underdeveloped countries of the Third World have refused, generally speaking, to stand for either one or the other of these sets of values. Therefore, whenever these countries are faced with a major problem, both the East and the West can say, "If they would only abide by our values, they would have no such problems."

It is, of course, only natural for Western man to feel that his system of government is the ideal one. It seems to him that the secret of his country's development lies in its superior form of government and institutions and that the Third World is always in such trouble and confusion because it refuses to apply this perfectly valid and proven system of government.

This attitude comes mainly from lack of knowledge of the facts and of the problems of these countries and also from an oversimplification of the situation. Western man is unaware that underdeveloped countries are not recently discovered "new worlds" with vast treasures, waiting to be transformed by science into model states. These countries sometimes include within their borders primitive societies starting from scratch, as in parts of Africa; they sometimes encompass ancient civilizations heavily burdened by long histories and traditions, which may at times be either an inspiration or a heavy burden. Western man is unaware that the values now prized so highly in the West were themselves challenged in Europe until very recently and that they did not come easily to maturity. Until World War I the predominant system of government in Europe was royal oligarchy; until World War II fascism was the predominant form of government in Germany, Italy, Spain, Portugal, Greece, Romania, and Hungary. And some of these aspects remain in Europe even today.

In 1870 Egypt had a strong beginning of political parties; it had a parliament, limited in its powers but with strong popular demands. It had a growing industrial movement and a trained generation of technicians and experts long before most European countries had anything similar. With the British occupation in 1882, which was part of the tide of European colonization of the world, these developments in Egypt were crushed and reversed.

This ideological difference, then, can be used by world media to stress the difference between the developed and the underdeveloped countries; it confirms in Western man the belief that people of the Third World do not want to learn and are on the wrong side.

The fourth source of bias is *bias against the Arabs as such*. Islam is a dominant factor in the cultural tradition of the Arab countries since most of the inhabitants are Muslim. This, of course, is not to deny the presence of millions of Christian Arabs, who have played an important role in preserving Arab culture and unity and have spiritually and actively led various movements calling for Arab unity and nationalism. Since Western culture, on the other hand, is basically Christian, with Judaism and the Old Testament included in its cultural heritage, it firmly excludes Islam.

Christianity has never felt threatened by any religion but Islam. For several hundred years Islam seemed intent on replacing it, gaining vast lands with millions of inhabitants, from China in the east, to Spain in the west, to the Balkans in the north. Christian civilization has recorded in detail the Crusades and welcomed with joy the return of Andalusia to the fold of Christianity and the national struggle against the Muslim Turks in the Balkans.

During the Algerian crisis, a French *pied noir* said: "Algeria is the Andalusia of Europe; losing it is the beginning of the end, just as Andalusia was for the Arabs." He was not predicting a historical event but was touching on a deep-rooted cultural gap shared by many Europeans.

Zionism, on the other hand, carefully considering the cultural roots of Christianity, tries hard to revive the common heritage of Judaism and Christianity—namely, the Old Testament. At the same time it attempts to wipe out the stigma of shedding Jesus Christ's blood that has been left on the Jews by the Christians. Apart from purely academic studies, Arabs have not drawn enough attention to the cultural and historical ties between Islam and Christianity. Too little attention has been paid to the heritage of western civilization preserved by Islam during the Middle Ages.

Political Biases

After listing these various sources of bias, we must notice that, for the mass media, political factors play the main role in presenting the Arab problem. The media generally show more sympathy and understanding to the traditional Arab regimes; an understanding is rarely extended to the so-called revolutionary Arab regimes, which are attempting to modernize their countries and catch up with world civilization. It suits the policy of Western nations better to deal with feudal rulers, who are in a sense more compliant and, having less popular support, have more need for the backing of foreign powers. In exchange, they can be trusted to look after Western interests—oil, military bases, or whatever.

When Western media attempt to evaluate various revolutionary or modernizing regimes in the Third World, they apparently never apply to them a purely academic test. Some rulers are approved and others are not, even if their systems of government are not much different. The criterion is commitment to imperialist interests.

Most of the nations of the Third World complain that their problems are misrepresented in world mass media; the Arabs, furthermore, have an enemy dedicated to the misrepresentation of the Arab problem and the disfiguration of the Arab image, an enemy with very strong influence over world media whether it be the press, the cinema, radio, or television. Israel and world Zionism do not choose their targets haphazardly but strike where they are certain to find a response, having carefully noted the cultural receptivities, prejudices, and complexes of both the Arabs and the Western world.

Israel has always identified itself with the West; it views itself as an advanced Western outpost in the heart of the Third World. From this vantage point it has branded as anti-West—meaning in a sense anticivilization—any position not to its advantage. Any triumph for Israel is quickly identified as a triumph for Western culture, civilization, and way of life. Israel has taken advantage of the notion prevalent in the West that the Third World is hopelessly underdeveloped to introduce itself as a nation of pioneers who have settled in a wasteland and, by performing agricultural miracles, have transformed it into green fields and gardens, and the Western mass media have relayed this image. The truth is that Israel occupies lands with ancient towns that have been inhabited for thousands of years and fields that have been sown and tilled for ages. Western media have failed to point out that the only agricultural miracle is the one performed by the Palestinians, who, having been expelled from their cultivated lands and thrown out into the desert, transformed the desert into groves of orange and olive trees without the help of millions of dollars in aid every year.

Israel also has taken advantage of the fact that the Arab countries, after centuries of political stagnation, are painfully creating national political and economic systems consistent with the modern world. Israel has used this situation to further increase the sense of alienation between the West and the Arabs and to point out its own complete identification with the West by presenting the Arab-Israeli problem as an Arab-West problem not only on the political level but on the cultural one as well.

Israel, being a small state composed mainly of immigrants and living off foreign aid and capital, finds it quite logical to be completely identified with a powerful foreign ally. The Arab world, with its size, wealth, and traditions, finds that it is its lawful right to have its independence, even if it must pay a heavy price for it. Therefore it is to Israel's advantage to create in the area a complete polarization between the Eastern and Western powers. In world opinion this will make Israel synonymous with the West, and the Israeli frontiers, extended by armed invasion, will be considered as sacred as the other frontiers of the cold war.

When Israeli Phantom jets continued month after month to bomb the Egyptian front and Egyptian villages, killing and wounding thousands, it was reported only in small print in the Western newspapers. But, when the Egyptian Air Defense brought down three Phantoms in one day, the world shook; world peace was at stake. Long articles and reports loudly and hysterically screamed at this new menace threatening Israel.

If Israel has professional supporters in the media, it also has the help of volunteers who, suffering from inherent biases, do their own little bit of harm. When I first visited the United States in 1960, I was interested in the literature of the Beat Generation and read *On the Road* by Jack Kerouac. I was struck by a sentence saying "We were like a band of Arabs coming to blow up New York" and another saying "Dean drove into a filling station . . . noticed that the attendant was fast asleep . . . quietly filled the gas tank and rolled off like an Arab." I thought then that Kerouac had probably never met an Arab in his life, and this image had been dragged up from the pit of his subconscious.

On my second visit to the U.S., I saw the film "Ben Hur," whose main point was that the Arab owns the horses but does not know how to train or control them and has to call on the Jew to show him how to train his horses and run his affairs. Lawrence Durrell, in his *Alexandria Quartet,* has built a plot around the Coptic minority in Egypt smuggling arms to the Zionists in Palestine. This idea is historically incorrect; not one incident of this nature has ever occurred.

A few weeks after the June War *Time* published a long article in which the defeat of the Arabs was explained in terms of the nature of Islam. The magazine failed to mention that Islam kept the torch of civilization burning in the Middle Ages. But in *My People* Abba Eban concedes this point to Islam; he admits that throughout its three thousand year history Jewish civilization never flourished so well as under Islamic rule in the eleventh and twelfth centuries, from Baghdad in the east to Andalusia in the west.

European Media and the Arabs

Michael Adams

WHAT PEOPLE SPEAK OF rather vaguely as the Middle East prob-
lem or, more specifically, as the Arab-Israeli conflict is essentially a dispute
between two rivals, each claiming rightful ownership of the land of Palestine. By stating the problem in these simple and straightforward terms, it
becomes much easier to understand, though not to solve. But it is very seldom presented in this way. Instead, and often deliberately, the fundamental
issue in the Middle East is clouded and confused by all kinds of largely
irrelevant side issues. The result, all too often, is that the world loses sight
of the main issue, and an enormous amount of time and energy is expended
in trying to resolve minor difficulties that would be of no importance if a
solution were found to the problem itself.

That this should happen is, of course, not accidental. If ordinary men
and women in every country were to realize that all the turmoil in the
Middle East is due to the fact that a small nation has been elbowed off its
land by aliens who came from overseas and imposed themselves by force,
there would, I feel sure, be a general feeling of antipathy toward the intruders. It is important to those who support the intruders to prevent the world
from seeing this. Consequently, they have used every effort to present the
world with a totally different explanation for the origins of the Middle East
problem. In doing so, with a skill that is as remarkable as their lack of
scruple, they have created and propagated a number of myths that have
gradually taken on the semblance of fact for much of the educated world.

There is, for instance, the myth that the Jews were the original inhabitants of Palestine, with its corollary that they had some ill-defined "right" to occupy the country in modern times, even though this occupation involved the dispossession or the subjection of the existing Arab population. There is the myth that Israel is a model of social democracy, where the members of other racial and religious communities enjoy equal rights with the Jewish inhabitants. There is the myth that any critic of Israel or of the Zionist philosophy is *ipso facto* anti-Semitic—and this is a particularly unjustifiable and dangerous myth. There is the myth that Palestine, before the invasion of the Zionists, was an empty and barren land.

None of these myths will stand up under close examination. The history of Palestine is reasonably well documented, and the story of the original Jewish invasion of what was then called Canaan is set out in grim detail in the one book that modern Zionists are not likely either to suppress or rewrite—namely, the Bible. The historical record clearly shows that there was a properly articulate Jewish political presence in Palestine for only some five hundred years out of the last four thousand. As for the twentieth-century picture, we know that at the time of the Balfour Declaration the Jewish community in Palestine accounted for well under 10 per cent of the total population and that the Palestinian Arab majority had been in undisputed possession of the land for more than thirteen hundred years.

The point about these myths is not that they are untrue but that they are believed—and believed not just by the ignorant majority but also by large numbers of otherwise literate adults. They have influenced the thinking and the actions of men in high places in Western society, men who either did not know any better or, if they did, were cynically prepared to stifle their knowledge in order to further policies that they knew to be morally indefensible.

The press is much to blame for this unhappy state of affairs—and, when I speak of the press in this context, I include radio and television, which have to some extent taken the place of the newspaper as the principal and certainly the most immediate source of information about current affairs. The fault lies not only with the press, however; great harm is done (sometimes unwittingly) by clergymen and others whose misinterpretation of the biblical prophecies has enabled unscrupulous politicians to exploit the ignorance, and sometimes the prejudice, of many ill-educated Christians. But that is another story. In regard to the question of how far the press is responsible for the Western world's failure to see the truth about the Middle East, one fact is striking: the press treats the Middle East problem quite differently from the way in which it treats other topics of international controversy.

Reasons for Pro-Israeli Bias

Of the questions of foreign policy which have divided Western opinion in recent years, the most obvious is the war in Viet Nam. Others have been the civil war in Nigeria, the rule of the colonels in Greece, and the sale of arms to South Africa. Widely divergent opinions on these issues have been expressed in the Western press, and they have been expressed freely and without apology. There has not been, so far as I know, any concerted attempt to suppress or muzzle the views of one side or the other in these highly controversial situations. Nor, I believe, has there been any concerted attempt to blacken the character or to damage the reputation of those who have sought to present the arguments for or against any of the parties involved. But the dispute between the Arabs and Israel presents a very different picture. In that situation there *has* been such a concerted attempt to prevent the free expression of the views of one side.

There are many reasons for this suppression. Outstanding among them, I think, is the fact that the Western world—rightly, I believe—has a bad conscience about its past treatment of the Jewish communities. There is a healthy instinct to make amends for past faults of intolerance and misunderstanding; but the instinct has been distorted into a willingness to transfer the sense of guilt to others and so to make others pay the penalty for sins which they did not commit. This is an ignoble form of escapism—and it characterizes the attitude of a large section of the Western press toward the controversy in the Middle East.

Editors and commentators too often lend sympathy to Israel and criticize the Arabs not because justice dictates such an attitude but because they are afraid that if they criticize Israel they will be labeled anti-Semitic. This is an empty argument. Any government or people which demands respect should also be prepared to accept criticism. But unfortunately this argument produces results and will continue to do so until there are enough editors and commentators with the courage to resist this kind of intimidation, which an Arab friend of mine has aptly called "intellectual terrorism."

Another powerful reason for the one-sided approach to the Middle East is a legacy of the age of imperialism. This reason applies much more to European, and especially to British, attitudes than to American. It is not so long since Britain played a commanding role in the Middle East; less than twenty years ago there were still British garrisons in Egypt, Jordan, Iraq, Libya, and Aden. Human nature being what it is, it is not surprising that many Englishmen have not yet adapted themselves to the notion that they no longer have much of a role to play in that part of the world. At any rate, those like President Nasser who have devoted much effort to persuading the British of the need for such an adjustment have aroused the anger and resentment of the more stiff-necked Englishmen. There has been a state of enmity between that kind of Englishman and the leaders of the Arab nationalist movement, and this, of course, has had an effect on the attitudes adopted toward Arab nationalism by a certain section of the British press. To some extent the same has been true in other European countries which at one time had imperial or colonial interests in the Middle East.

In general it has been my experience to find that those individuals who have lived and worked in the Arab world have developed a sympathetic understanding of the Arab attitude toward the Palestine problem. I know of no newspaper correspondent who has served for any length of time in the Middle East who has not been convinced of the essential justice of the Arab cause. Unfortunately, foreign correspondents very seldom become editors, and at the editorial level it is still rare to find men who have the practical experience in this area that would enable them to form balanced judgments about it. Working in London or Paris or New York and depending on the reports of others, they are not well placed to appreciate the strength of the arguments put before them. They are far more likely to come into close contact with people who, for one reason or another, are predisposed to Israel than they are to meet or develop any lasting association with Arabs. And here, I believe, we come close to a fundamental reason for the failure of the Western press to pay equal attention to the views of the two sides in the Middle East.

Soon after the 1967 June War I was talking to a young and highly intelligent clergyman of the Church of England. He admitted that he knew very little about the controversy in the Middle East and asked me to explain it to him. For perhaps half an hour I tried to do so and to make him see why the Arabs felt so bitter about the injustice that had been done to them in Palestine. When I finished, he said that I had told him many things of which he had been quite simply unaware—and then he made a revealing comment. "You know," he said, when people like myself think about the Middle East, the Jews seem, well, quite like ourselves. But the Arabs . . . " (and here he was searching for the right way to express himself), "the Arabs seem . . . somehow different."

That comment reveals much of the difficulty in persuading the Western world to take a more sympathetic view of the Arabs. Whereas the Jews live among us and share many of our social and intellectual patterns, most of us do not have such a direct relationship with the peoples of the Arab world. There are indeed barriers to understanding. Most obviously, there is a difference in language; and, although social patterns are growing steadily more alike, their differences are still more striking than their similarities. There are historical factors—for example, the influence of the Crusades, have done a great deal to condition Western attitudes toward the Islamic world, as well as the more recent contacts between the West and the Arab world during the colonial period. This is not the place to explore this interesting field of ideas; but these factors are mentioned because they affect the mental and intellectual background against which the ordinary westerner views events in the Arab world. And of course one must not overlook the influence exerted on the minds of young Western Christians by the Old Testament, in which the divine power appears always on the side of the Israelites, even when they behave in ways which today earn them the condemnation of the United Nations Security Council.

If such factors affect the thinking of the ordinary, moderately well educated westerner, they also influence those who write the editorials and the magazine articles he reads. Before any question of deliberate bias is considered, there tends to be in the minds of those who write for Western newspapers and television programs, as well as of those who read and watch them, a preconditioned preference—quite likely an unconscious preference—for the Israeli rather than the Arab point of view.

Zionist Influence on the Press

If this were all, it would be serious enough and would call for a substantial effort to right the balance and to win an equal hearing for the Arab case. But, of course, this is not all. This preference has been for many years reinforced by pressure from a well-orchestrated Zionist information machine, which works in two ways. On the one hand it provides for the journalist, with minimum effort on his part, material which is carefully prepared and skillfully directed to a particular audience. It is very easy for those who are engaged in the information field to detect this kind of material as it appears in the press, with its inspired leaks, its "informed sources," and its careful cultivation of the kind of mythology I referred to earlier. After continued exposure to such information, the uncritical reader sooner or later becomes convinced that the Palestinian refugees left Palestine of their own accord (surprising as that might seem to anyone who stopped to think about it) and that hijacking an airplane is somehow worse than hijacking a whole country.

But this kind of propaganda, although the sophisticated may find it distasteful, is, at least in a technical sense, legitimate. Those who practice it are merely taking advantage of the weaknesses in the modern system of communications and the gullibility of their readers. What is much worse, and equally widespread, is the constant attempt by those claiming to have Israel's interests at heart to silence anyone who dares to speak up for the interests of the Arabs. This is the more deplorable aspect of the subject we are discussing, for it touches on something to which all of us in the Western world pay lip-service: the right of any man to speak his mind in defense of his principles and his opinions. Where discussion of the Middle East is concerned, this right is very frequently infringed. Indeed, I would go further and say it is a conscious and deliberate part of Zionist strategy to prevent, whenever possible, the publication of material sympathetic to the Arabs or critical of Israel. To resist this attempt in societies which, as I have shown, are predisposed to giving greater weight to the arguments in Israel's favor and where the Zionists command both social and economic influence, which they are not slow to use, requires a degree of courage that not all editors possess.

There are many examples of how pressure has been exerted to prevent the publication of an article or a book. One has only to look at most American newspapers to realize how much more one-sided is the treatment of Middle East affairs than is the case in Europe. But in Europe, although there has been a steady improvement over the past couple of years, the situation is still unsatisfactory. Recently, for instance, it was announced in Britain that a new magazine was to be launched which would deal with the affairs of the Middle East. It was to be edited by a known authority on Arab affairs; the announcement added that the project had the backing of a group of people, one of whom was a member of Parliament. At once there were letters of protest in the press, and a deputation called on the member of Parliament asking him to withdraw his support for such a subversive undertaking as a magazine that could be expected to give a hearing to Arab supporters. This is characteristic. The protesters did not wait to see if there would be something to protest about; they objected simply to the fact that someone might try to give the Arab point of view about something. Faced with this dreadful possibility they at once brought pressure to bear on an elected representative to try to prevent him from lending the project his support. It would be hard to find a more obvious denial of the principle of free speech, and yet this was part of a very familiar pattern of operations.

I have suffered from this kind of thing myself. After spending some years as Middle East correspondent for the *Manchester Guardian*, I was working at the time of the 1967 June War as a free-lance writer. Soon after the war

I wrote a series of articles for the *Guardian* about conditions in the Arab territories occupied by Israel. I described a situation, in Gaza and elsewhere, which has since become notorious but which at that time was still unknown to the general public. The *Guardian* was courageous enough to publish four articles, in the face of a rising tide of protest from Zionist sympathizers in Britain. The editor preferred not to publish a fifth article, dealing with the Israelis' destruction of three villages in the Latrun area, and this was published instead in the *London Times*. (The facts it contained have since become well known and were most recently recapitulated in a report by the International Committee of the Red Cross in Geneva.) As a result of these articles, every editor for whom I was working, my publishers, and an organization for which I used to lecture (and still do) about the Middle East received letters, telephone calls, or personal interventions from Zionists in London, suggesting that they discontinue their association with me. I am happy to say that most of them refused to do so, although other writers have been less fortunate than I was.

Still the story was not ended. A few months later, when I accepted an invitation to become director of the newly formed Council for the Advancement of Arab-British Understanding, a Jewish newspaper told its readers that after seeing those articles of mine in the *Guardian* it would not be surprised to learn that I had accepted the appointment of public-relations consultant to the United Arab Republic. Of course, when they received a letter from my solicitors, they were happy to publish a correction—a week later—and by now, some two years later, I can say with some confidence that the editor of this particular newspaper knows quite clearly what the Council for the Advancement of Arab-British Understanding is and that it represents a growing body of British opinion.

Naturally enough, few details of the pressures exerted against publishers and newspaper editors find their way into print. It is only by word of mouth, for instance, that one learns that John Davis, the former commissioner general of UNRWA, had to find a British publisher for his excellent book on the Middle East, *The Evasive Peace* (London: John Murray Ltd., 1968); none of the many publishers he approached in the United States was prepared to take on this dangerous task. But not long ago an English weekly newspaper, the *Listener,* published a most interesting article detailing some of the instances in which pressure had been brought to bear to prevent the publication of material unfavorable to Israel.

Conclusion

While many are aware of the pressures to which I have referred and of the fact that Zionist sympathizers are well placed to exert them, we should remember the extent to which simple ignorance accounts for the biased presentation of news from the Middle East. There are publishers and editors who are prepared to resist the pressures and to let their readers have the truth. The pressures are very similar to the weapon of the blackmailer—effective as a threat but useless once the bluff has been called. Finally, in trying to put right a state of affairs that is so obviously wrong and that runs counter to such a central principle as the principle of free speech, the Arabs and their friends have one substantial advantage: they are in the right.

By contrast, the Zionists—with all their advantages of organization and their invaluable international connections—have to contend with the fact that their case is fundamentally a weak one. They have done wonders with this weak case; for many years it appeared that their myths had successfully obscured the facts of the Palestine problem. But since 1967 these facts have obstinately begun to claim the attention of the world. The press has not inspired this process of reassessment, but it has reflected, hesitantly and reluctantly, the success of the Palestinians in creating for themselves a new image in the eyes of the world—the image, not of a nation of refugees, but of people bent on liberating themselves from alien domination. And that is an image to which none of us in what we like to call the free world can remain indifferent.

The situation, then, is improving. The European press is presenting a much more balanced view of developments in the Middle East than was the case a year or two ago. While this is some cause for satisfaction, it should more properly remind those of us who care about justice in the Middle East of our obligations and opportunities. Whatever editorial writers may be saying, the suffering and the injustices persist. If opinion in the West has begun to shift, it is our duty to shift it further, and faster, to the point where Western governments feel impelled to undertake some constructive initiative to repair the mistakes of the past and to insist that the principles of justice and humanity, which are upheld elsewhere, be upheld also in the Middle East.

A Content Analysis
of American Newspapers

Janice Terry

THIS PAPER IS A STUDY OF the attitudes of three United States newspapers over a twenty-year period with regard to the Arab-Israeli conflict. The attitudes of the U.S. press toward this conflict are important, owing to the press's influence on public opinion, which in turn influences politicians in both executive and legislative branches of the government in shaping foreign policy. In addition, the press may also have a direct effect on politicians and other officials responsible for forming U.S. policies. Furthermore, newspapers are often used as recorded history by academics. Therefore, the way in which the Arab-Israeli conflict is presented by the United States press affects public opinion, decision-makers, and, in a larger sense, students of the conflict.

There have been several studies of the attitudes of the U.S. press toward the Middle East. The most important of these are Michael Suleiman's two surveys of seven newsmagazines, including the *New York Times*, from July to December, 1956, and in June, 1967; the special report by the American Institute for Political Communication on the coverage in June, 1967; and Leslie Farmer's less complete survey, "All We Know Is What We Read in the Papers," on the 1967 June War.[1] These and other studies conclude that

---

1. See Michael W. Suleiman, "An Evaluation of Middle East News Coverage in Seven American Newsmagazines, July–December 1956," *Middle East Forum*, XLI (Autumn, 1965), 5–30; American Institute for Political Communication, "Domestic Communications Aspects of the Middle East Crisis, A Special Report" (Washington, D.C.: APIC, July, 1967); and Leslie Farmer, "All We Know Is What We Read in the Papers," *Middle East Newsletter* (February, 1968), pp. 1–5.

the coverage of the Middle East in the U.S. press has generally been biased in favor of Israel. This analysis attempts to discover in quantitative terms if such a bias does exist and, if so, if it has been evident since the creation of Israel in 1948 and consistent over the twenty-year duration of the Arab-Israeli conflict. This study also attempts to discover if such a bias is uniform throughout the American press.

Method

The *New York Times,* the *Washington Post,* and the *Detroit Free Press* were chosen as the newspapers to be investigated. The *New York Times* was selected because of its prominence, its widespread distribution, and its general reputation; the *Washington Post,* because it is published in the capital and is, therefore, generally more sensitive to political decisions; and the *Detroit Free Press,* a midwestern newspaper with fairly large distribution, because it reflects the attitudes of so-called Middle America.

The study began with the coverage in 1948, the year in which Israel was created, and followed for every fourth year until 1968 (1948, 1952, 1956, 1960, 1964, and 1968). The quadrennial survey was adopted since it offered a workable amount of material and at the same time included key years of the conflict as well as election years in the United States. However, only articles dealing directly with the Middle East were considered. A study of candidates' statements on the Middle East during election years would be an extremely informative and valuable research project.

Articles pertaining to the Middle East, other than those containing entire speeches and those from foreign newspapers, were coded on IBM coding forms on a scale from one to ten. In each case, the title of the newspaper, the date, the type of article, and the attitudes revealed in it were coded. The general attitude toward the conflict and various breakdowns on attitudes toward Nasser, the United Nations, specific Arab nations, and Palestinians were included on the coding form. The form also provided a space to indicate whether the article linked the Middle East conflict to the conflict between the United States and the U.S.S.R. Articles were classified as news articles, editorials, features, or cartoons, and only major articles were coded.[2]

2. In the case of the *New York Times,* which had massive coverage in 1948 and 1956, articles under one headline were coded as one article. Due to a lack of library holdings and newspaper strikes, I was unable to code coverage in the *Washington Post* from January to March, 1968, and in the *Detroit Free Press* for January, 1956; from July 14 to November 25, 1964, and from January 1 to August 10, 1968.

The attitudes were coded as being either for or against Israel or Arab nations. An article was considered to be for one side if its attitude toward the action that side had taken was favorable or if it described that side in favorable terms. An article was coded as being against one side if it displayed a hostile attitude to the actions of that side or described the nation or its leadership in unfavorable terms. An article was coded as neutral if it lacked biased terms, presented both sides of the case, or merely provided information or news coverage of events.

Once all the articles had been coded, the information was transferred to IBM punch cards. The computer was then fed the information and was programed to tally the number of articles and types of attitudes revealed and to provide statistics comparing the attitudes of the three newspapers by year and by type of article. Tabulations were obtained on the frequency of occurrence of those questions dealing with attitudes toward the Arab-Israeli conflict, Nasser, the United Nations, Palestinians, and commandos, by newspaper and by year. Percentages of occurrence were also tabulated. Secondly, tabulations were obtained on those columns dealing with attitudes as dependent variables, using the type of article and count by year and by newspaper as the independent variables.

One of the problems in this method concerns the reliability of the coding system and of the reader. Due to the volume of material and the time factor, it has thus far proven impossible to obtain an adequate reliability check.

The volume of material available presents numerous possibilities for grouping and analysis, while the coding form allows for many other questions to be programed through the computer. The nuances of some articles are necessarily lost because of the broad categories that are demanded by the volume of material. A word tabulation would be an extremely informative study and would provide more concrete verification of the bias evidenced in the United States press. In spite of these drawbacks the present study documents the point of view adopted by three U.S. newspapers on the Arab-Israeli conflict and also the fluctuations of that stance over the twenty-year period of the conflict.

Results

The greatest volume of coverage was in 1948 and 1956, the years of the most violent conflict in the Middle East. The coverage in 1948 was overwhelmingly pro-Israeli. Much of the coverage in editorials and features dwelt on the themes of the new nation, the suffering of the Jews during World War II, and the unreasonable hostility of the Arab nations. The *New York Times* in 1948 published a total of 735 major articles on the conflict (see Table 1). Of this number, 54 were editorials, of which 38.9 per cent were pro-Israeli and 18.5 per cent were anti-Arab. Thus 57.4 per cent of the *New York Times*'s editorials favored Israel. At the same time there were no pro-Arab or anti-Israeli editorials. The same sort of bias is evidenced in the feature stories of 1948 in the *New York Times,* in which 28.6 per cent were pro-Israeli and 4.3 per cent anti-Arab, making a total of 32.9 per cent favoring Israel. The percentage of political cartoons in the anti-Arab category is much higher, with 24 per cent being anti-Arab (see Table 13). The cartoons in the *New York Times* appear only in the Sunday edition, which has a higher distribution rate; they are taken from other U.S. newspapers and therefore reflect the attitudes of numerous news sources. In the field of cartoons the anti-Arab attitude, with distinct racist overtones, is prevalent throughout the twenty-year period. The *New York Times* also printed numerous appeals for aid to Zionist organizations directly under news articles so that they appeared to the casual reader to be an integral part of the news item.

Although the volume of coverage in 1948 was much less in the *Washington Post,* much the same kind of bias is apparent. In all, 58.1 per cent of its editorial coverage in 1948 was pro-Israeli or anti-Arab. Interestingly, 19.4 per cent of the editorial coverage was anti-Arab, while 40 per cent of the cartoon coverage was anti-Arab (see Tables 8, 14).

The coverage in the *Detroit Free Press* in 1948 was about equal in volume to that in the *Washington Post;* however, the *Detroit Free Press,* which consistently displayed a more isolationist stand with regard to the Middle East, published a smaller number of pro-Israeli articles and, in fact, did not publish any pro-Israeli editorials in 1948 (see Tables 6, 9). On several occasions the *Free Press* announced its opposition to partition and severely criticized President Truman for his support of Zionism.

The role of the United Nations was viewed with favor in all of these newspapers. In the *New York Times,* 78.6 per cent of its editorials on this matter were pro-United Nations in 1948; in the *Washington Post,* 87.5 per cent; and in the Detroit Free Press, 66.7 per cent. The lower percentage in the *Detroit Free Press* reflects its attitude toward the partition scheme. Attitudes toward the United Nations continued to be favorable throughout the twenty-year period. However, had the coding included 1967, the results undoubtedly would have indicated an increase in the number of anti-United Nations editorials and features. That the attitudes in 1968 were again generally favorable reveals, perhaps, a willingness to let the United Nations handle a situation that the great powers seemed unable to resolve (see Tables 18, 19).

All of the newspapers virtually ignored the existence of the Palestinians as a separate group, referring to them as "Arabs," "Muslims," "Muslim Arabs," or "refugees." In the *Washington Post* the Palestinians were referred to as the "non-Jewish population," and Palestine as the "Holy Land." In fact, the Palestinians as a recognizable group, separate from Arabs and from other nations, were mentioned only six times in the *New York Times* in 1948 and not at all in the other two newspapers. In the following years, references to "Palestinians" disappeared altogether from the coverage; the refugees were referred to as "Arabs." "Palestine" did not appear in the 1960 index of the *New York Times*. Sympathy was shown to the refugees in two editorials in the *New York Times,* one in 1952 and the other in 1956. The *Detroit Free Press* also printed sympathetic editorials in these years (see Table 20).

The coverage of the Middle East dropped in 1952 to 6 per cent of that in 1948. Even feature articles on Israel and the Arab nations practically disappeared; the press appears to have made few if any attempts to publish follow-up articles on the conflict or to engage in an educational or propagandist program either in support of or against one side. It appears that the conflict is covered most widely during violent periods or when United States interests appear to be threatened. Following this trend the coverage in 1956 rose to a level similar to that of 1948, with much the same breakdown in the number of news articles, features, and editorials.

During 1956 Nasser began to be mentioned in major articles, and the coverage he received was uniformly unfavorable. He was frequently depicted as being pro–U.S.S.R. and as the cause of the 1956 crisis. In 1956 the *New York Times* published twenty-five editorials on the Middle East, of which 75.8 per cent were anti-Nasser in tone. The *Washington Post* printed twenty editorials, of which 80 per cent were hostile to Nasser, while the *Detroit Free Press* published eleven, all of which were hostile to him (see Table 16). The last two papers also contained numerous editorials and features which maintained a pro–U.S. and anti–U.S.S.R. posture. Anti-Nasser cartoons were particularly prevalent in the *Washington Post.*

During the tripartite aggression, the role of Israel was minimized. Several *Times* and *Post* editorials depicted Israel's participation as being in self-defense. Only 4.7 per cent of the *New York Times* editorials on this matter were anti-Israeli, while 27.9 per cent were pro-Israeli. In the *Post,* 22.2 per cent were pro-Israeli, while 3.7 per cent were anti-Israeli. The

Free Press took a slightly different stand; 15 per cent of its editorials were anti-Israeli, none were pro-Israeli or pro-Arab, 10 per cent were anti-Arab (see Tables 7–9). Together with other attitudes displayed, it appears that the *Detroit Free Press* advocated that position which would be most favorable to U.S. interests and showed little or no sympathy for either party to the conflict in the Middle East. Editorials in all three newspapers were also frequently anti-British or anti-French in tone, although the coding does not reveal this fact.

The coverage on Nasser tended to remain unfavorable to him after 1956, although his portrayal improved slightly in the *Washington Post* in 1964; this indicates a small improvement in relations during the Kennedy era. However, the *New York Times* remained hostile. Its editorials and features reflect not only an anti-Nasser stand but also an anti-Arab one. For example, an editorial published in September, 1960, lauded the arrival in the United States of the Israeli Philharmonic Orchestra and discussed at some length its accomplishments and Israeli culture. During this same period no mention was made of the sending of Egyptian art treasures to the United States, although this had been announced three days prior to the editorial on the Israeli orchestra.

The most notable change in the 1968 coverage was, of course, the recognition of the Palestinians as a separate group. The commandos also emerged as "newsworthy" and generally received neutral coverage. Indeed, 90 per cent of the coverage in the *New York Times,* 75 per cent in the *Washington Post,* and 100 per cent in the *Detroit Free Press* was neutral. However, the *New York Times* published three anti-commando editorials, 75 per cent of their total on this matter (see Table 21). The hostility notably increased in December, when the hijacking of airplanes began. The Israeli attack on the Beirut airport was minimized, although editorials on the subject may have appeared early in 1969.

Conclusion

The results of this study reveal a rather consistent pro-Israeli and anti-Arab bias in the three newspapers studied. This bias has been particularly clear in editorials and cartoons and, to a lesser extent, in feature stories. The *New York Times*'s coverage in 1968, compared with that in 1948, shows a definite drop in the total number of articles—from 735 to 211. In 1948, 126 of the 735 articles were either pro-Israeli or anti-Arab, making a total of 17.1 per cent of the *Times*'s coverage in 1948 clearly biased in favor of Israel. In 1968 the *Times* published 211 articles, of which 20 were either pro-Israeli or anti-Arab, making a total of 9.5 per cent of the coverage favorable to Israel (see Table 3). Statistics on the *Washington Post* are similar. However, the *Detroit Free Press,* while not publishing the same volume of material as the *Times,* tended to give much less biased coverage to the conflict.

It is important to note that much of the biased coverage in the three papers was anti-Arab in nature; much of this was purely racist in tone, as a word-coding study would reveal statistically. This becomes particularly evident in the coverage and descriptions of Nasser during and after 1956, which were generally hostile in attitude. It is also clear that the press ignored the existence of the Palestinians until 1968, when the commando movement emerged. Some sympathy was accorded the refugees, but only as Arabs and only in terms of some settlement that would not disturb Israel. Of all the facets of the Middle East conflict, the most neutral coverage was initially on the commandos; much of this coverage tended to be purely informative in nature.

The findings of this study reveal the need for more in-depth analysis, particularly in feature stories. It also shows that bias does exist, even in those papers which rather consistently maintain that they present objective accounts. Since the survey covered a twenty-year period, it shows that this bias is not a temporary one and that it is apparent not only in times of open hostility.

The study also uses new research techniques, particularly the computer, enabling the researcher to handle a great volume of material and to make complicated comparisons. The coding form is designed for widespread use and could easily be applied to other years and newspapers.

TABLE 1.
NUMBER OF ARTICLES ON THE ARAB-ISRAELI CONFLICT

	1948	1952	1956	1960	1964	1968	
New York Times							
News Articles	586	30	299	21	34	164	
Editorials	54	5	43	7	4	16	
Features	70	8	64	8	6	29	
Cartoons	25	2	25	-	1	2	
Total	735	45	431	36	45	211	
Washington Post							
News Articles	190	5	200	7	17	38	
Editorials	31	3	27	1	2	4	
Features	12	-	16	-	3	7	
Cartoons	10	1	7	-	-	-	
Total	243	9	250	8	22	49	
Detroit Free Press							
News Articles	135	3	112	7	6	9	
Editorials	11	-	20	1	1	5	
Features	10	-	17	1	6	1	
Cartoons	6	-	8	-	-	-	
Total	162	3	157	9	13	15	

TABLE 2.
DISTRIBUTION OF ARTICLES ON THE ARAB-ISRAELI CONFLICT*

	1948	1952	1956	1960	1964	1968
New York Times						
News Articles	79.7%	66.7%	69.4%	58.3%	75.6%	77.7%
Editorials	7.3	11.1	10.0	19.4	8.9	7.6
Features	9.5	17.8	14.8	22.2	13.3	13.7
Cartoons	3.4	4.4	5.8	-	2.2	0.9
Washington Post						
News Articles	78.2	55.5	80.0	87.5	77.3	77.6
Editorials	12.8	33.3	10.8	12.5	9.1	8.2
Features	4.9	-	6.4	-	13.6	14.3
Cartoons	4.1	11.1	2.8	-	-	-
Detroit Free Press						
News Articles	83.3	100.0	71.3	77.8	46.2	60.0
Editorials	6.8	-	12.7	11.1	7.7	33.3
Features	6.2	-	10.8	11.1	46.2	6.7
Cartoons	3.7	-	5.1	-	-	-

*Detail may not add to total due to rounding.

TABLE 3.
PRO-ISRAELI ANTI-ARAB COVERAGE IN THE NEW YORK TIMES (1948, 1968)

Type of Coverage and Attitude	1948		1968		1948	1968
	No.	%	No.	%	% of Total	% of Total
Total, Four Categories	735	-	211	-	-	-
News Articles	586	-	164	-	79.7	77.7
Pro-Israeli	62	10.6	3	1.8	-	-
Anti-Arab	3	0.5	-	-	-	-
Total	65	11.1	3	1.8	-	-
Editorials	54	-	16	-	7.3	7.6
Pro-Israeli	21	38.9	4	25.0	-	-
Anti-Arab	10	18.5	2	12.5	-	-
Total	31	57.4	6	37.5	-	-
Features	70	-	29	-	9.5	13.7
Pro-Israeli	20	28.6	11	37.9	-	-
Anti-Arab	3	4.3	-	-	-	-
Total	23	32.9	11	37.9	-	-
Cartoons	25	-	2	-	3.4	0.9
Pro-Israeli	1	4.0	-	-	-	-
Anti-Arab	6	24.0	-	-	-	-
Total	7	28.0	-	-	-	-

TABLE 4.
ATTITUDE TOWARD THE ARAB-ISRAELI CONFLICT IN NEWS ARTICLES OF THE <u>NEW YORK TIMES</u>

Attitude	1948		1952		1956		1960		1964		1968	
	No.	%	No.	%	No.	%	No.	%	No.	%	No.	%
Total	586	-	30	-	299	-	21	-	34	-	164	-
Neutral	515	87.9	29	96.7	297	99.3	21	100.0	34	100.0	161	98.2
Against Both	2	0.3	-	-	-	-	-	-	-	-	-	-
Pro-Israeli	62	10.6	1	3.3	1	0.3	-	-	-	-	3	1.8
Pro-Arab	1	0.2	-	-	1	0.3	-	-	-	-	-	-
Anti-Israeli	1	0.2	-	-	-	-	-	-	-	-	-	-
Anti-U.S.S.R.	2	0.3	-	-	-	-	-	-	-	-	-	-
Anti-U.S.	-	-	-	-	-	-	-	-	-	-	-	-
Anti-Arab	3	0.5	-	-	-	-	-	-	-	-	-	-
Sympathy to Refugees	-	-	-	-	-	-	-	-	-	-	-	-

TABLE 5.
ATTITUDE TOWARD THE ARAB-ISRAELI CONFLICT IN NEWS ARTICLES OF THE <u>WASHINGTON POST</u>

Attitude	1948		1952		1956		1960		1964		1968	
	No.	%	No.	%	No.	%	No.	%	No.	%	No.	%
Total	190	-	5	-	200	-	7	-	17	-	38	-
Neutral	186	97.9	5	100.0	200	100.0	6	85.7	17	100.0	38	100.0
Against Both	-	-	-	-	-	-	-	-	-	-	-	-
Pro-Israeli	4	2.1	-	-	-	-	1	14.3	-	-	-	-
Pro-Arab	-	-	-	-	-	-	-	-	-	-	-	-
Anti-Israeli	-	-	-	-	-	-	-	-	-	-	-	-
Anti-U.S.S.R.	-	-	-	-	-	-	-	-	-	-	-	-
Anti-U.S.	-	-	-	-	-	-	-	-	-	-	-	-
Anti-Arab	-	-	-	-	-	-	-	-	-	-	-	-
Sympathy to Refugees	-	-	-	-	-	-	-	-	-	-	-	-

TABLE 6.
ATTITUDE TOWARD THE ARAB-ISRAELI CONFLICT IN NEWS ARTICLES OF THE <u>DETROIT FREE PRESS</u>

Attitude	1948		1952		1956		1960		1964		1968	
	No.	%	No.	%	No.	%	No.	%	No.	%	No.	%
Total	135	-	3	-	112	-	7	-	6	-	9	-
Neutral	133	98.5	3	100.0	110	98.1	7	100.0	6	100.0	9	100.0
Against Both	-	-	-	-	-	-	-	-	-	-	-	-
Pro-Israeli	-	-	-	-	-	-	-	-	-	-	-	-
Pro-Arab	1	0.7	-	-	1	0.9	-	-	-	-	-	-
Anti-Israeli	1	0.7	-	-	-	-	-	-	-	-	-	-
Anti-U.S.S.R.	-	-	-	-	1	0.9	-	-	-	-	-	-
Anti-U.S.	-	-	-	-	-	-	-	-	-	-	-	-
Anti-Arab	-	-	-	-	-	-	-	-	-	-	-	-
Sympathy to Refugees	-	-	-	-	-	-	-	-	-	-	-	-

TABLE 7.
ATTITUDE TOWARD THE ARAB-ISRAELI CONFLICT IN EDITORIALS OF THE NEW YORK TIMES

Attitude	1948 No.	1948 %	1952 No.	1952 %	1956 No.	1956 %	1960 No.	1960 %	1964 No.	1964 %	1968 No.	1968 %
Total	54	-	5	-	43	-	7	-	4	-	16	-
Neutral	15	27.8	1	20.0	15	34.9	-	-	2	50.0	2	12.5
Against Both	8	14.8	-	-	3	7.0	-	-	-	-	6	37.5
Pro-Israeli	21	38.9	1	20.0	12	27.9	7	100.0	-	-	4	25.0
Pro-Arab	-	-	-	-	1	2.3	-	-	-	-	-	-
Anti-Israeli	-	-	-	-	2	4.7	-	-	-	-	1	6.3
Anti-U.S.S.R.	-	-	-	-	7	16.2	-	-	-	-	-	-
Anti-U.S.	-	-	-	-	-	-	-	-	-	-	-	-
Anti-Arab	10	18.5	1	20.0	1	2.3	-	-	2	50.0	2	12.5
Sympathy to Refugees	-	-	2	40.0	2	4.7	-	-	-	-	1	6.3

TABLE 8.
ATTITUDE TOWARD THE ARAB-ISRAELI CONFLICT IN EDITORIALS OF THE WASHINGTON POST

Attitude	1948 No.	1948 %	1952 No.	1952 %	1956 No.	1956 %	1960 No.	1960 %	1964 No.	1964 %	1968 No.	1968 %
Total	31	-	3	-	27	-	1	-	2	-	4	-
Neutral	9	29.0	2	66.7	13	48.1	-	-	-	-	1	25.0
Against Both	1	3.2	-	-	4	14.8	-	-	-	-	1	25.0
Pro-Israeli	12	38.7	1	33.3	6	22.2	1	100.0	-	-	-	-
Pro-Arab	1	3.2	-	-	1	3.7	-	-	2	100.0	1	25.0
Anti-Israeli	-	-	-	-	1	3.7	-	-	-	-	1	25.0
Anti-U.S.S.R.	-	-	-	-	2	7.4	-	-	-	-	-	-
Anti-U.S.	2	6.5	-	-	-	-	-	-	-	-	-	-
Anti-Arab	6	19.4	-	-	-	-	-	-	-	-	-	-
Sympathy to Refugees	-	-	-	-	-	-	-	-	-	-	-	-

TABLE 9.
ATTITUDE TOWARD THE ARAB-ISRAELI CONFLICT IN EDITORIALS OF THE DETROIT FREE PRESS

Attitude	1948 No.	1948 %	1952 No.	1952 %	1956 No.	1956 %	1960 No.	1960 %	1964 No.	1964 %	1968 No.	1968 %
Total	12	-	-	-	20	-	1	-	1	-	1	-
Neutral	4	33.3	-	-	8	40.0	-	-	1	100.0	-	-
Against Both	3	25.0	-	-	3	15.0	1	100.0	-	-	-	-
Pro-Israeli	-	-	-	-	-	-	-	-	-	-	-	-
Pro-Arab	1	8.3	-	-	-	-	-	-	-	-	-	-
Anti-Israeli	2	16.7	-	-	3	15.0	-	-	-	-	1	100.0
Anti-U.S.S.R.	-	-	-	-	3	15.0	-	-	-	-	-	-
Anti-U.S.	2	16.7	-	-	-	-	-	-	-	-	-	-
Anti-Arab	-	-	-	-	2	10.0	-	-	-	-	-	-
Sympathy to Refugees	-	-	-	-	1	5.0	-	-	-	-	-	-

TABLE 10.
ATTITUDE TOWARD THE ARAB-ISRAELI CONFLICT IN FEATURES OF <u>THE NEW YORK TIMES</u>

Attitude	1948 No.	1948 %	1952 No.	1952 %	1956 No.	1956 %	1960 No.	1960 %	1964 No.	1964 %	1968 No.	1968 %
Total	70	-	8	-	64	-	8	-	6	-	29	-
Neutral	35	50.0	4	50.0	49	76.6	7	87.5	6	100.0	17	58.6
Against Both	6	8.6	-	-	2	3.1	-	-	-	-	-	-
Pro-Israeli	20	28.6	4	50.0	3	4.7	-	-	-	-	-	-
Pro-Arab	3	4.3	-	-	5	7.8	1	12.5	-	-	11	37.9
Anti-Israeli	-	-	-	-	-	-	-	-	-	-	1	3.4
Anti-U.S.S.R.	1	1.4	-	-	4	6.3	-	-	-	-	-	-
Anti-U.S.	-	-	-	-	-	-	-	-	-	-	-	-
Anti-Arab	3	4.3	-	-	-	-	-	-	-	-	-	-
Sympathy to Refugees	2	2.9	-	-	1	1.6	-	-	-	-	-	-

TABLE 11.
ATTITUDE TOWARD THE ARAB-ISRAELI CONFLICT IN FEATURES OF THE <u>WASHINGTON POST</u>

Attitude	1948 No.	1948 %	1952 No.	1952 %	1956 No.	1956 %	1960 No.	1960 %	1964 No.	1964 %	1968 No.	1968 %
Total	12	-	-	-	16	-	-	-	3	-	7	-
Neutral	3	25.0	-	-	10	62.5	-	-	3	100.0	7	100.0
Against Both	-	-	-	-	1	6.3	-	-	-	-	-	-
Pro-Israeli	9	75.0	-	-	2	12.5	-	-	-	-	-	-
Pro-Arab	-	-	-	-	-	-	-	-	-	-	-	-
Anti-Israeli	-	-	-	-	-	-	-	-	-	-	-	-
Anti-U.S.S.R.	-	-	-	-	3	18.8	-	-	-	-	-	-
Anti-U.S.	-	-	-	-	-	-	-	-	-	-	-	-
Anti-Arab	-	-	-	-	-	-	-	-	-	-	-	-
Sympathy to Refugees	-	-	-	-	-	-	-	-	-	-	-	-

TABLE 12.
ATTITUDE TOWARD THE ARAB-ISRAELI CONFLICT IN FEATURES OF THE <u>DETROIT FREE PRESS</u>

Attitude	1948 No.	1948 %	1952 No.	1952 %	1956 No.	1956 %	1960 No.	1960 %	1964 No.	1964 %	1968 No.	1968 %
Total	10	-	-	-	17	-	1	-	6	-	1	-
Neutral	6	60.0	-	-	11	64.7	1	100.0	2	33.3	1	100.0
Against Both	-	-	-	-	-	-	-	-	-	-	-	-
Pro-Israeli	2	20.0	-	-	3	17.6	-	-	2	33.3	-	-
Pro-Arab	2	20.0	-	-	-	-	-	-	2	33.3	-	-
Anti-Israeli	-	-	-	-	-	-	-	-	-	-	-	-
Anti-U.S.S.R.	-	-	-	-	1	5.9	-	-	-	-	-	-
Anti-U.S.	-	-	-	-	-	-	-	-	-	-	-	-
Anti-Arab	-	-	-	-	1	5.9	-	-	-	-	-	-
Sympathy to Refugees	-	-	-	-	1	5.9	-	-	-	-	-	-

TABLE 13.
ATTITUDE TOWARD THE ARAB-ISRAELI CONFLICT IN CARTOONS OF <u>THE NEW YORK TIMES</u>

Attitude	1948 No.	1948 %	1952 No.	1952 %	1956 No.	1956 %	1960 No.	1960 %	1964 No.	1964 %	1968 No.	1968 %
Total	25	-	-	-	25	-	-	-	1	-	2	-
Neutral	8	32.0	-	-	5	20.0	-	-	-	-	2	100.0
Against Both	9	36.0	-	-	3	12.0	-	-	-	-	-	-
Pro-Israeli	1	4.0	-	-	3	12.0	-	-	1	100.0	-	-
Pro-Arab	-	-	-	-	-	-	-	-	-	-	-	-
Anti-Israeli	-	-	-	-	1	4.0	-	-	-	-	-	-
Anti-U.S.S.R.	-	-	-	-	9	36.0	-	-	-	-	-	-
Anti-U.S.	1	4.0	-	-	-	-	-	-	-	-	-	-
Anti-Arab	6	24.0	-	-	4	16.0	-	-	-	-	-	-
Sympathy to Refugees	-	-	-	-	-	-	-	-	-	-	-	-

TABLE 14.
ATTITUDE TOWARD THE ARAB-ISRAELI CONFLICT IN CARTOONS OF THE <u>WASHINGTON POST</u>

Attitude	1948 No.	1948 %	1952 No.	1952 %	1956 No.	1956 %	1960 No.	1960 %	1964 No.	1964 %	1968 No.	1968 %
Total	10	-	1	-	7	-	-	-	-	-	-	-
Neutral	1	10.0	-	-	3	42.9	-	-	-	-	-	-
Against Both	1	10.0	-	-	1	14.3	-	-	-	-	-	-
Pro-Israeli	1	10.0	-	-	1	14.3	-	-	-	-	-	-
Pro-Arab	-	-	-	-	-	-	-	-	-	-	-	-
Anti-Israeli	-	-	-	-	-	-	-	-	-	-	-	-
Anti-U.S.S.R.	2	20.0	1	100.0	2	28.6	-	-	-	-	-	-
Anti-U.S.	1	10.0	-	-	-	-	-	-	-	-	-	-
Anti-Arab	4	40.0	-	-	-	-	-	-	-	-	-	-
Sympathy to Refugees	-	-	-	-	-	-	-	-	-	-	-	-

TABLE 15.
ATTITUDE TOWARD THE ARAB-ISRAELI CONFLICT IN CARTOONS OF THE <u>DETROIT FREE PRESS</u>

Attitude	1948 No.	1948 %	1952 No.	1952 %	1956 No.	1956 %	1960 No.	1960 %	1964 No.	1964 %	1968 No.	1968 %
Total	6	-	-	-	8	-	-	-	-	-	-	-
Neutral	5	83.3	-	-	4	50.0	-	-	-	-	-	-
Against Both	1	16.7	-	-	2	25.0	-	-	-	-	-	-
Pro-Israeli	-	-	-	-	-	-	-	-	-	-	-	-
Pro-Arab	-	-	-	-	-	-	-	-	-	-	-	-
Anti-Israeli	-	-	-	-	-	-	-	-	-	-	-	-
Anti-U.S.S.R.	-	-	-	-	2	25.0	-	-	-	-	-	-
Anti-U.S.	-	-	-	-	-	-	-	-	-	-	-	-
Anti-Arab	-	-	-	-	-	-	-	-	-	-	-	-
Sympathy to Refugees	-	-	-	-	-	-	-	-	-	-	-	-

TABLE 16.
ATTITUDE TOWARD NASSER IN EDITORIALS

Newspaper and Year	Pro-Nasser		Anti-Nasser		Neutral		Total
	No.	%	No.	%	No.	%	No.
1956							
New York Times	-	-	25	75.8	8	24.2	33
Washington Post	-	-	20	80.0	5	20.0	25
Detroit Free Press	-	-	11	100.0	-	-	11
1960							
New York Times	-	-	5	83.3	1	16.7	6
Washington Post	-	-	-	-	-	-	-
Detroit Free Press	-	-	-	-	-	-	-
1964							
New York Times	1	33.3	2	66.7	-	-	3
Washington Post	-	-	1	100.0	-	-	1
Detroit Free Press	-	-	-	-	-	-	-
1968							
New York Times	-	-	2	100.0	-	-	2
Washington Post	1	100.0	-	-	-	-	1
Detroit Free Press	-	-	-	-	-	-	-
Total	2	-	66	-	14	-	82

TABLE 17.
ATTITUDE TOWARD NASSER IN FEATURES

Newspaper and Year	Pro-Nasser		Anti-Nasser		Neutral		Total
	No.	%	No.	%	No.	%	No.
1956							
New York Times	2	16.7	4	33.3	6	50.0	12
Washington Post	2	12.5	12	75.0	2	12.5	16
Detroit Free Press	2	28.6	5	71.4	-	-	7
1960							
New York Times	1	33.3	-	-	2	66.7	3
Washington Post	-	-	-	-	-	-	-
Detroit Free Press	-	-	1	100.0	-	-	1
1964							
New York Times	-	-	-	-	-	-	-
Washington Post	2	100.0	-	-	-	-	2
Detroit Free Press	-	-	1	50.0	1	50.0	2
1968							
New York Times	1	33.3	1	33.3	1	33.3	3
Washington Post	-	-	-	-	-	-	-
Detroit Free Press	-	-	-	-	-	-	-
Total	10	-	24	-	12	-	46

TABLE 18.
ATTITUDE TOWARD UNITED NATIONS IN EDITORIALS

Newspaper and Year	Pro-U.N.		Anti-U.N.		Neutral		Total
	No.	%	No.	%	No.	%	No.
1948							
New York Times	22	78.6	3	10.7	3	10.7	28
Washington Post	14	87.5	2	12.5	-	-	16
Detroit Free Press	4	66.7	1	16.7	1	16.7	6
1956							
New York Times	15	93.8	1	6.3	-	-	16
Washington Post	16	100.0	-	-	-	-	16
Detroit Free Press	3	75.0	1	25.0	-	-	4
1960							
New York Times	-	-	1	100.0	-	-	1
Washington Post	-	-	-	-	-	-	-
Detroit Free Press	1	100.0	-	-	-	-	1
1964							
New York Times	-	-	-	-	-	-	-
Washington Post	1	100.0	-	-	-	-	1
Detroit Free Press	-	-	-	-	-	-	-
1968							
New York Times	7	77.8	2	22.2	-	-	9
Washington Post	-	-	-	-	-	-	-
Detroit Free Press	-	-	-	-	-	-	-
Total	83	-	11	-	4	-	98

TABLE 19.
ATTITUDE TOWARD UNITED NATIONS IN FEATURES

Newspaper and Year	Pro-U.N.		Anti-U.N.		Neutral		Total
	No.	%	No.	%	No.	%	No.
1948							
New York Times	5	83.3	1	16.7	-	-	6
Washington Post	3	100.0	-	-	-	-	3
Detroit Free Press	1	100.0	-	-	-	-	1
1956							
New York Times	11	100.0	-	-	-	-	11
Washington Post	-	-	-	-	1	100.0	1
Detroit Free Press	1	33.3	2	66.7	-	-	3
1960							
New York Times	2	100.0	-	-	-	-	2
Washington Post	-	-	-	-	-	-	-
Detroit Free Press	-	-	-	-	-	-	-
1964							
New York Times	-	-	-	-	-	-	-
Washington Post	-	-	-	-	-	-	-
Detroit Free Press	-	-	-	-	-	-	-
1968							
New York Times	1	100.0	-	-	-	-	1
Washington Post	-	-	-	-	-	-	-
Detroit Free Press	-	-	-	-	-	-	-
Total	24	-	3	-	1	-	28

TABLE 20.
MENTION OF PALESTINIANS AS SEPARATE ENTITY

Newspaper and Year	No. of News Articles	No. of Editorials	No. of Features	Total
1948				
New York Times	6	2	3	11
Washington Post	-	-	-	-
Detroit Free Press	-	-	1	1
1952				
New York Times	2	1	-	3
Washington Post	-	-	-	-
Detroit Free Press	-	-	-	-
1956				
New York Times	-	-	4	4
Washington Post	-	-	-	-
Detroit Free Press	-	-	-	-
1960				
New York Times	1	2	1	4
Washington Post	-	-	-	-
Detroit Free Press	-	-	1	1
1964				
New York Times	-	-	-	-
Washington Post	-	-	-	-
Detroit Free Press	-	-	-	-
1968				
New York Times	8	2	7	17
Washington Post	1	1	2	4
Detroit Free Press	2	-	-	2
Total	20	8	19	47

TABLE 21.
ATTITUDE TOWARD COMMANDOS IN 1968

	Pro		Con		Neutral		Total
	No.	%	No.	%	No.	%	No.
New York Times							
News Articles	-	-	2	10.0	18	90.0	20
Editorials	-	-	3	75.0	1	25.0	4
Features	-	-	4	57.1	3	42.9	7
Washington Post							
News Articles	2	25.0	-	-	6	75.0	8
Editorials	-	-	1	100.0	-	-	1
Features	-	-	1	33.3	2	66.6	3
Detroit Free Press							
News Articles	-	-	-	-	2	100.0	2
Editorials	-	-	1	100.0	-	-	1
Features	-	-	-	-	-	-	-
Total	2	-	12	-	32	-	46

American Policy
and the Arab World

Richard Cottam

A GENERATION AGO parlor analysts of American foreign policy liked to say that Americans had an attitude that was paralyzing in foreign policy: they wanted to be loved. The disappearance of this attitude marks a loss of innocence. Most Americans assumed that other peoples of the world would see them as Americans saw themselves: a great, disinterested, and beneficent nation. Since then too many American flags have been burned, anti-American demonstrations held, and USIS libraries leveled for Americans to maintain the illusion that others recognize their beneficence and love them for it. But, except among some of the younger generation, the American self-image remains. When many Americans hear Arabs impassionately denouncing American imperialism and its Zionist ally, they can only conclude that the speakers are either mad or dupes of communism.

Influences on American Policy

Much of the reality of present Arab-American relations can be seen by juxtaposing the two images of America: on the one hand the beneficent, disinterested, and peaceful nation, and on the other hand the leader of capitalist-Zionist-Western imperialism. Prior to World War II Arabs did have a somewhat favorable image of the United States, whereas Americans were only vaguely aware of the existence of an Arab world. How was it possible that within a generation America was pushing aside France and even Britain for the honor of being the least-popular world power in the eyes of the Arab world? The answer is not likely to be found in pointing to a list of men who through stupidity, greed, or malevolence led the United States along the path of error. Stupidity and greed have certainly been present, but a policy as complex as the American policy toward the Arab world has deeper roots. American policy in this area has been—and most likely will continue to be—determined primarily by three factors. One of these is the American Jewish community. A second is American economic interests in the Middle East, particularly oil. A third is the sense on the part of the American foreign-policy and defense communities that events in and around the Arab world are of concern to American national security. In other words, in a study of the making of American policy toward the Arab world the groups to look to are an ethnic interest group, an economic interest group, and one section of the bureaucracy.

The activities of the ethnic interest group are often highly visible. Periodically, for example, three-quarters of the United States Senate signs a statement prepared for them by lobbyists of this interest group. It is by now a ritual for congressional and presidential candidates to address Jewish gatherings and to say what the audiences wish to hear. Arabs looking at this behavior are likely both to underestimate and overestimate the importance of this group. They underestimate its size in assuming that it is composed only of Zionists. A great many American Jews who have no real interest in Zionism do fear that another Jewish community, this time the one in Israel, is threatened with genocide. Their determination that this time the American government must not stand by in helpless passivity is intense whenever they perceive, as they presently do, that the danger is serious.

The importance of this ethnic pressure group is overestimated to the extent that it is assumed the surface activity reflects the group's influence. In fact, as reaction to the Rogers Plan has illustrated, United States policy frequently is bitterly opposed by lobbyists for this group. One point is clear, however; American politicians do not believe any serious political price will be incurred by giving extravagant verbal support to the Israeli position. Apparently Americans who identify with the Arab cause are not voting on this issue in sufficient numbers for any verbal note to be taken of their sensitivities.

Since neither the oil interests not the bureaucracy conduct their activities in the public eye, their influence on policy is even more difficult to assess. That does not mean the oil interest group's activities are underestimated. Pro-Israeli lobbyists and Americans of the left, in fact, may well overestimate the impact of oil interests on policy. To believe, for example, that oil interests are pleased with current American policy, much less responsible for it, requires a large measure of faith in the proposition that oil interests are part of the great military-industrial establishment which makes all policy. In fact, American policy has placed American oil investments in the Middle East in clear jeopardy, and American business is not generally noted for its masochistic drive. If the role of oil interests is overestimated by some, the role of the bureaucracy is underestimated by almost everyone.

American Policy before 1948

An assessment of the relative importance of these three factors can best be made by looking at actual policy in the present and in the recent past. American policy first became active on a sustained basis following World War II. At that time the American public and President Truman alike were strongly predisposed to look at the area in terms, simply, of the unspeakable crime that a Western and Christian people had committed against European Jewry. Consequently the Truman administration acted to put pressure on the British, whom Truman found to be unaccountably resistant, to admit first 100,000 refugees and then to allow unlimited Jewish immigration to Palestine. Later, the United States became the chief advocate of the United Nations majority plan for the partitioning of Palestine.

But this was an inexpensive policy. As the British pointed out, Washington paid no price in putting pressure on the British to admit the refugees, but British troops had to deal with the outrage of the Arab population. Pushing the partition plan was equally inexpensive. Israel would come into being; although Arab indignation at the loss of territory regarded as part of the Arab heartland might well be translated into armed resistance, the newborn Israel would have to face that problem. American assistance would be limited to the exhortations of Warren Austin, ambassador to the U.N., that the Arabs accept the decision.

At the eleventh hour the Truman administration did have some second thoughts on the partition plan. Secretary of Defense Forrestal had earlier tried to convince Truman that the plan was a direct threat to American security. He saw the decision leading to instability in the Middle East and Arab hostility toward the United States, both of which would play into the hands of the Soviet Union. Within the State Department there was agreement with that position. Furthermore, there was a realization within the bureaucracy that a fierce armed conflict would follow Israel's independence and that the United Nations would lack the means to enforce its decision. Zionist leaders, confident of their own ability to overcome Arab military resistance and skeptical of ever receiving any real military support from the plan's sponsors, wanted the decision to stand. But the Truman administration decided that the security implications and lack of enforcement provisions were too serious and offered in place of the partition plan a trusteeship proposal. It was estimated that over 100,000 troops would be required to enforce even the trusteeship decision, and quite clearly the United States was prepared to consider contributing heavily to that security force. However the new proposal attracted no support, produced an anguished opposition from the Zionists and a contemptuous rejection from the Soviet Union, and was allowed to die quietly.

The behavior in this episode of the three major forces involved in formulating American policy toward the Arab world followed patterns that have persisted ever since. Zionist efforts were energetic and open. Truman has recorded the intense pressures he was under from Jewish lobbyists, and Forrestal claimed that some of Truman's closest advisers were dedicated supporters of the Zionist dream. Congress responded on cue as it would many times thereafter. But the Zionists' ability to reach the bureaucracy was much more limited. Clear indication of the difficulty they were having in this area is given by their singling out and publicly attacking individual bureaucrats—in particular Loy Henderson—who, they believed, were obstructing their efforts. However, the very visibility of this campaign tends to conceal the Zionists' modest objective. They made no real effort to gain American material assistance for the yet-to-be-born Israel—although their activities in supplying the Jewish forces with illegal arms from the United States were epic. This too is typical. There seems to be a conviction among pro-Israeli lobbyists that they can get assistance from the United States but that it will always be limited assistance.

Oil interests at this time were out of public sight. No senators or congressmen from oil-producing areas with small Jewish populations opposed the partition policy. But in this case, thanks to *The Forrestal Diaries,* there is evidence that the public silence corresponded to a private lack of deep concern. Forrestal's recorded conversations with oil representatives are remarkably lacking in suggestions that oil interests might be jeopardized by the long conflict almost certain to follow execution of the partition plan.

The bureaucratic response to the partition plan was sluggish to begin with, but these were only the opening months of the cold war. Forrestal, who led the attack in the beginning, was far ahead of others in the Truman administration in foreseeing a prolonged and serious confrontation with the

Soviet Union in the Middle East. Once his position did gain substantial bureaucratic support, the administration was willing to risk paying a considerable political price in reversing itself and furthermore was ready to make an expensive policy decision, one involving the possible commitment of men and material. This underlines the central thesis of this essay, which is that intense American involvement in the Arab world in this period has occurred only when American security interests were seen to be directly and adversely involved. In this case the bureaucratic triumph came much too late, but it did portend vigorous American involvement in the affairs of the Arab world.

American Policy from 1948 to 1958

There were many bizarre aspects to American policy toward the Arab world in the years immediately following Israel's independence. Although Miles Copeland's *The Game of Nations* has been denounced as inaccurate, it does provide a first-hand account of the events in this period by a major American participant in policy. His memory surely is fallible, and his cloak-and-dagger role was very different from that of one of his detractors, John Badeau. But the flavor is alive and real and tells of the combination of scientism and ignorance, of innocence and arrogance, which were as much a part of American policy as was the wise and conservative counsel of the Badeaus. Anyone who deals with American policy toward the Arab world at any length without discussing U.S. involvement in the coups and counter-coups in Syria during this period, the role (minor though it was) in the overthrow of King Faruk, and the vigorous efforts to overturn the Arab revolutions in 1957–58 is guilty of unconscionable distortion. American policy in the Middle East during the 1950s was characterized by interest so intense and activity so widespread that the United States intervened in the internal affairs of most of the states in the Arab world.

It would be a mistake to spend much time and effort looking for *the* American policy toward the Arab world. There was no single policy, well planned and carefully orchestrated. American policy is better seen as a series of decisions, some minor and some major, made by very different men and usually designed to meet some urgent and specific crisis. But if an effort is made to see if the hundreds of specific decisions add up to some general policy, it is likely to be discovered that they do. Throughout the cold-war era American policy-makers tried to achieve three objectives. First—and, in the view here, most important—they sought to contain the advance which they clearly perceived of as an aggressive international Communism centered in Moscow. This objective required most of all that Arab regimes be stable, non-Communist, and willing to resist the Communist advance. Second, the policy-makers wanted to preserve and protect American interests, especially oil interests, and to make certain that oil continued to flow into European and Japanese industry. Third, they wanted to see Israel independent, secure, and able to live in peace with the surrounding Arab world.

But what kind of Arab regimes would be most capable of resisting Communist aggression? Would the United States be best advised to support a government such as that of Iraq before July, 1958? That government, dominated by the clever, ultraconservative Nuri al-Said, was anti-Communist and willing to suppress ruthlessly any internal opposition. Or should the United States associate itself with revolutionary Arab leaders such as those in the military junta that was leading in Egypt in 1952? That government was also severe with local Communists and in addition sought to bring internal stability by satisfying the demands of the Egyptian people for a better and more dignified life. For a time the United States was favorable to both governments, even though they represented opposite ends of the Arab political spectrum. The more consistent British did not conceal their preference for Nuri al-Said and their anger at American sympathy for Nasser. Both policies appeared to be sensible means to achieve stable non-Communist regimes. Furthermore, the other objectives were either advanced or not endangered by American support for the Egyptian and the Iraqi poles of the Arab world. Although both regimes were rhetorically vigorous in their opposition to Israel, until Israel attacked the Gaza Strip in 1955 they were equally acquiescent in Israel's existence. With regard to oil, the Iraqi regime was solicitous of American interests, and Egypt was not an important oil-producer. Therefore the three major influences on American policy were reasonably well satisfied.

In 1955, however, the situation began to change. The Gaza raid of February 28, 1955, led to an Israeli-Egyptian confrontation. Then almost simultaneously the Baghdad Pact was formed, with Iraq joining Turkey, Iran, Pakistan, and Great Britain. The idea behind the pact was an American one, and, although the United States did not formally join, it did participate informally. The objective of the pact was ostensibly to contain the advance of Communism, but in the minds of many middle easterners—not only Arabs—the real purpose was to provide a vehicle for the military presence of the Western imperial powers. Nuri al-Said of Iraq was seen as a tool of Western imperialism in the Arab world. Suspicions that the revo-

lutionary elements in the Arab world were the targets of a Western imperial effort in which the Zionists and Arab reaction would act as local agents
had always been present but now were revitalized. Nasser's prominent role
at the Bandung conference later that year reflected these suspicions.

For the first time there was serious conflict among the groups influencing
American policy toward the Arab world. The unease which leaders of the
Jewish ethnic interest group felt toward a policy of support for the Egyptian regime was transformed into open hostility. At the same time, a serious
conflict developed within the bureaucracy. One element believed that the
United States must remain friendly with the leaders of revolutionary Arab
nationalism or risk seeing those leaders turn to the Soviet Union; another
felt that the United States was deserting its natural allies, the conservative
Arab leaders, and was in danger of encouraging a revolution which would
almost inevitably prefer the East to the West. Evidence of that intrabureau-
cratic conflict, which continued at least until 1967, can be found in the near
insubordination in 1956 of Henry Byroade, American ambassador to
Egypt; in the CIA–State Department conflict over recognition of the
Yemeni republic; and in the resignation and public remarks of Ambassa-
dor-designate Richard H. Nolte and members of his staff in 1967. The role
of oil interests in all of this can only be conjectured; but, since oil investments were in the states controlled by conservative Arab leaders and since
the revolutionary leadership was socialist in its thinking, it is plausible that
oil-investors sided with the anti-Nasser section of the bureaucracy. Policy
wavered violently. The cancellation of the offer to finance the Awsan Dam,
for example, must have pleased the same American decision-makers who
later were horrified by the adamant opposition of Dulles and Eisenhower to
the Anglo-French-Israeli operation against Egypt in 1956.

However, the policy-wavering ceased in 1957. Although the Eisenhower
Doctrine was worded so vaguely that observers had difficulty in interpreting its direction, as events developed in 1957 it became clear that those in
the bureaucracy who favored a policy of friendship with the leaders of revolutionary Arab nationalism had been soundly defeated. The defection of
Saudi Arabia from its alliance with Egypt was seized upon as an indication
that the tide had swung against revolutionary nationalist regimes. With
Iraq and Saudi Arabia as new-found allies leading the movement, the
United States began a campaign to modify, overturn, or isolate the revolutionary Arab regimes.

First to go was the Nabulsi government of Jordan, the victim of an
American-backed royal *coup d'état*. American economic and technical
support for the royal dictatorship in Jordan reveals much of the direction

evolving in American policy. As it had done in Iran several years earlier, the United States sought to induce the royalist Jordanian regime to inaugurate strong economic-development programs. It would be a serious mistake to describe American policy as simply supportive of reactionary leadership. On the contrary it was always well understood within the American government that the rising expectations of the Arab population of Jordan must be satisfied, at least to the extent necessary to prevent dissatisfaction from leading to revolution. American policy favored replacing the traditional bureaucracy, which was seen to be inefficient, corrupt, and based on nepotism, with a new breed of technocracy, which would be efficient, competent, and non-ideological. The revolutionary nationalists, described as extremist agitators, had to be suppressed, even if as a result there could be no pretense of permitting any real political freedom for many years. Jordan was indeed to join Iran as one of the most successful models of this policy.

This policy of using American influence to strengthen conservative regimes and to overturn or isolate radical ones had the great advantage as well of meeting the objectives of the other two major groups interested in American policy toward the Middle East. The type of regime favored was almost certain to try to attract Western investments and to provide a favorable atmosphere for existing investments. Such regimes also would be far more likely to restrict their hostility toward Israel to the rhetorical level while in fact acquiescing in Israel's presence in the Middle East. Consequently, of all the major influences on American policy in the area, only that section of the bureaucracy which regarded the conservative regimes as fundamentally unstable was dissatisfied. Within the politically liberal sections of the American public, which might have been expected to oppose the suppression of what was a national liberation movement, there was not a ripple of opposition.

By the end of 1957, however, this new American policy was in serious difficulty. A plot to overturn the Syrian government was uncovered, and evidence of American complicity, published in Damascus and later in Baghdad, is most persuasive. In any case, American complicity is widely accepted as fact in the Arab world. As a consequence the swing to the left in Syria was so strong that Syrian President Quwatli turned to union with Egypt in order to protect his country from being victimized by either Eastern or Western imperialism. Arab public opinion generally moved sharply against the United States.

The Syrian fiasco did not produce a reversal in American policy however. The defeat seems to have been seen as an unsuccessful episode in the struggle to stop Soviet infiltration. The military intervention in the

Lebanese civil war the following summer was fully in tune with the policy of containment. But the intervention in Lebanon came on the heels of what was for United States policy a disastrous development: the Iraqi revolution, in which Nuri al-Said, the chief supporter of American policy in the Arab world, was overthrown. A major alteration in American policy was inevitable, and it came within a few months of the American intervention in Lebanon.

Evidence of change was shown clearly in Lebanon itself. At the time of the American intervention, the Lebanese insurgents and their United Arab Republic supporters had been characterized as being closely allied with the Soviet Union. But only a few weeks later a compromise government emerged, with full American support, in which Rashid Karami, one of the most noteworthy rebel leaders, was premier. This amounted to implicit American recognition that Communist influence in the civil war had been exaggerated to an extraordinary degree. This coincided with a series of sharp attacks by President Nasser on Communist activities in the Arab world. The result was a significant decline in the estimate of threat from Communist expansion in the Arab world.

American Policy since 1958

In retrospect the American intervention in the Lebanese civil war seems to have been the climax of American involvement in the Arab world. In the years that followed there was not necessarily a change in policy. In fact, as will be discussed later, in the Johnson years the formula of 1957 seems to have been applied again: conservative regimes were supported, and the more revolutionary ones were opposed. But after 1958 there was a difference in the intensity of involvement. Active intervention in the internal affairs of Arab states no doubt continued, but not on a level that was visible to the interested observer with no access to classified information. Compared with the events of 1948–58, American policy appeared to be almost disinterested.

Seen in terms of the three influences on American policy, this indicates that the bureaucracy concerned with American national security was far less fearful of Communist expansion in the area than it had been. As a result, it was less interested in trying to wrench heavy appropriations from Congress for use in the Middle East, especially as the situation in Southeast Asia deteriorated.

In the Kennedy years there was a tentative shift toward rapprochement with President Nasser and the Arab nationalists. The Kennedy-Nasser correspondence reflected President Kennedy's general sympathy toward the efforts of peoples long the victims of imperialism or of their own traditional elites to reassert their national dignity. His government's recognition of the Republic of Yemen reflects this. But, generally speaking, the Kennedy years were uneventful with regard to American-Arab relations. Neither the Jewish ethnic interest group nor the oil interests were visibly active in trying to alter American policy. It was widely assumed that *de facto* acceptance of Israel was occurring. The oil interests were not seriously threatened in the area. In fact only the Cyprus issue was seriously upsetting to American policy in the Middle East generally. Both Turkey and Iran drifted toward improved relations with the Soviet Union and away from their exceptionally close relationship with the United States. Perception of threat from international Communism had declined precipitously in the entire area.

This assessment of the situation coincides in general with that of the emerging leadership of the Palestine movement. They too believed that there was a trend toward *de facto* acceptance by the Arab world of the loss of the Palestinian homeland. Their efforts to fight this strong, seemingly irreversible trend were remarkably successful. By 1966 they had succeeded in annoying Israel to the point of launching serious retaliatory raids, including especially the one on Samu in Jordan. They had in addition compelled those Arab regimes which were the most acquiescent in Israel's existence as a Jewish state to reconsider their policy. This was accomplished largely through the excitement their activities generated, especially among the young, throughout the Arab world.

American policy began to respond to these changes at the time when the Johnson administration was reversing the Kennedy policy of seeking friendship with the Arab revolution. Whereas Kennedy had recognized the Yemeni republican regime, Johnson can be fairly accused of seeking to destroy it. Two recipients of extensive American military aid, Saudi Arabia and Iran, were supplying the royalist forces in Yemen. There were, in addition, many American mercenaries attached to the royalist forces, and the suspicion among revolutionary Arabs of clandestine official American involvement is understandable. American relations with all revolutionary Arab regimes had deteriorated. The widespread belief among Arabs that the American involvement in Yemen was coordinated with Israeli aggressive plans is based more on deduction from previous Western behavior than on evidence. If American interest in overturning Arab revolutionary regimes had been comparable in intensity to that of 1957, it is difficult to believe that the resulting activities would not have been highly visible.

Coinciding with the intensifying Palestinian conflict was the increase in Soviet naval strength in the Mediterranean. In 1966 this was more of a nuisance or portent of the future than a threat; but, with the substantial Soviet arms assistance to revolutionary Arab regimes, American security worries were beginning to return.

By the spring of 1967, the American national security bureaucracy was mildly concerned about the Arab world. Oil interests were engaging in no visible activity to influence American policy, but the Jewish interest group suddenly was deeply concerned. There was by May, 1967, fear that Israel might be defeated in a new round of the conflict, and this fear was communicated to the government. However it was unclear what action the United States was expected to take other than letting the Soviet Union know that any intervention on its part would not be tolerated. In 1956 the conservative Arab regimes had managed to resist serious involvement in the Suez crisis. But when King Hussein brought Jordan into the Egyptian-Syrian defense pact at the height of the new crisis, the American formula of supporting both Israel and the conservative Arab regimes suddenly collapsed. American ability to influence the course of Arab affairs had evaporated.

The Arab charge of fundamental American-Israeli collusion in the 1967 June War should not be dismissed lightly. Since it is assumed that the collusion occurred at the highest policy-making levels and was part of an informal policy process, the charge cannot be disproved by anyone lacking direct access to this process. However, the assumption that there was a highly rational, purposeful American policy, worked out in careful detail by Israeli and possibly oil interest collaborators, is contradicted by visible American policy at this time, which appeared confused, uncertain, and directionless.

The proposition accepted here is that the visible confusion reflected a basic uncertainty. The Arab-Israeli conflict is one of several which are in part independent of the East-West conflict but which could lead to accidental war between the great powers. By May, 1967, events had gone well beyond the control of the United States and the Soviet Union, and the possibility of an escalation into a great-power conflict, even a nuclear conflict, was a real one. As has been contended, a perception of threat to national security takes precedence over any other interest, and the conflict of June, 1967, is a classic example. A determination not to permit the conflict to spread to the great powers was the one clear feature of American policy. The hot line was used, and both great powers sought energetically to bring the fighting to an end. It is difficult to imagine American decision-makers actually planning a conflict in which the threat of great-power involvement was so great.

Soviet-American cooperation during the war and the Glassboro Conference with its suggestion of mutual interests in stability in the area had unanticipated results. Fears of Soviet aggression in the area, far from being confirmed, were considerably lessened. This meant that, of the three influences on American policy in the area, two were to be little concerned. Neither national security interests nor economic interests were seriously threatened. Consequently the Jewish ethnic group, which remained deeply concerned about the security of Israel, became relatively more influential. This appears to have been reflected in policy. An important Israeli diplomatic objective was that the United States not support an international approach to resolving the Arab-Israeli conflict. Israel, having no faith in the willingness of the United Nations or the great powers to provide for its security, was therefore of the opinion that an international effort would offer only the illusion of support. Such an effort, Israel believed, could only subvert the central Israeli task, which was to demonstrate to the Arabs that the price that Israel could charge for its elimination as a Jewish state was greater than the Arabs could ever pay. The American diplomatic stance, one of responding sluggishly if at all to suggestions of energetic international efforts, was clearly in tune with this objective. Later, when Israel sought to replace France with the United States as the leading source of Israeli arms, the American government again complied. The final months of the Johnson administration were a period of close American-Israeli relations, but it should be noted that once again the policy was an inexpensive one.

The election of Richard Nixon as president of the United States brought about some alteration in the relative influence of the three groups. The Republican party is generally less responsive to representatives of the Jewish community, which is strongly Democratic. Conversely, the influence of the oil interests on this party are considerably greater. Finally, Nixon had been one of the most intransigent cold warriors; even though he had announced, in accepting the Republican presidential nomination, his intention to negotiate with the Communist powers, the probability that he would interpret Soviet military activity as threatening was a strong one.

The policy of the Nixon administration toward the Arab world appears to reflect such an alteration of influence. Policies have been advanced, particularly by Secretary of State Rogers, which have done considerable damage to Israeli tactical planning. The administration appears to be willing to take political risks with the Jewish electorate in order to try to achieve a settlement of the conflict. Reflected here is a general interest in achieving stability in the area, in lessening the chances of an accidental war, and in avoiding serious risks to American investments. Ironically, if this analysis is valid, the Israeli effort to convince the United States that the Soviet Union is highly aggressive in the Middle East could have the opposite effect of that intended. If fear of Soviet aggression grows, it is likely that the United States will move energetically to re-establish some influence with 100 million Arabs occupying vast and strategic territories. It would make little sense for the United States to look to 3 million Israelis occupying a tiny territory to blunt a Soviet advance that presumably would take the form of internal subversion in the Arab countries. Renewed fears, equal in intensity to those of the 1950s, would very likely result in an equally intense involvement in the affairs of the Arab world.

What seems less likely every day is the possibility, should American activity in the Arab world intensify, of returning to the old formula of 1957. Inexorable change is reaching even the sheikdoms of the Arabian Peninsula. The day of the traditional Arab leader who solicited Western support has largely passed. An American policy based on support from King Hussein in the east and King Hasan II in the west is not likely to give the United States great influence in the Arab world. It is a policy more in keeping with the picture presented in this paper—of a United States which no longer is intensely interested in influencing developments in the Arab world. The community of interest which the conservative wing of the national security bureaucracy, the oil interests, and the lobbyists for the Jewish interest group fell upon in the 1950s no longer exists. The United States has already been warned that, if it continues to side with Israel in a worsening Arab-Israeli conflict, American economic interests in the area will suffer. If this threat is granted credibility, there is every reason to believe that the ethnic and economic interest groups will place sharply conflicting pressures on Washington policy-makers.

A projection of this picture into the immediate future suggests something of a standoff between these two interest groups, with Israel and the Arabs in turn angered by particular American responses. The factor which is likely to be decisive in determining the outcome is American fear of the Soviet Union and, in the years to come, of China. If the present world trend, despite the sometimes spectacular but temporary reversals, toward accommodation of the United States and the Soviet Union continues, the American national security bureaucracy is likely to be less and less willing to commit American resources to an active policy in the Arab world. The contest then will settle on such questions as American willingness to sell arms and grant generous credits to Israel. Whether it does so depends on the bargaining skill of the competing interest groups. Certainly evidence to date suggests primacy for the Jewish ethnic interest group, but the Arabs have not yet placed serious pressure on the oil interests to use their influence on United States policy to greater effect.

If American fears of either or both great Communist powers increase substantially, the national security bureaucracy is likely to be willing to commit major resources to the Middle East. The pattern of the 1950s, with heavy involvement in Arab internal affairs, is likely to be repeated; but the formula of supporting and attempting to bring stability to Arab traditional regimes almost certainly will not work. Competition with the Communist powers for influence within the Arab world must of necessity focus on the centers of Arab power, such as Cairo, Damascus, and Algiers. Such an effort would grant the Arabs a vastly improved bargaining position with the United States and conversely would weaken the Israeli one. This closely parallels the extraordinarily disadvantageous bargaining position in which the Zionists found themselves during World War II, when they were competing with the Arabs to influence British policy.

This prospect is a grim one for the United States internally. It would only add to the Jewish community's sense of isolation and fear, which, solidly based as it is, is father to the Arab-Israeli conflict.

West Germany And The Arabs

Mahmoud el-Shazly

BEFORE WORLD WAR II the Arab people viewed Germany with sympathy and admiration. Germany represented a challenge to the pre-eminence of Britain and France, the countries occupying the majority of Arab territories. Young Egyptian nationalists, including Nur al-Din Tarraf and Fathi Radwan of the old nationalist party and Ahmad Hussein of Masr al-Fatat, in a violent reaction to the signing of the Anglo-Egyptian Treaty of 1936, attended the 1936 Nuremburg rally.

The drive by Field Marshal Rommel to El Alamein, some fifty miles west of Alexandria, in January and February, 1942, was viewed by many Egyptians as a prelude to the liberation of Egypt from British occupation. General Aziz el-Masri, the Egyptian chief-of-staff, was removed from office in 1942 by the British for alleged contacts with the Germans. On February 24, 1945, the Egyptian premier, Ahmad Maher, was assassinated because he planned to declare war on the Axis powers. In Iraq the nationalist premier, Rashid Ali, appealed to Hitler for help in expelling the British and received planes and arms from Germany. Any charge, however, that Arab nationalists knew and approved of Nazi crimes against the Jews of Europe is unfounded. Information about such atrocities was made public only toward the end of the war.

The Luxemburg Agreement

Perhaps the most important event in the postwar relations between the Arab world and the Federal Republic of Germany (West Germany) was the Luxemburg agreement of 1953, concluded not between West Germany and any Arab state but between West Germany and Israel. This treaty climaxed a campaign which the Zionists had been waging against Germany for nearly eight years and in which they had capitalized on world-wide condemnation of Nazi war crimes.

Nahum Goldmann had raised the question of restitution as early as 1941, at the World Jewish Congress. On September 20, 1945, Chaim Weizmann, speaking on behalf of the Jewish Agency, addressed a letter to the governments of the United States, Great Britain, the U.S.S.R., and France in which he defined restitution "as embracing the buildings, plant equipment, money, securities and valuables of various kinds taken from Jewish institutions and individuals, as well as Jewish cultural treasures, religious articles and communal properties."[1] In 1951 Israel addressed several notes to the four Allied occupation powers requesting that they urge the Federal Republic of Germany to satisfy Israeli claims. The United States suggested that a settlement of Israeli claims be effected through direct negotiations between the Israeli and the German governments, thus recognizing the legality of Israel's claim to German restitution funds.

Judging by what appeared in the Germany press during 1945 and 1946, the Germans strongly resisted any suggestion that they alone were responsible for the war; at the same time, however, the *Neue Zeitung,* the newspaper published by the American occupation authorities, consistently stressed German war crimes. In the Zionists' assessment of the period in Germany, "no re-education program instituted through the Allied Powers was able to bridge the mental gap."[2]

On the other hand, world Jewry was to be discouraged from going to the extreme of refusing to deal with the Germans altogether. Nahum Goldmann wrote in the *Zionist Quarterly* in 1952 that

> the passage of time will have to bring about profound changes in the German national character. . . . However, there is quite another aspect to the problem. This has to do with the simple fact that the Nazi Regime stole from Jews all over Europe tremendous amounts of property. To take the position that we don't want our property returned to us by the Germans would be absolutely immoral.[3]

1. Quoted in Kurt R. Grossmann, *Germany's Moral Debt* (Washington, D.C.: Public Affairs Press, 1954), p. 7.
2. *Ibid.,* p. 2.
3. Nahum Goldmann, "Direct Israel-German Negotiations? Yes," *Zionist Quarterly,* I, no. 3 (Winter, 1952), 9–13.

This attitude was finally to gain the upper hand over the attitude of those who opposed any direct negotiations with Germany.[4]

It is doubtful whether the German leadership recognized from the start the magnitude of the Zionist's objectives. On the Jewish New Year holiday in 1949, Chancellor Konrad Adenauer expressed his readiness to give DM 10 million (about $2.5 million) to Israel. About three years later, on September 10, 1952, Chancellor Adenauer, Foreign Minister Moshe Sharret of Israel, and Nahum Goldmann, acting as president of the Conference on Jewish Material Claims against Germany, signed the Luxemburg agreement. It was ratified on March 18, 1953, by the Bundestag (the lower house of the West German parliament). The agreement obligated West Germany to pay, over a period of twelve to fourteen years, $822 million in goods to the state of Israel and substantial sums to various Jewish groups and individuals.

Reaction to the Agreement

The Arab reaction to the Luxemburg agreement was predictably violent. Arab delegations set up headquarters in Germany and used every means conceivable to present their case against the agreement to the German people. They arranged press conferences and managed to secure editorial backing from some newspapers previously in favor of the agreement. They received favorable responses from some members of the Bundestag. Franz Joseph Strauss, a leading figure in the Christian Social Union, the Bavarian wing of Adenauer's party, wrote on February 16, 1953:

> The Bundesrepublic of Germany must value the traditional good relations of Germany with the Arab States, which must be maintained and fostered. I do not consider it impossible that a way can be found to fulfill the duties of restitution toward the Jews and at the same time maintain friendly relations with the Arabs.

Strauss also criticized the German government for failing to advise the Arabs of its intention to conclude the agreement with Israel.[5] Furthermore, Strauss wrote in January, 1953, in *Chemische Industrie* that ratification of the agreement might cause Germany to lose a potential Arab market of

4. See Joseph B. Schectman, "Direct Israel-German Negotiations? No," *Zionist Quarterly,* I, no. 3 (Winter, 1952), 14–20.

5. Quoted in Grossmann, *Germany's Moral Debt,* pp. 27–28.

DM 5 billion over the next ten years.[6] The strongest opposition from within the West German cabinet came from Fritz Schaefer, the finance minister, and from Heinrich Hellwege, the minister for the Bundestag.

Hjalmar Schacht, the financial architect of the Third Reich, declared that Germany had been pressured into the agreement by the Allies. The validity of this statement was best demonstrated by the behavior of Hans Seebohm, the minister of transportation, who voted for the agreement in the Bundestag but subsequently attacked it at his party's convention in May, 1953.

To soften Arab reaction, the West German government announced that it was sending a special trade mission to Cairo. The mission, headed by Ludgar Westrich of the ministry of economics, arrived in Cairo early in February, 1953. West German-Arab relations, however, seemed to have reached the point of no return; an East German trade delegation, invited by the Egyptian government, arrived in Cairo shortly after the West Germans had started negotiations.

From the beginning, the Communist bloc strongly opposed the payment of reparations to Israel. Of the four Allied powers, the U.S.S.R. alone did not reply to the repeated notes from the Israeli government. The Communists opposed first the West German negotiations with Israel and then the ratification of the agreement. They declared at this time that Israel was a tool of the United States and that the agreement was nothing more than a capitalist scheme from which only the Americans would benefit.

Effects of the Agreement

To appreciate the significance of the agreement, let us review the reparations as they apply to nine major economic areas.

1. *Industry:* New or replacement machinery was supplied to 1,275 plants. By the time the agreement was fulfilled, more than 200,000 workers were employed to operate this machinery.

2. *Shipping:* Forty-nine ships were built and delivered, including bulk carriers, tankers, mixed cargo vessels, and two passenger liners, for a total of 466,000 tons; these ships opened markets for Israel in Africa, Asia, and Latin America. More than 50 per cent of the reparations goods were carried in ships flying the Israeli flag.

3. *Port facilities:* The port of Haifa was modernized and enlarged to more than twice its former capacity. Equipment received included a 7,500-

6. Quoted in *ibid.,* p. 31.

ton-capacity floating dock worth $2 million to handle ship repairs; a dry dock capable of raising 18,000 tons; a 25-ton-capacity floating crane; fourteen rail-operated mobile cranes; a 200-ton-capacity dredger; and building materials to begin construction of the Israeli shipyard on the Kishon River.

4. *Transportation:* New railway equipment valued at $11.5 million was imported, including automatic signaling devices (making express trains possible in Israel for the first time), 12 passenger-car sets, 400 freight cars for hauling potash and phosphate from the Negev, and rails for the new line to Beersheba and for the replacement of the Tel Aviv-Jerusalem line. Modern aviation equipment was also supplied for the air terminal at Lydda.

5. *Communication:* More than $6 million in equipment was supplied, including automatic telephone exchanges for all major cities, a radio-telephone hookup to remote settlements, and a ring of telex stations for Tel Aviv, Jerusalem, Haifa, and Beersheba.

6. *Power:* West Germany provided turbogenerators totaling 560,000 kilowatts; a 110-kilovolt high-tension station; and power-correcting generators, transformers, and cables. The electrical energy supply in Israel increased from 885 million kilowatt hours in 1953 to 2 billion kilowatt hours in 1963.

7. *Mining:* Equipment worth $3.5 million was supplied to the Timna copper works, which in 1963 was treating 500,000 tons of copper ore annually.

8. *Housing:* Construction materials worth $80 million were used to replace the hut cities of the early 1950s with permanent homes for close to a million new immigrants.

9. *Fuel:* Israel purchased 9 million tons of oil in England under a special sterling account set up by the West German government.

At the time the agreement became effective (1953) the ratio of Israel's imports to exports was about five to one. The influx of German goods under the agreement represented approximately 30 per cent of Israel's general revenue and covered close to 40 per cent of Israel's expenditures under its development budget. With reparations assuming the burden of industrial development, the Israeli government was able to devote funds to problems that otherwise would have received little attention—for example, absorption of a million immigrants, reclamation of the Negev, inauguration of a national road-building program culminating in the Beersheba-Eilat highway, expansion and modernization of hospitals and medical facilities, refinancing of the national debt, and purchasing large quantities of food and other consumer items.

West German-Arab Relations

In an effort to counterbalance the effects of the Luxemburg agreement, West Germany tried to develop trade and promote economic and cultural ties with the Arab states. The government extended capital credits to the Arab countries totaling, as of December 31, 1964, $247.7 million. Algeria received $17.6 million; Jordan, $12.7 million; Morocco, $22.7 million; Sudan, $31.1 million; Syria, $88.1 million; Tunisia, $15.1 million; the U.A.R. (Egypt), $57.9 million; and Yemen, $2.5 million.[7]

The parties involved in these transactions interpreted them in different ways. While West Germany considered the project to be one of financial aid, President Nasser did not agree: "We have received no aid from West Germany. [It has] taken part in some industrial projects, and we pay their cost in full. We have already repaid the larger part at 6 per cent interest. Do you call this aid?"[8]

West German loans, nevertheless, supported important projects in many Arab states. In Jordan the port of Aqaba was developed; in Egypt a dry dock was constructed and in Alexandria bridges over the Nile and ships to navigate the river were built; in Tunisia three dams for irrigation, a textile factory, and the Melitta airport were constructed, a high-tension line was installed, and the fishing harbor at Mahdia was developed; in Algeria pipelines for irrigation projects were installed, modern farm equipment was introduced, and the harbor of Annaba was developed; in Morocco the chemical industry based on phosphate received financial backing, and port and other transportation facilities were developed.[9] In addition West Germany attempted to support some projects of a technical nature: in Egypt the Institute for Technical Education, the Institute for Trade School Teachers, and the Center for Precision Mechanics in Cairo, the Polytechnical Institute in Helwan, and the Petroleum Institute in Suez; in Morocco a metal-workers school in Nador and a center for training in the use of agricultural machinery in Rabat; in Tunisia a cotton institute, a model dairy farm, an experimental station for sugar beets, and a mobile veterinary station; and in Saudi Arabia a trade school. The West German government gave Algeria, in honor of its independence, four Volkswagen ambulances and an X-ray diagnostic apparatus.[10]

---

7. Karl Holbik and Henry Allen Myers, *West German Foreign Aid 1956–1966* (Boston: Boston Univ. Press, 1968), p. 48.

8. "West Germany, Caving In," *Time,* February 19, 1965, p. 28. *Time* contended that the interest was only 3 per cent.

9. Holbik and Myers, *West German Foreign Aid,* p. 83 n.

10. *Ibid.,* p. 85.

By the end of 1964, West German–Arab relations seemed to be slowly recovering from the effects of the Luxemburg agreement. The Federal Republic imported three-quarters of its oil from the Arab world (40 per cent from Libya alone). An estimated 25,000 West German tourists visited Egypt during 1964. At the same time, over one-third of the 1,900 Egyptians with professional experience who had been sent to Europe for further training had gone to West Germany. Shortly after President Boumedienne of Algeria took office, he included West Germany on his list of preferred trading partners. West German–Arab relations suffered a setback, however, when a secret gift of arms from West Germany to Israel was made known and, later, when the two countries established full diplomatic relations.

In a 1960 meeting in New York between Chancellor Adenauer and Prime Minister David Ben-Gurion, the former, always sensitive about Germany's past, arranged to give military equipment worth approximately $80 million to Israel, with the approval—and most likely the urging—of Washington. This included both American-made and German-made tanks, two used British submarines, helicopters, and light artillery. The operation was so secret that Bonn's foreign ministry discovered it only by accident late in 1964.

Nasser reacted by inviting Walter Ulbricht, head of state for the German Democratic Republic, to visit Cairo. Since the policy of Bonn was to sever relations with any country that recognized East Germany, the invitation started a diplomatic chain reaction. After complex diplomatic maneuvers and propaganda exchanges, Spanish mediators arranged a settlement in which West Germany promised immediate cessation of arms shipments to Israel and an end to the training of Israeli army officers, and in return Nasser promised not to recognize East Germany in the near future. Nevertheless, Nasser received Ulbricht with all the honors normally reserved for heads of states.

In May, 1964, Israel and West Germany formally established diplomatic relations. Consequently, Algeria, Iraq, Jordan, Lebanon, Saudi Arabia, the U.A.R., and Yemen severed their relations with Bonn, and the West German–Arab situation came under considerable strain. German tourism in Egypt and the training of Egyptians in West Germany declined in 1966 and 1967. Today, in the eyes of some observers, West German–Arab relations are no better than they were two decades ago.

The election in October, 1969, of the Social Democrats, headed by Willy Brandt, gives new hope for better relations between Germany and the Arab countries. Brandt's more imaginative *Ostolitik* has been demonstrated by his meeting in March, 1970, with East German Premier Willy Stoph in Erfurt, by his various contacts with Eastern European capitals, and finally and most significantly by his signing of a treaty with the Soviet Union in August, 1970. In the treaty the Soviet Union and West Germany pledged to renounce the use of force and agreed to accept the national boundaries in Eastern Europe that resulted from Germany's defeat in World War II. These events may enable West Germany to establish a foreign policy that is more independent of Washington. In addition, Brandt's anti-Nazi past makes him less susceptible to Zionist pressures than his predecessors.

Zionism and International Politics

Theological and Religious Implications of Zionism in Palestine

Elmer Berger

THIS IS NOT THE FIRST period of history in which the dichotomy between theology and religion has been overtly admitted by many and hailed as a virtue by some. The only theologians who seem to find no agonizing spiritual discrepancies between dogmatics and life in the context of Israel and Palestine are the apocalyptic determinists and the "God is dead" advocates. Jews who are apostles of either or both of these schools are not in the main current of Judaism's tradition. Those who call themselves Zionists and who revere the *authentic* tradition have—particularly since 1967—overtly wrestled with the undeniable contradictions between the facts of national Zionism, sovereignized in the state of Israel, and the dream of Zion invested with varying degrees of sanctity in Judaism's several denominations. I think of Judah Magnes and Martin Buber and, in a somewhat more secular context, of Jacob Talmon and even Nahum Goldmann. Whatever such men believed about the merit or necessity of the physical presence of Zionism in Palestine, they have raised increasingly insistent doubts about the "fulfillment" of the dream.

Whose Theology or Religion?

My intention is not to deny the tradition of a return to Zion which as a creed is important to many—but not all— Jews. Nor is it to deny that this legitimate spiritual aspiration has been vulgarized and prostituted by both the political propagandists of Zionist Israel and the politico-religious parties within Israel itself. Reform Judaism was a product of the Enlightenment and the liberal revolutions in Europe and America. It repudiated the concept of Jewish nationality. Perhaps the most unequivocal statement to this effect was made in 1885 in what came to be known as the Pittsburgh Platform. In that statement a group of the most distinguished Reformist rabbis declared:

> We consider ourselves no longer a nation but a religious community, and therefore expect neither a return to Palestine, nor a sacrificial worship under the administration of the sons of Aaron, nor the restoration of the laws concerning the Jewish state.[1]

This straightforward repudiation of the Zionism that Theodor Herzl had delineated a decade and a half earlier has been watered down in the more recent years of pro-Zionist influence. Modern Reform Jews will profess to be pro-Israel, whatever this means either religiously or theologically. I submit that, despite all the Zionist movement's propaganda and organizational success in the United States, it has lacked both the candor and the confidence to argue forcefully that American Jews are a political nationality which is recognized in international law to possess a functional second nationality with respect to the state of Israel. In fact, I can testify from personal experience that a fair part of the Zionist propaganda budget has been spent in attempting to camouflage this issue whenever those of us who understand the phenomenon have raised it.

The problem is somewhat different in more traditional or Orthodox Judaism. There are probably good psychological and emotional reasons why many traditional Jews, as such, have been more militant in their public expression of anti-Zionism than those of the Reformist school. The idea of Zion as a sacrament is immeasurably more important to them. Any desecration of that sacrament, therefore, evokes a much more emphatic response. These traditional Jews are also religiously more immersed in general creed and observance than Reform Jews. My spiritual ancestors selectively shed traditional observances when, rightly or wrongly, they intellectualized their understanding of the tradition. Traditional Judaism, too, has changed; but change is resisted and is more the result of erosion and a reluctant surrender to rapidly changing life-patterns. This psychologically different attitude to change may account for the fact that some of the

---

1. Isaac Landman, *Universal Jewish Encyclopedia* (New York: Ktav, 1941), VI, 241.

most vehement denunciations of Zionism have come from the most traditional and observant elements of contemporary Judaism. For example, this advertisement appeared in the *New York Times:*

ALL JEWS

who are truly loyal to the Torah, abhor and disclaim the recent Zionist political meddling. . . . The Zionist political leaders have, once again, revealed themselves as the *arch-enemies of the Jewish people.*[2]

In somewhat less shrill terms, an organization of devout Jews calling itself Friends of Jerusalem recently offered the following advice in a small pamphlet:

Contemporary Zionism, which since its inception considers Jewish religious practice and observance as a private and voluntary matter and which has substituted modern secular nationalism for the divine covenant, is completely incompatible with Judaism. Zionism is a radical break with the Jewish past and Jewish tradition, a perversion of the true nature of the Jewish people and a most dangerous development in Jewish history. . . .

STATE OF ISRAEL
The fact that the country, which is the result and embodiment of Zionism, has adopted the name of Israel, tends to spread utter confusion within the Jewish community and in the outside world because its policies and actions are carried out under the name of Israel, which is the historic designation of the Jewish people, even when those policies and actions are diametrically opposed to Jewish tradition, Jewish religious (Torah) laws and the real interests of the Jewish people. Indeed, the very establishment of this secular national "Jewish" state constitutes a break with Jewish tradition and with the norms laid down for the Jewish people in talmudic and rabbinic laws.[3]

Nor is this position new—a result of disillusion with pragmatics or a tactical revulsion at Zionist-Israeli excesses since the 1967 June War.

With regard to the Zionists what shall I say and what am I to speak? There is great dismay also in the Holy Land that these evil men who deny the Unique One of the world and His Holy Torah have proclaimed with so much publicity that it is in their power to hasten redemption for the people of Israel and gather the dispersed from all

2. *New York Times,* March 12, 1970, p. 12.
3. *Pamphlet #*1, Friends of Jerusalem, 545 Fifth Ave., New York, N.Y., 1968.

the ends of the earth. . . . The chief of these ruffians (*biryonim*) in
our Holy Land has uttered terrible words, full of denial of the Most
High, promising that Dr. Herzl will neither rest nor be silent until the
foot of Israel ceases from the lands of the Exile, and mocking at the
saying of the Sages that the day of the Gathering of the Exiles will be
as great as the day on which heaven and earth were created. . . . And
had I intended to describe to your honour the storm that was aroused
among the masses of Arabs and Christians, I would have had insufficient paper and been too weak to elaborate, since when he entered the
Holy Land, hell entered with him, and we do not yet know what we
have to do against the destroyers of the totality of Israel, may the Lord
have mercy. For us in the Holy Land it is a sure sign that Dr. Herzl
comes not from the Lord but from "the side of pollution," for we say,
anyone who pleads in defense of Israel is exalted in the world by the
Holy One, Blessed be He, while this evil man pleads in condemnation
and multiples accusation.[4]

These are not the words of Gamal Abdel Nasser or even of the Grand
Mufti. Nor are they quoted from a pamphlet of the national guidance or
information ministry of Iraq or Syria. These are the words of a devout
rabbi in Palestine, written in 1898 in a letter to a colleague in Hungary.

With complete integrity, therefore, I submit that national Zionism and
the state it spawned are not only alien to the Jewish tradition—both theologically and religiously—but must be considered as a desecration of the
tradition. *Desecration* is an applicable term precisely because for political
purposes Zionism has fostered the belief that it is a religious movement,
sanctified by Jewish theology, and that it has produced a state which fulfills
theological concepts and enriches religious experience.

But I return to my contention that Zionism does not argue this case with
very much enthusiasm to Jews. That is the irony. In the West the exploitation among Christians of these religious and theological pretensions has had
important political consequences. A brilliant Arab scholar and nationalist
once confided to me, after spending a year at an Ivy League university, that
in his mind the theological predilections of the Bible Belt were a greater
threat to an understanding of the Palestine question than the Zionist lobby.
I am not prepared to agree unreservedly with that judgment, but the observation deserves great consideration; and it can be applied as well to those
Western European countries where Calvinist Christianity is a predominant
force.

I am not sure whether what I have said so far can be classified as theolo-

4. Quoted from *Der Yid,* a New York Yiddish newspaper, in 1965, in Emile
Marmorstein, *Heaven at Bay* (London: Oxford Univ. Press, 1969), p. 79.

gy, religion, or neither. But our interest here in theological—or even religious—concepts is for their relevance to a grave political problem. I devoutly wish that there were more Bubers and Marmorsteins to speak up for the authentic Jewish tradition. But no less earnestly do I wish that there were more Christians—particularly among those who profess the more fundamentalist creeds—who would be as outspoken about the counterfeiting of their Messianism by Zionist Israel as these traditional Jews have been. That would not of itself solve the Palestine problem, but it would materially diminish the distortion of the historic debate in which so much of the Western world has engaged. To put it bluntly, Christian fundamentalists who give their religious and theological endorsements to the Zionist state of Israel are being "had." Religiously, they are giving a racist, discriminatory kind of nationalism the blessing of God. I do not, in any sense, excuse or attempt to exonerate those of my own faith who acquiesce in this confidence game. But I am bound to say that if Christian dissent had been historically as consistent and as extensive as has Jewish dissent, the Palestine problem would today be of considerably smaller dimensions.

"The Jewish People"

It is possible to examine thoroughly in this paper all of the theological concepts in Judaism which the Zionists have used at one time or another to support their case. I propose to make a few categorical statements and to examine in some depth the theological question which I believe to be the core of the confusion: namely, the concept of "the Jewish people."

It must be said, first of all, that there is a legitimate Zionism in the authentic Jewish tradition. But that legitimate tradition was repelled by what Herzl's Zionism did in Palestine. There is probably no more authoritative or eloquent expression of that aversion than the words written by Ahad Ha-am, the architect of what has been called "cultural Zionism," in 1922. In that year, during one of the earliest riots in Palestine, Ha-am learned of the death of an Arab at the hands of Zionists. His reaction was, "If this be the Messiah, let him come and me not see him."[5]

Another matter that might be classified as a religious implication is the humanitarian problem created by centuries of prejudice against Jews, the climactic chapter in that phenomenon occurring under Hitler. I will not repeat here the arguments demonstrating that Zionism is not in conception,

5. *Haaretz*, no. 840 (Elul 8, 5682 [1922]).

and never was, a humanitarian program to counterbalance this inhumanity. Nor is it necessary to raise and answer here the moral question involved in the general agreement of the Western world—Christian and Jew alike—to meet this human problem with a plan that violated the human and political rights of what the Balfour Declaration euphemistically called "the non-Jewish communities in Palestine." I understand the cynicism of politicians who advocated and acquiesced in this political formula. Speaking for myself—and admitting the integral place of compassion and of providing relief for human suffering in the value system of almost any religion—I cannot endorse the callous transfer of political injustice from one group to another as a religious act. The business of choosing the lesser of two evils is for the politicians of the world—not for the religionists, whose business ought to be morally inspired indignation at all evil.

Charity also claims a high priority in the Western ordering of religious values. But I cannot find anywhere in Judaism the license to sanctify orgies of "million-dollar-a-minute" campaigns, which masquerade as charity but whose proceeds subsidize the occupation by force of territories and property taken by the sword. I do not find anything either in Judaism's theological commitment to the idea of one God for all humanity or in its religious mandate to do unto others what you would have them do unto you which justifies the second-class citizenship assigned to the Arab minority in Israel.

I can understand all of these phenomena—and others which need not be detailed here—in the context of a tough revanchist nationalism fostering an exclusivist and discriminatory base. But I cannot reconcile them, by any criteria I know, with religious acts; and I know of no genuine interpretation of any Jewish theological concept which can justify them as religion.

These problems all derive from the theological and religious distortion of the central political and demographic problem in Palestine—the character and purpose of what is called "the Jewish people." This question, in turn, is related to the character of Judaism. Here again, I propose to argue theological and religious questions with some political and sociological facts. One of these facts is that, left to their own volition, no substantial number of Jews have demonstrated a compulsion to reconstitute their lives as either a separate secular or a theocratic nation in a political sovereignty of their own. I say this despite the presence in Israel today of nearly three million Jews. As the world well knows, they came, for the most part under duress. In the years before Hilter there was little immigration to Palestine, even though conditions in Eastern and Central Europe were less than ideal and the immigration policy in Palestine was regulated only by a flexible limitation described as "the economic absorptive capacity" of the country.

The impact of the establishment of the state of Israel upon Arab societies, together with the economic, political, and social revolutions in the Arab world in which—to some extent—all non-Muslims have been made more self-conscious of minority positions, had an effect on Jews and resulted in the immigration of more than half of Israel's present Jewish population. The considerable sums of money that were spent on indoctrination and the more considerable sums that were spent on a variety of economic subsidies in Israel are now being used to recruit immigrants from what the Zionist-Israeli establishment calls "the affluent countries." Some results are observable. But my point is that, even accepting the Zionist interpretation of Judaism as a potpourri of religion and nationality and even admitting that many Jews pray—or are enjoined to pray—three times a day for a return to Zion, few are moved to any positive action in response to this allegedly religious commandment.

Ideologically, then, it becomes necessary for Zionists to offer a rebuttal to those of us Jews who argue that Judaism is a religious discipline of essentially universal dimensions. Many Zionists or pro-Zionists are reluctant to join the issue at this level and instead argue that it is immaterial what Jews think about their faith and the identity of "the Jewish people" deriving from this faith. These Zionists and/or Zionist apologists point to the history of persecution and argue that, even if Jews claim that their identity as Jews derives from profession of such a universal faith and wish to practice this faith while enjoying full acceptance and integration at all secular levels of their lives, the people of the world will not permit this. This case is usually confused by an oversimplified approach to history and to the meaning of full integration in terms of the varied societal systems in which Jews live.

I will state one moral equation, and, again, it seems to me that the essence of the answer is a responsibility greater for Christians than for Jews, since—as I have indicated—I think Jews have historically given their answer. If—and I underline many times the *if*—the Christian world does in fact believe that Jews are unsuited to full acceptance in the societies in which they are minority groups, then Jews are entitled, at the hands of this same world, to a place where their acceptance—at least theoretically—may be complete. That does not mean, however, that the sociopolitical equation is morally or religiously justified if the Christian world, out of a sense of guilt, assigns such a place at the expense of people who are known as Arabs.

There is, of course, the standard Zionist answer to my formulation of this choice. Zionists today fundamentally reject the equation. The future of "the Jewish people," they argue, is something that Jews are no longer willing to leave to the caprices of those who are not Jews. In Zionism—buttressed by the sovereignty of Zionism's Middle Eastern state—Jews, they say, will exercise the same right of self-determination as other peoples.

Inspired largely by the Palestinians' claim to the right to liberate their homeland, a new semantics has been added to the controversy. Zionists and even official representatives of the Israeli government are now speaking of "liberating the Jewish people." The Israeli ambassador to the United Nations recently declared, for example: "The world must understand that Zionism is as sacred to the Jewish people as the national liberation movements are to the nations of Africa and Asia." This is, of course, simply dressing the old Zionist pitch for "ingathering the exiles" in the garb of new semantics. The ambassador exhorted American Jews to accept immigration as "not merely an idea, but a well organized, efficient, constant process from every city and town, every family."[6]

But, as with virtually all Zionist-Israeli actual programing—and rhetoric—this is political, not theological and/or religious. And even if, for some Jews, there are muted and reverberating overtones that seem to echo the great prophetic sermons of Judaism's past, calling for redemption and then restoration, the similarities are more apparent than real. And in any event, for half a century of what Zionists have called "practical Zionism," Jews have not responded.

The Question of Survival

I believe there cannot be the slightest doubt that the massive support for Israel offered by the Jews of the free world is motivated essentially— whether generally justified or not—by the most elemental desire for survival. Gottlieb Hammer, the executive vice-chairman of the United Israel Appeal, the largest Zionist fund-collecting agency in the world, said with astonishing candor, "When the blood flows, the money flows."[7] Many of us who know the Zionist-Israel phenomenon from less strategic locations concluded long ago that Zionism is a "crisis" movement. The

6. *Jewish News* (Newark), April 7, 1970, p. 28.
7. Lawrence Mosher, "Zionist Role in U.S. Raises New Concern," *National Observer* (Washington, D.C.), May 18, 1970, p. 1.

state is a crisis state. In the ten years from 1957 to 1967, which was Israel's longest period of even relative quiet, most of its economic artificialities and internal social and demographic inconsistencies became clear. Put another way, in a period relatively free of the threat of disestablishment by outside forces, the Zionist momentum of the union of state and movement showed unmistakable signs of slowing.

No one has yet demonstrated in a responsible way that anything like a majority of those involuntarily embraced in Zionism's "Jewish people" nationality concept consider themselves to be proper subjects of international law and a recognized separate national entity endowed with a functional system of rights and obligations with respect to the state of Israel. Certainly, there is nothing in Jewish theology to support this claim; and, in my opinion, if religion has any relevance to the humanity of men, to their visible aspirations and voluntarily expressed values, there is no religious justification for the abnormal political stance on Zionist Israel taken by most of the so-called Christian nations of the world.

Conclusion

Those who wish to argue the case for "Jewish survival" or to justify it either for themselves or for others—and here I refer again and directly to the fundamentalist Christian theologians—should reread the history of this survival. Emil L. Fackenheim, a modern theologian who is at least centrist enough to be quoted frequently by the Zionist news service (the Jewish Telegraphic Agency) and by the so-called Anglo-Jewish press, recently summarized that history:

> To account for Jewish survival is possible only in terms of the Jewish faith. All the other supposed causes of Jewish survival, such as tradition or feelings of group loyalty, can themselves be explained only in terms of the Jewish faith.

Fackenheim then makes the obvious point that we live in an age of profound religious questioning. He says the Jew today, like everyone else, "is unsure whether, and if so to what extent, he can accept the faith which was handed down to him." Fackenheim has no more certain answer to this question than any of the rest of us. If the Jew determines to survive as a Jew, he says, he will accept as authentic the ancient encounter of his people with the living God.

He will then accept himself as part of a people constituted by an encounter with the Nameless and still extant as a people only because it continues to be committed to that encounter.[8]

That, I submit, is little more than the old verity, presented in the semantics of the world of confrontation and dialogue. But it is an answer to the golden calf worship of the Zionist-Israeli establishment and the effort to make that establishment look like Zion by pasting the old and revered names on what is just another ethnically centered, antidemocratic Middle European nationalism transplanted to Western Asia.

I have suggested a number of times that the political problem which motivates our consideration of these theological and religious questions is, in the final analysis, a problem more for Christians than for Jews. But by no means do I exonerate my coreligionists from contributing to this struggle or to the theological and religious confusion which has intensified the political problem. Jews are no more guilty or innocent than Christians or Muslims who find their religious disciplines inadequate, or at least inadequately articulated, for this agonizing and agonized world. In distressing numbers many from all faiths have turned to secular creeds—communism, fascism, the New Left, the radical right, or whatever new ideological crutch for tottering self-discipline and substitute for personal morality may flash on the television screen tomorrow. Zionism is a substitute of this kind for Jews, appealing to the part of their nature which is consciously Jewish. But, measured by the authentic tradition, it is a theological and religious heresy. And it will take a supratheological but intensely religious effort on the part of all to prevent the cataclysm that can follow from the Palestine problem—the result of substituting a secular, unauthentic "Jewishness" for the encounter with God which has been the core of Jewish collectivity.

I end with the majestically significant words of one of Christianity's great theologians. In 1939 Dietrich Bonhoeffer was living in the United States, having gone there to remove the ugliness of Naziism from the range of his daily vision. Suddenly he realized that he had made a demeaning spiritual error. In a letter to Reinhold Niebuhr he announced his intention of returning to Germany:

Christians in Germany will face the terrible alternative of either willing the defeat of their nation in order that Christian civilization may

8. Emil L. Fackenheim, "The Religious Duty of Survival," *Jewish News,* September 25, 1970, p. 76.

survive or of willing the victory of their nation and thereby destroying our civilization. I know which of these alternatives I must choose, but I cannot make that choice in security.[9]

This eminent Christian has, with or without the sanctification of theology, stated the religious dilemma of our age, and therefore of my coreligionists, with painful accuracy. There is neither theological nor religious sanction in Judaism for either national Zionism or its sovereign state in the Middle East. The Jews of our age face the terrible alternative which Bonhoeffer delineated for the Christians of Germany. These Jews must either will the defeat of the present theocratic and racist sovereignty they have acquiesced in—and even supported—or face the total functional eclipse of Judaism's values within any Jewish collectivity. Zionist propaganda and a world generally uprooted from its spiritual tradition—or worse, hypocritical about it—have encouraged the absolutely untenable proposition that the two traditions are not only compatible but constructively nourish each other and humankind. The moral cowardice of many Christians who know better, and the ignorance of their tradition plus the moral cowardice of many Jews, are parts of the religious implication which I, as a religionist, see in the Palestine crisis. I leave the theological systematization to the future. Peace *can* come to Palestine if both Christians and Jews in the nations most inclined to advertising their spiritual indebtedness to both traditions would urge their governments to follow the religious injunctions of justice and righteousness and the brotherhood of man.

9. Robert McAfee Brown, "What Kind of Patriotism," *Christianity and Crisis,* XXX, no. 11 (June 22, 1970), 1.

Zionism and
United States Foreign Policy

Emile A. Nakhleh

IN DEFINING AMERICAN INTERESTS in the Middle East, Secretary of State Rogers said in 1969 that the United States remains "interested in good relations with all states in the area. . . . We remain prepared to work with others . . . so long as they sincerely seek the end we seek: a just and lasting peace."[1] Two months later, President Nixon viewed the American posture in the Middle East from a clearly cold war perspective. In his report to the Congress in February, 1970, he declared:

1. The interests of the great powers are involved in the contests between local forces, but we also have a common interest in avoiding a direct confrontation.
2. The United States has long-standing obligations and relationships with a number of nations in the area.
3. But the United States would view any effort by the Soviet Union to seek predominance in the Middle East as a matter of grave concern.
4. I now affirm our total intention to maintain careful watch on the balance of military forces and to provide arms to friendly states as the need arises.[2]

1. U.S., Department of State, *A Lasting Peace in the Middle East: An American View* by William P. Rogers (Washington, D.C.: Government Printing Office, 1969), p. 10.
2. U.S., Department of State, *U.S. Foreign Policy for the 1970's: A New Strategy for Peace,* report to the Congress by President Nixon, February, 1970 (Washington, D.C.: Government Printing Office, 1970), pp. 80–81.

President Nixon returned to this theme in a special television interview in July, 1970, and once again pledged to preserve a military balance favorable to the United States and some "friendly states" in the region. He emphatically stated that "it is in the U.S. interests to maintain the balance of power [between Israel and the Arab states], and we will maintain that balance of power."[3] This view is essentially similar to the cold war policy pursued by Secretary of State Dulles, under the Eisenhower administration, although it is more committed to a *status quo* of which Israel has been the primary beneficiary. In spite of frequent disclaimers of a pro-Israel leaning on the part of the United States government in the last few years, actual policy has constantly pointed toward closer political and military cooperation with and support of Israel. This pattern could not have been more evident than in the fighting which occurred in Jordan in 1970. A joint American-Israeli plan was contemplated which envisioned an American-backed Israeli military intervention in Jordan to make certain that King Hussein would not be overthrown.

An examination of the preceding statements in the light of United States policy and action concerning the Middle East in the last twenty-five years reveals that American policy has miserably failed to comprehend the forces of change in that region and the most elemental desires, demands, and aspirations of the people involved. The basis of this policy, according to Sen. J. William Fulbright, is "not . . . the overall good of the United States, but . . . the existence of a pressure group in the United States who seeks to inject the Arab-Israeli dispute into domestic politics."[4]

U.S. Policy toward the Middle East

Political relations between the United States and the Arab world since World War II have been primarily influenced by three concerns: Israel and Palestine; oil; and Soviet-American ideological rivalries. These concerns have contributed to an intimate American involvement in the region—an involvement marked by controversy, colossal misunderstandings, and a distorted sense of priorities. Literature on the attitude of the United States toward these concerns and the response to challenges arising from them during the last two decades is abundant. This paper, however while not

3. U.S., Department of State, *A Conversation with the President* (Washington, D.C.: Government Printing Office, July, 1970), Publ. 8545, p. 33.
4. U.S., Congress, Senate, *Congressional Record*, 86th Cong., 2d sess., April 28, 1960. A special copy of this was obtained from Senator Fulbright's office.

purporting to minimize the obvious magnitude of such foreign-policy determinants as Arab oil and Russian influence, examines the question of Arab-American political relations from another perspective. It attempts to point out a more subtle yet more crucial determinant: the role that domestic influence—in this case Zionist activity in the United States—has on policy-making and the interpretation of the national interest. It is precisely this role that Arab policy-makers have failed either to comprehend or handle adequately. The intricate interaction between a domestic political factor and the process of foreign policy-making is of utmost significance. Although American policy-makers in the last twenty-five years have attempted to establish broad long-range national objectives in the Middle East, they have often failed to differentiate these objectives from those espoused by American Zionists; the former clearly represent an American policy, while the latter are somewhat more particular in scope.

Recalling the pressure put on him by Zionist partisans in 1947, former President Truman wrote: "Many Jews, however, chose to believe that our Palestine policy was the same as the Zionist program for Israel. . . . The simple fact is that our policy was an American policy rather than an Arab or Jewish policy." Concerning the intensity of the pressure, he wrote: "I do not think I ever had as much pressure and propaganda aimed at the White House as I had in this instance. The persistence of a few of the extreme Zionist leaders—actuated by political motives and engaged in political threats—disturbed and annoyed me."[5] Truman's statements are symptomatic of the interaction between American and Zionist policy processes concerning the Middle East. Although he was describing the events surrounding the creation of the state of Israel, his statements apply as well to what has happened since. In addition, Zionist partisans in the United States have succeeded in identifying the Arab-Israeli conflict with the East-West cold war.

Determinants of Foreign Policy

The diplomatic quagmire of the Middle East has been sustained by at least three factors: a well-coordinated Zionist political program on behalf of Israel; the decline of the Senate as a formulator of foreign policy and a corresponding rise of the executive as the initiator of public policy; and the rise of ideology, especially in the 1950s, as the primary criterion in foreign

5. Harry S. Truman, *Memoirs* (Garden City, N.Y.: Doubleday, 1956), II, 157–58.

policy. On the surface these three factors may appear independent of one another; yet, when viewed from the perspective of that nebulous entity, the national interest, they show remarkably similar qualities.

Since the national interest is the prime criterion and propellant force behind a state's foreign policy, the sources of the national interest in a particular situation are of paramount importance. National interest is usually defined in terms of two elements: a national ideology ("those mass-shared values in foreign policy whose maximization by government is demanded by a broad consensus"), and the way in which a small group of decision-makers or policy-making practitioners who are directly involved in a particular policy interpret the national interest. It is generally agreed that any such interpretation should reflect a desire for self-preservation, security, and well-being. Any commitment the United States makes to other nations, whether explicitly or implicitly, must serve one primary interest: the security of American territory and institutions—and this criterion has not been applied in the case of American policy toward Israel.

Another important determinant of foreign policy in a democracy is the role of public opinion and the way it can be manipulated by a well-organized pressure group—in this case, the Executive of the World Zionist Organization/Jewish Agency. In the words of V. O. Key, Jr., public opinion "may simply be taken to mean those opinions held by private persons which government finds it prudent to heed."[7] As an input into the political system, public opinion can be, and has been, influential in determining policy output. The degree of effectiveness is determined by the type of individuals expressing the opinion, how their views are translated into political input, and on what level within the political system such an input is being fed. Gabriel Almond has distinguished three "publics" in the United States: a general public, an attentive elite, and a policy elite. In Almond's view, it is the elite segment of the public, and not the general public, that determines the so-called public opinion. The elite public is "informed and interested in foreign policy problems" and is therefore the only public that has any relevance in the policy-making process.[8] It "plays the most important role in making up the mass mind by telling it what to think."[9]

6. Charles O. Lerche, Jr., *Foreign Policy of the American People* (Englewood Cliffs, N.J.: Prentice-Hall, 1967), pp. 5, 6, 11.

7. V. O. Key, Jr., *Public Opinion and American Democracy* (New York: Knopf, 1961), p. 14.

8. Gabriel Almond, *The American People and Foreign Policy* (New York: Harcourt, 1950), p. 138.

9. Lerche, *Foreign Policy,* p. 32.

Zionist propaganda has successfully manipulated public opinion in the United States, especially those selective "publics" and "opinions" which are significantly influential and powerful. In addition, the Zionist lobby in Washington has established effective contacts with Congress as well as with the White House and other agencies of the executive branch. This lobby has also strongly supported the 1967 United States Supreme Court decision upholding the right of dual citizenship (*Afroyim* v. *Rusk*).

Nature and Methods of Zionist Propaganda

Zionist propaganda in the United States has had one specific end—to achieve support for Israel—and in this effort American Zionists have mounted an aggressive, unrelenting, and overpowering campaign. Propaganda has been aimed at high officials within the executive branch; lawmakers in the United States Congress (through direct and indirect lobbying); church organizations; the media; and human rights associations. The theme of this propaganda has varied according to the intended target. For instance, invoking the principle of democracy, Zionist partisans have appealed for support on the ground that Israel is a bastion of democracy surrounded by semifeudal, monarchal, nondemocratic Arab states. Similarly, they have appealed to the American Protestant ethic of hard work on the ground that, by developing the land in Palestine, Zionist settlers have proved themselves. To religious groups in America, Catholic and Protestant alike, Zionists have emphasized the special relationship between the Jews and Palestine and the role of God's Israel in the development of the New Testament. In the area of human rights, in order to legitimize their status in Palestine, Zionists have constantly pointed to the six million Jews who were killed during World War II. Hence charges of anti-Semitism and treason have been made against Jewish and non-Jewish American officials who view American interests from a non-Zionist perspective. One example of this is the smear campaign and the charges of anti-Semitism that were made against Secretary of Defense Forrestal.[10] The traditional American penchant for supporting the underdog has also been frequently exploited by Zionist propagandists, although this tactic has been somewhat less effective since 1967.

According to Samuel Halperin, Zionist appeals have focused on nine themes:

10. Walter Millis, ed., *The Forrestal Diaries* (New York: Viking, 1951).

1. Zionism is the Jewish badge of honor. . . . Jewish pride and self-respect are enhanced by what happens in Palestine.
2. The Jews everywhere constitute one people. . . . The Jew who cares about his people is a Zionist, for Palestine depends on him.
3. . . . The Zionist cause is Dramatic, for it combats the enemies of the Jewish people while it re-creates the Jewish state and nation.
4. Zionism is a constructive way to solve the Jewish problem. . . . No country wants Jewish refugees except Palestine.
5. Zionism perpetuates Judaism and provides for Jewish survival as a distinctive grouping. . . .
6. Zionism will help end anti-Semitism by ending the abnormality of the Jewish national homelessness. . . .
7. The Jewish state is inevitable—biblical prophecy, a crying world need, and the impressive achievements of Palestinian Jewry all require a statehood solution.
8. Assistance for Palestine is consonant with the loyalty to the United States. . . .
9. The Zionist solution proposed historic justice—a Jewish state is just compensation for innumerable massacres, especially for the 6,000,000 European martyrs of Nazism and Fascism.[11]

It is common knowledge that the White House was subjected to intense pressure from Zionist partisans just prior to the establishment of the state of Israel and that the Zionists constantly attempted to entangle the United States in Palestine. That President Truman and succeeding presidents attempted to formulate a policy toward the Middle East that would conform to American foreign policy throughout the world may also be a tolerable hypothesis. What is bewildering is the support that Israel has enjoyed since 1948 in party platforms, in the United States Congress, and in the White House, as well as in the lower echelons of the national government. All of this indicates a solid *de facto* American commitment to Israel consonant with Israel's *de facto* existence for the past two decades. This commitment is unprecedented in the diplomatic history of the United States, and, potentially at least, it creates grave dangers for the future course of American global policy.

The militancy of Zionist propaganda in the United States can be traced to 1943, when Abba Hillel Silver, a rabbi from Cleveland, assumed the cochairmanship of the Zionist Organization of America. Silver's approach toward soliciting American support for Zionist plans in Palestine, unlike the approach of such other Zionist leaders as Chaim Weizmann, was

---

11. Samuel Halperin, *The Political World of American Zionism* (Detroit: Wayne State Univ. Press, 1961), pp. 255–56.

direct, aggressive, and unrelenting. In a letter to Weizmann in March, 1944, Rabbi Silver rejected quiet diplomacy as being ineffective. His formula for success was expounded in a message to Zionist leaders in 1944:

> Put not the future of our movement in the sole keeping of individuals, however friendly, however great; appeal to the masses . . . ; talk to the whole of America; . . . carry on an active educational propaganda in your circle, within the sphere of your influence, among your own friends. That will be reflected in the higher political circles.[12]

The propaganda machine which the Zionists have put to full use since the middle of the 1940s has been charged with the fulfillment of Silver's injunctions.

Structurally, Zionist propaganda has been channeled through a well-coordinated structure called the Jewish Agency, Jerusalem, and its American arm, the Jewish Agency, American Section; the latter is registered with the U.S. Department of Justice on behalf of the Executive of the Jewish Agency, Jerusalem. The Covenant between the government of Israel and the World Zionist Organization/Jewish Agency was filed with the Department of Justice in July, 1969, thereby making the Zionist Executive a foreign agent, operating on behalf of Israel. Other organizations within the Zionist structure in the United States which have intermittently received funds in the last two decades directly and/or indirectly from the Jewish Agency, American Section, and/or the Israeli consulate in New York include the American Israel Public Affairs Committee, the Synagogue Council of America, and the Hebrew Culture Foundation.[13]

Through this semicorporate structure, Zionists in America have been able to reach the public and win it over through lobbying, mass media, and grants to institutions of higher learning and religious organizations. Lobbying on behalf of the American Zionist Council has been conducted in the last two decades by I. L. Kenen, executive director of the American Israel Public Affairs Committee. The American Zionist Council has paid a group subscription fee to Kenen's publication, *Near East Report*, to be sent free of charge to members of the United States Congress. The *Israel Digest* published by the Jewish Agency, is another publication that is used to disseminate Zionist propaganda. In the field of higher education Zionist funds

12. Quoted in *ibid.*, p. 271.
13. U.S., Congress, Senate, Committee on Foreign Relations, *Activities on Non-diplomatic Representatives of Foreign Principles in the United States,* 86th Cong., 2d sess, 1963, pt. 12.

from the American Section of the Jewish Agency have often been channeled
to such universities as Harvard and Columbia through grants from the
Hebrew Culture Foundation "for the purpose of establishing chairs in
Hebrew language or Israeli studies or Jewish studies or Middle East studies." In the area of religious associations, the Synagogue Council of America has received funds from the American Section of the Jewish Agency for
the purpose of preparing and distributing "educational and cultural materials in connection with the upbuilding of Israel, particularly with regard to
the historic and spiritual relationship of the Jewish communities outside of
Israel to the Holy Land." The Synagogue Council of America has not limited its activities to the religious sphere; it also strenuously campaigned in
Washington for "continuing mutual security aid to Israel."[14]

In reference to this point, Rabbi Mark H. Tanenbaum, former executive
director of the Synagogue Council of America, sent a confidential letter on
June 21, 1960, to Gottlieb Hammer, then executive vice-chairman of the
Jewish Agency in New York, informing him of the services which the
Synagogue Council of America performed as a result of the generous grants
received through the offices of the Jewish Agency. The detailed report
which was enclosed in that letter clearly demonstrates that the activities of
the Synagogue Council of America transcended the religious, educational,
and cultural functions normally associated with such an organization. One
entry in that report follows:

> April 1959—Representatives from the Synagogue Council of America
> testified before the House Foreign Affairs and the Senate Foreign
> Relations Committees, on the moral imperatives underlying our for-
> eign aid program. Rabbi Theodore L. Adams, then president of the
> Synagogue Council of America delivered a keynote address on this
> theme with Bishop Fulton J. Sheen and the Reverend Dr. Edwin T.
> Bahlberg, president of the National Council of Churches, at the White
> House Conference on Foreign Aid and Trade, on a program featuring
> President Eisenhower, former President Truman, late Secretary John
> Foster Dulles, Dean Acheson, Vice-President Nixon, and Adlai Stev-
> enson. At this time, the mutual security grants to Israel were threat-
> ened with reduction. *During their testimony, the Synagogue Council
> leaders made a strong plea for continuing mutual security aid to Israel.*
> Observers (including S. *[sic]* L. Kenen) regarded the effect of these tes-
> timonies as greatly beneficial to the subsequently improved reception
> to Israel's request for maintaining status quo in grants.[15]

14. *Ibid.*, pp. 1754, 1758, 1764, 1765, 1767, 1779–80.
15. *Ibid.*, p. 1767. Italics added.

In the area of party politics, Zionist activities have shown tremendous organization. "Our good friends here," wrote Rabbi Silver in 1944 to Chaim Weizmann, "will not move on their own accord, inspired by the moral righteousness of our cause. . . . Our friends might be inspired to move and take some definite action as a result of the pressure of five million Jews in a critical election year."[16] In a special memorandum sent to local Zionist committees in 1943, Zionists were instructed to "work both sides of the political street." They were told it would be wise "to cultivate the local political leader, who is often a close friend of the Congressman or Senator . . . [who] might be . . . persuaded to throw the weight of his political influence and power behind our cause. . . . If your present Congressman is a Republican . . . he may be opposed in the next election by a Democrat. The latter prospective candidate should be cultivated."[17] For example, Rabbi Silver exploited his close relationship with Sen. Robert A. Taft and Sen. Robert F. Wagner, and Eddie Jacobson convinced President Truman, a close friend of his, to meet with Chaim Weizmann in 1948.[18]

The program of cultivating major political candidates and marshaling their support for the Zionist cause has been extremely successful. Since 1948 it has been customary for presidential candidates to speak at least once during the campaign at a Zionist meeting. Congress and the state legislatures have exhibited even more blatant support for Zionism and Israel than has the executive branch.[19] In 1948 President Truman recognized the state of Israel *de facto* exactly eleven minutes after its existence had been proclaimed. However, during the 1948 presidential campaign, President Truman and the Democratic party were accused by the Republicans of vacillation and indecision on the question of Palestine. The Republicans, though not explicitly in favor of the deployment of force to implement the partitioning of Palestine, called for full recognition of Israel with its bound-

16. Quoted in Halperin, *American Zionism*, p. 271.
17. Quoted in *ibid.*, p. 273.
18. Truman, *Memoirs*, p. 160.
19. For a comprehensive report on pro-Zionist Congressional resolutions prior to 1948, see Joseph B. Schechtman, *The United States and the Jewish State Movement* (South Brunswick, N.J.: Yoseloff, 1966), pp. 64–92. For complete information on recent pro-Zionist and pro-Israeli resolutions in Congress, see U.S., Congress, *Congress and the Nation: 1945–1964* and *Congress and the Nation: 1965–1968* (Washington, D.C.: Government Printing Office, 1965, 1969). See also U.S., Congress, Joint Committee, *Legislation of Foreign Relations with Explanatory Notes*, 89th Cong., 2d sess., 1966.

aries as sanctioned by the United Nations and for aid in developing its economy. Neither party mentioned the Palestinian Arabs.

Although in the 1952 election the Republican party platform did not include a plank on the Middle East, the plank in the Democratic platform read as follows: "We pledge continued assistance to Israel so that she may fulfill her humanitarian mission of providing shelter and sanctuary for her homeless Jewish refugees while strengthening her economic development." The Democratic party adopted a similar plank in 1956 and, in addition, called for the sale of arms to Israel. The Republican platform in 1956 included a forceful statement on behalf of Israel: "We regard the preservation of Israel as an important tenet of American foreign policy. We are determined that the integrity of an independent Jewish State shall be maintained. We shall support the independence of Israel against armed aggression." The positions taken by both parties in the 1960, 1964, and 1968 presidential election campaigns were variations of the support expressed in the 1950s, focusing on a clear American commitment to the survival of Israel.

Although this pro-Israeli stand by the two parties can be explained within the framework of the American political system, it is clear that the American commitment to Israel, based on ideological, emotional, or political grounds and resulting from party politics during and between national elections, has imposed a burden on the foreign policy of the United States—a burden which, when translated into reality as in Viet Nam, is often all too painful to bear. In the Middle East context the United States, for reasons of domestic politics and ideological shortsightedness, has blindly felt its way in foreign policy, stumbling from one blunder to another. In equating his policy with a mythical search for the good, Secretary of State Dulles could not intellectually comprehend that gray areas might possibly exist. He could not tolerate the form of Arab nationalism led by President Nasser of Egypt because it sought to break free from the Manichaean mold in which he had cast the world.

The ideological taboos which restricted Dulles' ability to view foreign policy from a macrocosmic perspective produced of necessity a new harmonizing factor in American-Israeli relations. This dipolar progression has continued to the present time. What is seen in the 1960s and 1970s proceeds from the ideological vision of the 1950s—a new yet similarly mythical notion that an archaic balance of power must be maintained between Israel and the Arabs. The illusion to which the Nixon administration clings is that the United States must be the only balancer. This twisted perception of the realties of power and the calculated refusal to accept the existence of a new Palestinian variable has placed American policy in a worse predicament than that created by Dulles' Manichaeanism in the 1950s. The rise of the Palestinian element has signaled the complete failure of the traditional American cold war policy toward the Arab world.

The Re-emergence of Palestine

Commenting on the future course of American policy in the Middle East, Sen. Mark O. Hatfield said on June 16, 1970:

> We must squarely confront the third rising force in the Middle East, the Palestinian movement. The issue of Palestine must be understood and its meaning in the eyes of all the Arab world must be grasped. Our viewpoints must become sensitive to the injustice that the Palestinians feel so deeply, and our policies must be constructed to deal with this sense of injustice.[20]

The senator seems to imply clearly that future American policy in the Middle East—especially in regard to Palestine—if it hopes to achieve any measure of success, must heed the new realities in the region. What are some of these realities?

First, the results which Dulles had hoped to attain through his cold war policy in the Middle East have never materialized. On the contrary, Dulles' policy has indirectly brought about a Soviet penetration into the region, and consequently American influence and prestige in the Arab world are presently at an all-time low.

Second, the conflict in the Middle East is no longer primarily between Israel and the Arab states but between the Zionist structure in Palestine and the Palestinian people themselves. The primacy of the Palestinian issue, especially since 1967, is a phenomenon that must be reckoned with. The Palestinian people have re-emerged from the misery of the camps, conscious of themselves as a people and desirous of redressing the injustices dealt them over the last generation by superior regional and international forces. The issue *is* Palestine and the Palestinians, not Jordan, Lebanon, Syria, Egypt, or Israel.

Third, by advocating armed struggle and by reasserting their national identity by violence, the Palestinians, through the Palestine Resistance Movement, have demonstrated the bankruptcy of traditional international

20. Quoted in *New York Times,* June 17, 1970.

law and have shown that the violent phenomenon is capable of effectuating political change. They are convinced of the effectiveness of violence because only through violence have they succeeded in getting the concerned powers (Arab governments, Israel, and others) to take notice of their existence as a Palestinian entity. Unfortunately the United States has continued to cling, for whatever reasons, to old myths and to make sterile peace initiatives while ignoring new realities. In effect the United States has told the Palestinians: we will be ready to talk to you when you are strong enough to upset the *status quo*. The lesson of the American experience in Viet Nam and the American *de facto* recognition of the Viet Cong has not been lost on the Palestinians.

Fourth, the prolonged warfare envisioned by the Palestinians as inevitable for the success of their revolution will prove detrimental to long-range U.S. interests in the area. The validity of this viewpoint is being slowly accepted in the United States. Among the American elite public an isolationist trend, which precludes long-range American involvement in foreign countries, is developing. The lesson of Viet Nam will be remembered for many years, and the mere possibility of a similar involvement will be strongly rejected, American-Israeli friendship notwithstanding.

In the light of the above, one question is properly raised: What course of action ought the United States to follow *via-à-vis* Palestine? John C. Campbell suggests two sound guidelines for developing future policy in the Middle East: "To keep in the forefront of thinking the basis on which a peaceful settlement in the Middle East must rest; and to move the level of military conflict downward and not upward."[21] In doing so, U.S. policymakers must primarily consider the real issues of American security as perceived by them and not by others. U.S. foreign policy must be an American policy.

In its issue for March 16, 1970, *Time* commented on whether there is a Jewish foreign policy in the United States: "The vehemence of the American Jewish community's support for Israel creates an impression in the minds of some that Washington is acting not on the basis of national interest but out of fear of Jewish wrath." A more serious question on the activities of Zionist propaganda agencies in the United States and their interaction with American foreign policy was raised in a special report in the *National Observer*. "Zionist activity is creating special concern in the American Jewish community and in U.S. Government circles. For Ameri-

---

21. John C. Campbell, "The Arab-Israeli Conflict, An American Policy," *Foreign Affairs,* no. 1 (October, 1970), 64.

can Jews, the Zionist insistence on prime allegiance to Israel sometimes raises personal problems of dual loyalty. For official Washington . . . there is genuine concern over the undoubted ability of the Zionists to influence U.S. policy in favor of Israel."[22] It seems that the only solution to this problem is that "sometime some President of the United States will have to review the entire American policy for the [Middle East], specifically considering whether the cost to the United States of support for Israel is worth the economic and political losses in the Arab world."[23]

Concerning Palestine, the United States, if it is sincerely committed to peace and justice, must develop new directions for its future policy, including the following: (1) a serious examination of a possible new political structure in Palestine in which both Palestinian Jews and Arabs can coexist; (2) a wholehearted effort to establish serious dialogue with the Palestine Resistance Movement; (3) an admission that the Zionist experiment in Palestine, as a solution to the "Jewish problem" created by anti-Semitism in Europe, has failed, for instead of solving the Jewish problem it has created a Palestinian problem; (4) an unequivocal backing of the multitude of U.N. resolutions which have constantly supported the right of the Palestinians to return to their homeland; (5) a recognition of the fact that, unless the Palestinian problem is solved, no enduring peace can ever be established in the Middle East; and (6) a rejection of the argument, supported by some American policy-makers, that the United States can tolerate a minimum state of tension in the area, for no state of tension can be kept under control forever.

22. Lawrence Mosher, "Zionist Role in U.S. Raises New Concern," *National Observer* (Washington, D.C.), May 18, 1970.
23. Drew Middleton, "The Arab World: U.S. Viewed as Friend of the Enemy, Israel," *New York Times,* July 17, 1968.

Settler States and Western Response: Israel and South Africa

Richard P. Stevens

AMONG THE DECISIONS of the Western world which have affected the peoples of the Third World, none has revealed more clearly the essence of Western ethnocentrism nor has demonstrated more conclusively the capacity of the Western world to transform, translate, and legitimize its basic power thrust under the cloak of international law and morality than two decisions reached in London—the South Africa Act (1909) and the Balfour Declaration (1917). These two documents, formulated without regard to the rights and aspirations of the peoples affected, were rationalized in terms of the highest moral principles and responsibilities of Western civilization. Thus, in the name of British liberalism the indigenous peoples of Palestine and South Africa have not only lost their homes, their lands, and their most basic natural rights but have also found themselves stripped of their own positive identities, subjected to the dictates of those capable of exercising massive power, and taxed and administered in keeping with a plan designed to insure the survival of the colonizers. The terms of "otherness"—*nonwhite* on the one hand and *non-Jewish* on the other—which have been used to describe the colonized peoples, reveal a psychological bias characteristic of the Western powers, a bias so completely assimilated into the prevailing international legal order that protests from those affected have been dismissed in terms of that same legal code. The principles of nonintervention, opposition to violence, and a host of others regarded as fundamental to the preservation of civilization and international order have all been used to defend decisions that were ratified by governments capable of determining the content of the international legal system.

Since the early 1960s in South Africa and the mid-1960s in the Middle East, new forms of resistance to the consequences of these decisions have been taking place. The subjected peoples of both areas, finally recognizing the reality of power behind the facade of legality, have undertaken through violence not only to resist the structures superimposed on them but also to challenge the sources of power that have controlled most of the world's resources. The methods of the resisters—indeed their basic intentions—not only offend Western sensibilities but pose a threat to vested Western interests. But it is not these events which I propose to discuss. Rather, my concern is with the formulation of the South Africa Act and the Balfour Declaration and the psychological climate which made them possible. The fact that the Western world finds it difficult to sever its ties with the racist South African state and to comprehend the demands of the Palestinian people indicates that Western ethnocentrism survives and points out the necessity of discussing both cases in a historical context. As William Howitt wrote in 1838:

> Nay, in such colours does the modern philosophy of conquest and diplomacy disguise the worst transactions between one state and another, that it is not for plain men very readily to penetrate to the vast enormity beneath.[1]

Palestine and South Africa were both sacrificed in the name of Western peoples and British imperial interests, and the details were arranged by the same British statesmen. In both cases, a perceived injustice committed by Western civilization, against Jew on the one hand and Boer on the other, was to be atoned for at the expense of those too "backward" to establish an equal moral claim. In both cases, the self-identification of Jew and Boer as a chosen people and inheritors of a promised land was explicitly or implicitly accepted by Britain and subsequently by the bulk of the Western world as proof of its own tolerance. In each case, it was for the "natives" to abide by legal and constitutional structures imposed by the West; resistance was considered not only illegal but in violation of the canons of international morality.

---

1. William Howitt, *Colonization and Christianity* (London, Longmans, 1838), p. 209.

The Balfour Declaration

In the context of imperialistic enterprise and psychology Zionism defined itself and established political goals that coincided with the power realities and the interests of the Western world. Although in the early days of Zionist activity it was understood that the ultimate question of Jewish sovereignty over Palestine and the political means of achieving it would not be debated, it was also understood that any legal or semilegal arrangement or subterfuge enabling Jews to immigrate to Palestine would be adopted, despite growing opposition from the Ottoman Empire. The fact that the Arabs, like other national groups within the Ottoman Empire, were challenging the basis of Constantinople's rule and denying its right to permit foreign immigration into the Arab heartland was ignored by the Zionists as they turned first to Germany and then to Britain in search of support for their plans. If Germany lacked the will or power to carry off a political scheme in Palestine, the same was not true of Britain. Both domestic and international considerations, it was perceived, could be used to gain British endorsement. Support of Zionism, argued Theodor Herzl before a Royal Commission in 1902, would not only spare the British government the distasteful necessity of imposing immigration restrictions on a swelling number of Eastern European Jews but would serve British imperial interests. Joseph Chamberlain, the colonial secretary, informed Herzl that "he liked the Zionist idea" and suggested that Herzl find "a spot among the British possessions which was not yet inhabited by white settlers."

At one time or another Herzl considered Cyprus, Sinai, and Uganda as colonial bases for the ultimate attainment of Palestine and was amenable to other suggestions. But whatever the strategy, his plan was to gain the support of outstanding Western leaders, both Jew and Gentile, for the general project of planned Jewish settlement. Only with such Western support could "public, international arrangements, formally establishing adequate legal rights in a suitable territory as well as suitable understandings concerning the transfer of emigrants and their property," be attained.[2]

Thus, without legal permission from the Ottoman authorities, the Zionists, assisted by the World Zionist Organization, opened the Anglo-Palestine Bank in 1903 and established the Jewish National Fund, which began purchasing land in 1905. The Palestine Land Development Fund was founded in 1908 to make land ready for the settlement of buyers still

2. Benjamin Halpern, *The Idea of a Jewish State* (Cambridge: Harvard Univ. Press, 1961), p. 127.

abroad. With these and other sources of financial assistance provided by the Jewish Colonization Association, the number of Zionist settlers in Palestine reached 12,000 by 1914 out of an estimated Jewish population of 60,000. In the same year the Arab population was 630,000. Jews owned 2 per cent of the land. The whole Zionist enterprise, in keeping with the prevailing political philosophy, was seen as self-justifying in its results. As the Zionist historian Israel Goldberg stated at a later time:

> The Jews, by race and origin an eastern people and by experience and skills a part of the west, were exceptionally qualified to bring the stagnant east into the orbit of western civilization. . . . Zionism was introducing a dynamic impulse into Palestine which promised to infuse new life into the entire Near East.[3]

Britain and the United States became the main areas of Zionist activity. American Zionist support was crucial for the survival of the Zionist movement and of the Palestinian Zionist communities, which were deprived, during World War I, of European funds. The raising of $10 million between November, 1914, and December, 1917, by the American-Jewish Joint Distribution Committee was an indication of the potential power and influence of the American Zionists. In both the United States and Britain, Zionists worked toward obtaining a guarantee from the Allies that, in the event of Ottoman defeat, Palestine would be recognized as a Jewish commonwealth open to unrestricted immigration.

The patient and persistent Zionist efforts gradually began to show signs of success. Victory in the British Cabinet was due in no small part to the role played by Herbert Samuel, who stated the case for the founding of a Jewish state with the help of Britain and the United States. In March, 1915, he advanced a memorandum which, according to one authority, "marked a turning point in the history of the Middle East and of the world." He proposed the annexation of Palestine and argued that a protectorate over that land would "enable England to fulfill in yet another sphere her historic part of the civiliser of the backward countries." Samuel's argument for a protectorate, which was eventually adopted as British policy, was:

> Its establishment would be a safeguard to Egypt. It is true that Palestine in British hands would itself be open to attack, and the acquisition

---

3. Israel Goldberg [Rufus Learsi], *Fulfillment: The Epic Story of Zionism* (Cleveland: World, 1951), p. 172.

would bring with it extended military responsibilities. But the mountainous character of the country would make its occupation by an enemy difficult, and, while this outpost was being contested, time would be given to allow the garrison of Egypt to be increased and the defences to be strengthened. . . .

A British protectorate, according to the Egyptian Intelligence Department report . . . , would be welcomed by a large proportion of the present population. There have been many previous indications of the same feeling. I am assured, both by Zionists and non-Zionists, that it is the solution of the question of Palestine which would be by far the most welcome to the Jews throughout the world.

It is hoped that under British rule facilities would be given to Jewish organizations to purchase land, to found colonies, to establish educational and religious institutions, and to co-operate in the economic development of the country, and that Jewish immigration, carefully regulated, would be given preference, so that in the course of time the Jewish inhabitants, grown into a majority and settled in the land, may be conceded such degree of self government as the conditions of that day might justify. . . .

The course which is advocated would win for England the gratitude of the Jews throughout the world. In the United States, where they number about 2,000,000, and in all the other lands where they are scattered, they would form a body of opinion whose bias, where the interest of the country of which they were citizens was not involved, would be favourable to the British Empire.[4]

Samuel's proposal fell on receptive ears in December, 1916, when David Lloyd George became prime minister and Arthur Balfour, foreign secretary. Balfour's association with Zionism went back at least a decade, roughly to the period in which his opinion was vital in another area of European settlement—namely, South Africa. At that time Balfour's basic philosophy was revealed in debates on the proposed Union of South Africa. Although that prospect was greeted with greatest enthusiasm as a testament to the liberal English tradition, it set the stage for the legal subjugation of the African majority. Balfour's defense of the proposed union was undoubtedly rooted in the same creed which later dictated his approach to an analogous situation in Palestine. He had argued:

If the races of Europe have really conquered, by centuries of difficulty and travail, great rights and privileges for themselves, they have given some of those rights and some of those privileges to men quite incapable, by themselves, of fighting for them at all, or obtaining them at all.

4. Quoted in John Bowle, *Viscount Samuel* (London: Gollancz, 1957), p. 170.

That is the plain, historic truth of the situation, which it is perfect folly for us to attempt to forget. It is this very fact of the inequality of the races which makes the difficulty.[5]

By July, 1917, Zionist conversations with the British government had reached an advanced stage regarding a proposed declaration that would commit Britain to Jewish settlement, if not a Jewish state, in Palestine. This declaration, supported by President Wilson, Sir Mark Sykes, Lord Rothschild, and Samuel, was then endorsed by Winston Churchill, Lord Milner, Lord Cecil, General Smuts of South Africa, Lloyd George, and Balfour. The result was that, on November 2, 1917, Balfour, on behalf of the Cabinet, addressed a letter to Lord Rothschild:

His Majesty's Government view with favour the establishment in Palestine of a national home for the Jewish people, and will use their best endeavours to facilitate the achievement of this object, it being clearly understood that nothing shall be done which may prejudice the civil and religious rights of the existing non-Jewish communities in Palestine, or the rights and political status enjoyed by Jews in any other country.

That Britain had not formally committed itself to the establishment of a Jewish state was patently clear; that such a state might eventually emerge seemed only logical. The ambiguity in the declaration was as much a concession to Jewish anti-Zionist sentiment as an attempt to overcome Arab protests of betrayal. But allusion to the more than 90 per cent Arab population as "non-Jewish communities" revealed the imperial government's capacity to tailor reality to its plans and to lay the ground psychologically for easy acceptance of the imperial interpretation. As Herbert Adams Gibbons, writing in 1919, observed, from the day of the declaration's appearance

the Zionists . . . looked upon the letter of Mr. Balfour to Lord Rothschild as official British sanction to the establishment of a Jewish state in Palestine by means of wholesale immigration and buying up of the land.[6]

5. Quoted in L. M. Thompson, *The Unification of South Africa (1902–1910),* (London: Oxford Univ. Press, 1960), p. 38.
6. Herbert Adams Gibbons, "Zionism and the World Peace," *Century,* XCVII, no. 3 (January, 1919), 369.

With their task in Britain accomplished, the Zionists had only to receive the sanction of international law. France, Italy, and the United States approved the declaration in 1918. Thereafter the Zionists were closely linked to the Allies and became an unofficial partner. With Allied endorsement it was assumed that the "legal" right of the Jews to build a national home in Palestine had been established; this argument was then employed to win over a larger segment of world public opinion to the Zionist cause. In the words of Bernard Rosenblatt, president of the Zion Commonwealth, Inc., and a leading figure at the 1918 Zionist conference in Pittsburgh:

> After convincing the powerful governments of Great Britain, France, and Italy; and after securing endorsement . . . from the President of the United States, we feel that we have won our case before the world, and that it is altogether unnecessary to expend valuable energy in order to convert a negligible opposition. The Jewish Commonwealth of Palestine is a fact and we are now fixing the boundaries of the state.[7]

After spending fifteen days in Palestine in 1919, the King-Crane Commission concluded that only the Zionist Jews, about one-tenth of the total population, favored the establishment of a Jewish national home. In its final report the commission advised "serious modification of the extreme Zionist program" of unlimited immigration. There was nothing on which the population of Palestine was more united, said the report, than its hatred of the entire Zionist program. "To subject a people so minded to unlimited Jewish immigration, and to steady financial and social pressure to surrender the land, would be a gross violation of the principle [of free acceptance], and of the people's rights, though it kept within the forms of law."

Although the Zionists of the period carefully refrained from mentioning a Jewish state, the call for unlimited immigration, powers of local government, and other privileges left little doubt as to the ultimate objective. Zionist writers graphically described the methods to be employed in securing that end, and their descriptions of the culture and disposition of the indigenous population are remarkable. It was noted that in buying land

> there is no reason why we should pour wealth into the hands of those who happen to hold title to the land of Palestine, when the increased value will be due, not to labor on the part of the landlords, but to the

---

7. Bernard Rosenblatt, "Zionism at the Peace Conference," *Public,* February 1, 1919, p. 112.

new government which Great Britain and the Zionists have established. . . . The land values should be taxed for the benefits received from the conquest of Great Britain and the Jewish mass immigration.[8]

As for the Arab population, Albert Hyamson concluded that

> there will be a new incentive, and a strong one, for a Moslem Arab emigration from Palestine. Close at hand there is to be a Moslem Arab State, organized under its own rulers. . . . This state should of itself be a magnet to Moslem Arabs settled in other lands. . . . It should be unnecessary to say that no Arab will be dispossessed or forced by any means to leave his home. If he does so, it will be of his own free will; and his removal will leave no cause for bitterness.[9]

In a more realistic vein, Israel Zangwill pointed out:

> The whole planet is in the grip of Allied Might and it needs but Allied Right to reshape all racial boundaries and international relations. . . . But a Hebrew Palestine, if it is to exist at all, must be a reality, not a sham. . . . The power in every country . . . always remains in the land-owning classes. Yet over 30,000 Arab landlords and some 600,000 fellahin are to continue in possession of the bulk of the Holy soil. . . . And hence we must suppose that this new system of creative politics . . . will be carried out in Palestine as elsewhere. Thus the Arabs would gradually be settled in the new and vast Arabian Kingdom. . . . Only thus can Palestine become a "Jewish National Home." . . . Only with a Jewish majority (not of course a Jewish totality), only with the land nationalized—and Jewish as well as Arab land must be expropriated with reasonable compensation—can Israel enter upon the task of building up that model State, the construction of which American Zionism, in its trustful acceptance of the [Balfour] Declaration, has already outlined. And it is now or never.[10]

The final Zionist victory came on April 24, 1920, when the Allied Supreme Council allotted Palestine to Great Britain. It was understood that the Balfour Declaration would provide the framework for British rule. Wilson had been forced to admit that there was an irreconcilable conflict

8. Mary Fels and Bernard A. Rosenblatt, "The Palestine Land Program," *Public,* May 24, 1919, p. 542.

9. Albert Hyamson, "Problems of the New Palestine," *Quarterly Review,* no. 459 (April, 1919), p. 324.

10. Israel Zangwill, "Before the Peace Conference," *Asia,* February, 1919, pp. 105–6.

between his belief that the Jews must be helped and his belief in self-government and self-determination. The decisions made at San Remo accorded neither with the wishes of the Palestinians nor with the purported objects of the war. Under the noble-sounding title *mandate,* Britain tried to reconcile the demands for some form of legality with the facts of imperial and political interest. The word, by contrast, dismayed the Arabs and became the very embodiment of Western hypocrisy. Not only had Palestine been handed over to a Jewish minority, but the Arab heartland was callously divided among the Allied powers.

The prospect that the Arab cause was lost, at least in terms of Western decision-making, brought about the April, 1920, riots in Jerusalem and Jaffa. Had the Arabs possessed the power to uphold their demands, the outcome might have been different; but power was clearly not in Arab hands. Instead of seeing the violence of April, 1920, as portending the future of Palestine, Britain chose to interpret the riots as "disturbances" which, it hoped, would not be repeated. Zionists attributed the violence to the work of a small group of Arab agitators. When clashes occurred between Jews and Arabs, said Goldberg, "they were not the result of national antagonism, but rather of a zest for plunder which harked back to remote times." With the arrival of the British high commissioner, he said, "the Arabs . . . would now accept the inevitable, and in place of the obstructive and unimaginative army officers" the foundations of a Jewish state would be laid.[11]

The shout, "Palestine for the Palestinians," was interpreted by the Arab press, however, as arising precisely from economic and national considerations. A Palestinian conference protested on December 27, 1919:

> If it is possible for France to establish Alsace-Lorraine as French land, when it had been annexed by the French for only two hundred years, before which it was German, how can it be possible to obliterate our sovereignty over this land, which has lasted for 1,200 years, and while its sons are still masters of it. How can the Zionists go back in history two thousand years to prove that by their short sojourn in Palestine they have now a right to claim it and to return to it as a Jewish home, thus crushing the nationalism of a million Arabs?[12]

Other voices were also raised on behalf of the Palestinians. Lord Sydenham of Comb noted that "a veil has since fallen between the British people

11. Goldberg, *Fulfillment,* pp. 171, 222.
12. "Syrian Protests against Zionism," *Literary Digest,* LXVI, no. 1 (July 3, 1920), 31.

and the rightful owners of Palestine, for whose welfare they have become responsible." Anstruther MacKay, writing in the *Atlantic* in July, 1920, noted that "the whole population will resist the Zionist Commission's plan of wholesale immigration of Jews." To fulfill their aspirations, he noted, "the Zionists must obtain the armed assistance of one of the European powers, presumably Great Britain, or the United States of America." Even more prophetic of events which now, some fifty years later, seem closer to realization, MacKay concluded that

> the theory that the Jews are to come into Palestine and oust the Moslem cultivators by "equitable purchase" or other means is in violation of principles of sound policy, and would, if accepted, arouse violent outbreaks against the Jewish minority. It would, moreover, arouse fierce Moslem hostility and fanaticism against the Western powers that permitted it. The effect of this hostility would be felt all through the Middle East, and would cause trouble in Syria, Mesopotamia, Egypt, and India. To this might be ascribed by future historians the outbreak of a great war between the white and the brown races, a war into which America would without doubt be drawn.[13]

The South Africa Act

MacKay's warning of the future war "between the white and brown races" due to Western imperialism in the Middle East paralleled the theme advanced in 1900 by W. E. B. DuBois, who, speaking at the First Pan-African Congress in London, asserted that "the problem of the twentieth century is the problem of the colour line—the relation of the darker to the lighter races of men in Asia and Africa, in America and the islands of the sea." DuBois's concern, however, was not race conflict narrowly construed but conflict between the possessors of power and those regarded as the objects of power—Arabs, Asians, blacks, browns—broadly speaking, all those who did not share in the power structures of Europe and its white offshoots. This first assembly of black spokesmen also urged the British government to redress the grievances of the Africans of South Africa and Rhodesia. Meeting during the Boer War of 1899–1902, the conference expected that Britain would surely seize the opportunity resulting from the imminent victory over the Boer settlers in South Africa to guarantee the

13. Anstruther MacKay, "Zionist Aspirations in Palestine," *Atlantic*, CXXVI (July, 1920), 123–25.

human and political rights of the African majority. By way of reply, Joseph Chamberlain affirmed that "Her Majesty's Government will not overlook the interests and welfare of the native races."

How did Her Majesty's government look after the welfare of the native races following the Boer War? When the Boer forces lay prostrate and their theories of racial supremacy, slavery, and chosen people appeared in disrepute, British "liberal" and "humanitarian" sentiment saved the situation. Out of possible victory for the African cause came defeat; it was not the African majority which was to receive liberal and humanitarian treatment but the defeated white minority. In 1909, when the South Africa Act was signed, it was hailed "as a great triumph of liberal magnanimity." At that moment the British government granted the white minority population of South Africa, which was brought together in a quasi-federal union, the capacity to rule without impediment from Westminster and without any obligation to respect the rights of the indigenous population, which was excluded from the parliament. British magnanimity for the vanquished Boers, while winning the loyalty of such defeated leaders as General Botha and General Smuts, was more aptly seen by a critic in 1908 as cause to say, "For the first time we are asked to write over the portals of the British Empire: 'Abandon hope all ye who enter here.'"[14]

The fact that Africans believed British victory would both improve their lot and lead to their systematic inclusion in the political process induced African spokesmen such as Dr. Jabavu to urge trust in British promises. Not only were these spokesmen optimistic, but they at first castigated their fellow Africans who wished to press demands for legal safeguards. "That the existing rights and privileges of the Natives of Cape Colony will be safeguarded [in the Union] we have no doubt," said Jabavu in 1908.[15] But in 1909 the South African Native Convention strongly and emphatically protested the nature of the color bar to be imposed in the Union; the convention then said that, while the imperial government had fulfilled its liberal promises to the defeated republics, "the natives and Coloured subjects of His Majesty have not been shown the same liberal and generous treatment despite assurance that His Majesty's Government would not purchase peace at their expense."[16] African protests against the South Africa Act had

14. Nicholas Mansergh, *South Africa 1906–1961, The Price of Magnanimity* (New York: Praeger, 1962), pp. 15, 61.

15. Quoted in Edward Roux, *Time Longer than Rope* (Madison: Univ. of Wisconsin Press, 1964), p. 70.

16. Quoted in Mansergh, *South Africa*, p. 94.

earlier been deflected by white liberals in South Africa, who, more anxious to effect union than to preserve the principles of democracy, acquiesced in the sacrifice of the Africans. In fact, throughout the history of the Union, liberal counsel urged the Africans not to put forward any extreme demands since this would play into the hands of the reactionaries. But the racists had no scruple about setting forth extreme demands, and compromise was always in their favor. Militant African organizations and leadership had been rejected in favor of compromise and trust; in the end all was lost.

Prevailing British attitudes, professedly "liberal" and indeed "Christian," held that the Africans were unable to form a realistic opinion as to where their future interests lay. This judgment was reinforced by England's highest ecclesiastical personage, the archbishop of Canterbury, who, while regretting the color bar in the proposed Union, stated he would not oppose it. For the present, said the archbishop, it is justifiable to impose restrictions and limitations on the Africans "which correspond to those we impose on our children." Balfour, whose sentiments on race were mentioned earlier, believed that "the only glimmer of hope of dealing successfully with the real race problem in South Africa, is not to attempt to meddle with it ourselves, but having made this Union Parliament, to trust the men of a like way of thinking as ourselves to rise to the occasion."[17] In language that was to become more familiar in imperial dealings, the British government argued that earlier promises to "consult" with local chiefs whose territory was coveted by the Union did not imply that the chiefs could exercise veto power. Similarly, British concepts of legality easily justified stripping the neighboring protectorate of Swaziland of its sovereignty as a result of European purchase. "This method of peacefully extending British dominion may well be as little generally understood, as it is (where it can operate) in law unquestionable." According to Lord Harley, Britain's early guarantees of Swazi independence were judicially meaningless, "since they were made to people subsequently brought under protection and cannot be allowed international force."[18]

17. Quoted in L. M. Thompson, *The Unification of South Africa 1902–1910* (London: Oxford Univ. Press, 1960), p. 428.
18. Quoted in Hilda Kuper, *An African Aristocracy* (London: Oxford Univ. Press, 1947), p. 31; and Lord Harley, *An African Survey* (London: Oxford Univ. Press, 1938), pp. 272–73.

Conclusion

In the final analysis, Britain's decision to sacrifice the rights of the indigenous peoples of South Africa and Palestine is perhaps traceable to imperial considerations. What dominated the thinking of the British government in 1909 was that in time of war the Suez Canal might be closed to British shipping, in which case the Cape route would resume its commercial and strategic importance; a friendly united South Africa would be a vital asset. Following the dismemberment of the Ottoman Empire, British control of Palestine with its Zionist settlers was seen as the best guarantee that Great Britain would never be denied access to the Suez route.

British trust in her new partners brought immediate rewards. General Botha, the distinguished veteran of the Boer War willingly occupied German Southwest Africa as World War I opened. General Smuts was put in charge of the whole imperial force in East Africa and eventually became a member of the British war cabinet. Although he declined to accept the Palestine command, Smuts was a staunch supporter of British control and Zionist settlement in Palestine; his friendship with Chaim Weizmann was one of the most important in his life. Indeed, Smuts was among the most influential in bringing about the mandate system, and it is of no small significance that he played a prominent role in the disposition of both Palestine and Southwest Africa under that system. As Europe strove to construct an international system that would preserve and extend traditional imperial interests, the Fourth Pan-African Congress, meeting in London in 1923 protested vainly:

> What more paradoxial figure today confronts the world than the official head of a great South African State [Smuts] striving blindly to build peace and goodwill in Europe by standing on the necks and hearts of millions of Black Africans.[19]

19. Quoted in Colin Legum, *Pan-Africanism* (New York: Praeger, 1963), pp. 29–30.

The Future of Palestine

A Humanistic Perspective

Maxime Rodinson

THE ARAB-ISRAELI STRUGGLE is properly viewed, I believe, as one of the many conflicts between two peoples which have occurred throughout history. There are those who hold that all human conflict can be reduced to class struggles; but, even though Marx himself once expressed this sentiment, I am of the opinion that the solid foundations of Marxist sociology prohibit this kind of interpretation. Human history has been characterized by conflicts between nations as well as those between social classes.

It is evident that the outcome of the Arab-Israeli conflict is contingent on the relative strength of each side and its allies. Furthermore, total victory on the part of one side is hardly certain, for many conflicts of this nature have ended in compromise.

It is the right of every individual in the world, every group, and every nation to offer a judgment on this conflict. One can judge on the basis of personal interest. A judgment of personal egoism is irrefutable, for it is impossible to convince someone that he is wrong to act or judge according to his personal interest. However, it is impossible for such an individual to convince others that he is right and to gain their support for his cause.

Beyond individual egoism is group egoism, where one judges a priori that his group holds the truth. This widespread type of judgment is well illustrated by the slogan "My country, right or wrong." To judge the value of this sentiment and the excesses to which it can lead, it is sufficient merely to recall that a German translation of this slogan was inscribed on the door to the Buchenwald concentration camp. It is as impossible to convince a group adherent that he is wrong to follow group dictates as it is for him to convince others to join him. If, for example, the Arabs are content to say, "We are Arab, and we fight with the Arabs whether they are right or wrong," they would have no right to ask for aid or sympathy from other nations. The response to such a request could very well be, "We are not Arab, and so we don't have to fight for you or give you aid or sympathy."

Not unrelated to the foregoing attitude is a common type of judgment wherein two conflicting groups are judged on the basis of sympathy toward one and antipathy toward the other. Again, it is impossible to convince someone who has formed such an opinion that he is in error. If, for example, I expressed partiality to the Arabs because they were more attractive than the Israelis, how would I reply to one whose sentiments, although similarly founded, were to the contrary? There are those who contend that the Israelis, as Jews, having been victimized throughout history, are the more deserving of sympathy. But history proves that there is nothing to prevent the victims of one period from becoming oppressors in another.

The only arguments which are capable of convincing others are those based on universal criteria, either religious or secular. For believers, the universal criterion is to know which of two conflicting parties is adhering more closely to the will of God. For nonbelievers (or believers who do not require the intervention of God in human affairs or who think that the good of man is God's will), the universal criterion will be to know which side better serves the interest of progress and the well-being of mankind or which side is the more just.

It is to this latter universal point of view, which is held by those called humanists, that I adhere. Human progress has consisted of going beyond individual and national egoism. It is an extremely fragile and precarious progress but one which, in my view, must be safeguarded with the greatest vigilance. Man's effort to disengage himself from the influence of personal interest and group membership in order to arrive at universal judgments is by no means a recent phenomenon; it has characterized the great universalistic religions.

Parenthetically, if one is to develop a worthy judgment of any conflict, it is important to distinguish between the demands of a people, group, or class, and the general idea underlying its struggle, on the one hand, and its program, strategy, and tactics, on the other. One can easily not sympathize with the program adopted by a movement, be critical of its strategy, condemn its tactics, and yet still be convinced of the essential appropriateness of its cause. Programs, strategy, and tactics are merely of a transitory nature. For example, when the proletariat began to advance its demands in the nineteenth century, one tactic was to destroy machines. Opposition to such condemnable behavior was completely justified; however, the tactic did not warrant a disregard of the demands of an exploited and frustrated class. This important distinction must be kept in mind when judging such problems as the Palestinian struggle.

How can one apply a universal judgment to a specific case such as the Arab-Israeli conflict? There are those who say that they believe in universal judgment but mechanically reduce this conflict to one involving a universal cause. For example, many Arabs maintain that the struggle is between the Israeli bourgeoisie or capitalism and imperialism, and the Arab people, or the proletariat. Many Israelis and pro-Israelis contend that the conflict is between the Israeli proletariat and the great Arab bourgeoisie. Both theses seem to me equally invalid; all of the Israelis, the capitalists as well as the workers and middle classes, have profited from their settling in Palestine, although in unequal measure, and, similarly, all of the Arabs have suffered from the colonization, although, again, unequally and although some individuals were able to profit from it. Thus, because of this oversimplified view, few Arabs or Israelis publicly deny their solidarity with their group, although many of them are disinterested parties to the conflict.

The conflict is not a question of the Israelis' struggle against Arab fanaticism, racism, or imperialism. The Arabs have mobilized against Israel only in revolt against an infringement on Arab territory. If the Arabs indulge in racism and fanaticism, as any people in conflict do, this is merely a secondary development. Similarly, it is not a question, as some Arabs often contend, of a struggle between the Arab people and the international capitalist bourgeoisie. Many Arabs have nothing against capitalism, which for them is merely one of several means of development. They are united against capitalist imperialism only to the degree that it threatens their full realization of independence.

Stressing the foregoing clarifications and contending that the Arab-Israeli conflict is fundamentally one between two peoples, I believe that the struggle can be judged on the basis of the simple humanistic—meaning judging from the point of view of humanity in general—principle that no people should oppress another or violate the rights of another. When a conflict involves two nations that have been in existence for a long time, like France and Germany at the time of World War I, the matter is simple. One nation can resist, from within or without, the excesses of another until an equilibrium has been achieved whereby each nation can exist without infringing on the other's right to an independent existence. That is essentially what transpired between France and Germany, and the reconciliation appears to be stable. The same principle can be applied in the case of colonization. Consider, for example, the relations between France and Algeria. Even though some French people had settled in Algeria and considered Algeria, to a certain degree, to be their country, it was clear that they felt a stronger loyalty to France. It was also clear that their constituting, as non-Algerians, the dominant minority prevented the Algerians from exercising their right to an independent existence. The reconciliation between the French and Algerian peoples dates from the abolition, in 1962, of the colonial situation. The return to France of most of the colonizers has restored normal relations between the two countries; they can coexist without infringing on each other's rights.

The difficulty in the case of the Arab-Israeli conflict results from the very existence or the creation of Israel, which was an attack on Arab rights. Therefore, one cannot take for granted Israel's right to existence. It seems to me completely incontestable that in 1890 Palestine was Arab territory, in the sense that England is English territory and France is French territory. I defy anyone to explain to me how the Zionist program of establishing a Jewish state on Arab land could have been realized without the Palestinian Arabs becoming either subordinated or chased away. It was inconceivable that the Palestinian Arabs would agree to having their rights to their own territory infringed on; in any case, the Zionists for the most part never sought such an agreement with arguments carrying even the slightest conviction.

Therefore, the Arabs have contested the very legitimacy of Israel. Outwardly, the Israelis are merely relying on the principle that each people has a right to existence, yet they do not wish to recognize in their reasoning that theirs is a special case—that they won their existence not long ago at the expense of another people's rights. It is true that similar processes have occurred in history, but they have been obscured by time. Nowhere is there a supreme tribunal that can say when a nation, established on the territory of another by force, may view its existence as respectable and legitimate. Even the authority of the U.N. is questionable because of the ways in which it is influenced by certain powers and certain groups of international interests.

I propose a humanistic judgment of this situation; I acknowledge the fragility of this proposal and that there are opposing arguments, yet it is one that seems reasonable to me. As I see it, Israel has no unconditional right to existence any more than there exists any unconditional duty to destroy this new entity. I believe, from the point of view of international and universal morality, that the existence of Israel (that is, the existence of the Israeli people as a new ethnic group, endowed by this title with rights to a specific political structure) can be accepted on certain conditions. It is up to the Israeli people to meet these conditions in view of the fact that they recently imposed themselves to the detriment of another people and did so without any provocation. The Zionists, at least in the beginning, never pretended that the formation of a Jewish state in Palestine was intended to punish the Arabs for committing some injustice against the Jews.

The following conditions seem to me to be justified from the point of view of a universally valuable international morality: it would be necessary, first of all, for Israel to make reparations for the material and moral injustices that it has inflicted on the Arabs and, second, for it to adopt new political structures of such a nature that further injustices would not be propagated. Only in this way can an ideal solution be reached: an egalitarian coexistence of the two ethnic groups. If the Israeli people do not meet these conditions, it seems clear to me that they will have no grounds for insisting that their right to existence be supported.

Although, as I stated earlier, the outcome of the Arab-Israeli conflict will depend primarily on the relative strength of each side, it seems to me nevertheless that the moral judgment which has been offered is not absolutely fruitless. Moral ideas can carry force. We have seen this occur to the detriment of the Arabs in June, 1967, when European and American public opinion, strongly convinced of the Israelis' rights, weighed heavily upon the attitudes of governments. This moral judgment will be of value if it has an effect on public opinion, which in turn will influence governments in integrating the solution to the Arab-Israeli conflict based on the relative strength of each side with a solution that is ideally just.

A Radical Perspective

Noam Chomsky

LET ME BEGIN by entering a disclaimer. What I have to say will not be particularly radical. I will be satisfied if it is somewhat realistic and more or less humane. There may be, some day, a program of action in the Middle East that is both radical and realistic. However, it seems to me that that day is still remote.

I would like to distinguish very clearly between predictions and recommendations. A plausible analysis of the present situation leads, I am afraid, to unpleasant conclusions. I frankly expect them but do not recommend them. It is possible to recommend more attractive alternatives. It may even be possible to work toward them. One can only be skeptical, however, as to whether such efforts will succeed.

The participants in the Palestine tragedy of the past half-century perceive it as a national conflict: Jews against Arabs. Each side sees itself faced with a threat to survival. Each sees itself as the victim of terror. Each sees its own acts as justified resistance or mere retaliation. I will not try to adjudicate these competing claims. Within the framework of national conflict each side can construct a case that is persuasive on its own terms, admitting little possibility for discussion or negotiation because the demands are seen basically as demands for survival. Furthermore, within the framework of national conflict virtually any act can—and generally does—receive some justification in terms of the demand for survival, of national destiny, or of historic needs. To such a conflict—or better, to a conflict so perceived—there is no solution except through force.

This conclusion is, of course, not unique to the Arab-Israeli conflict. Rather, it is typical of national conflicts. Consider the Franco-German conflict in World War I. Those who spoke out against that meaningless slaughter were regarded as traitors. When Karl Liebknecht opposed war credits he was denounced as a lunatic, a fanatic. These traitors and lunatics were right, of course. Both sides were following a losing strategy. Again, this is typical of national conflicts, which rarely serve the interests of those who are slaughtering or threatening one another.

In the present case, I think that each side is pursuing a losing strategy. Israel is, at the moment, the more powerful military force by a large margin. It is capable of striking far more serious blows. The fate of the city of Suez is a sufficient example. According to recent reports, Israel is the only Middle Eastern power possessing medium-range surface-to-surface missiles that can be fitted with conventional or nuclear warheads. From inside Israel they could reach Cairo and Alexandria. It seems likely that Israel is on the verge of producing nuclear weapons and may, in fact, already be doing so. Israel has been hoping that, by exercising military force, it can bring the Arab states to the negotiating table on its terms and can get them to suppress the Palestine guerrilla movement. Such plans are not likely to succeed. The Israeli scholar Y. L. Talmon writes that "Israel may be able to win and win and go on winning til its last breath, win itself to death. . . . After every victory, [it faces] more difficult, more complicated problems. . . . The abyss of mutual hatred will deepen and the desires for vengeance will mount." Though Israel has military superiority, it cannot administer a crushing blow. Such a capability might well lead to Russian intervention, destruction of Israel, and perhaps a nuclear war.

For example, those Israelis who believe that the way to achieve security is through military strength were pleased when the United States supplied Israel with Phantom jets, which the Israeli Air Force used in deep-penetration bombing raids on Egyptian targets. The result was a Russian intervention that re-established the earlier military "balance" at a much higher level of force and potential danger. In general, each military success simply reconstitutes the struggle at a higher level of bitterness and hostility, a higher level of military force (compare 1948, 1956, 1967, and 1970), a higher level of potential danger to all concerned. From the Israeli point of view, this is a losing strategy. Israel can win every conflict but the last. Sooner or later it is likely that at some moment, the international situation will be unfavorable. That moment, if it arrives, will be the end of Israel, though the catastrophe will probably be far greater in scale.

Even in the short run it is a losing strategy. Israeli democracy can hardly survive with one million Arabs in the occupied territories who cannot become citizens with equal rights because Israel insists on a dominant Jewish majority. The army will plausibily argue that the territories cannot be abandoned for reasons of security. Present Israeli policy speaks of secure and guaranteed borders. Everyone knows, of course, that there is no such thing as a guarantee of security. If Israel were to write the peace treaty itself and everyone were to sign on the dotted line, this would not guarantee security. The result is a hopeless impasse.

Furthermore, Israel is forced to be increasingly dependent on the world powers, in particular, the United States. It is common these days to hear Israel described as a tool of Western imperialism. As a description this is not accurate, but as a prediction it may well be so. From the point of view of American imperial interests, such dependence will be welcomed for many reasons. Let me mention one that is rarely considered. The United States has a great need for an international enemy so that the population can be effectively mobilized, as in the past quarter-century, to support the use of American power throughout the world and the development of a form of highly militarized, highly centralized state capitalism at home. These policies naturally carry a severe social cost and require an acquiescent, passive, frightened population. Now that the cold war consensus is eroding, American militarists welcome the threat to Israel. The Joseph Alsops, with supreme cynicism, eagerly exploit the danger to Israel and argue that only American martial spirit and American military power are capable of saving Israel from Russian-supported genocide. This campaign has been successful, even in drawing left-liberal support.

The Arabs are also following a losing strategy. Egypt, for example, has taken terrific punishment because of Israeli air superiority, and there is no reason to doubt that this will continue. It is likely that the technological gap will increase rather than decline. Similarly, the Palestinian movement cannot succeed in its present form. Israel is not Algeria. Its inhabitants will not be driven out or freely leave or abandon a high degree of self-government. Any policy directed to these ends will lead to continued destruction, to a strengthening of the reactionary and repressive forces on all sides, and perhaps to a form of recolonization by the great powers—in any event, to increasing dependence on the imperial powers, which have their own interests in maintaining such dependence.

The tragic irony is that each side, in fighting for national independence, is losing it in the course of the struggle. Since 1947 arms expenditures alone have surpassed $25 billion and are increasing. This in itself is a kind of recolonization, which may be followed by more direct forms. All of this can only be described as an enormous tragedy for the people of the Middle East. One recalls a warning of Rosa Luxemburg: "In the era of rampaging imperialism there can be no more national wars. [The assertion of] national interests can only serve as a means of deception, of betraying the working masses of people to their deadly enemy, imperialism."

The situation of the Palestinian Arabs is at the heart of the Arab-Israeli impasse. Their problems, their demands, their rights and prospects have not been seriously discussed in the West and are cynically disregarded. In fact, the Palestinians are at best an annoyance and an embarrassment to every powerful group in the Middle East and to the great powers as well. I think it is no exaggeration to say that all of the national states directly involved in the area are united in the hope, open or secret, that the Palestinians will somehow quietly disappear. Correspondingly, their efforts not to disappear as a political or social force lead them into conflict with the great powers and most of the Middle Eastern states. It is not surprising, therefore, that their national movement, or at least some elements in it, seems to be moving in a revolutionary direction. The development of this movement, which is a matter of enormous significance for the future of the Middle East, will also very largely determine the possibilities for a just peace.

It is difficult to be optimistic when considering the possibilities for a just peace in the Middle East. Peace and justice, though surely interlinked, are very different. At least we know what we mean when we speak of peace. When we speak of justice, matters are not so simple. There are, as I have noted, apparently just demands of conflicting national groups, demands that appear to be quite incompatible. But it is, nevertheless, surely true that the search for justice transcends national lines; some would argue that it requires abolishing and overcoming national divisions. For the left, in particular, the problem of justice is inextricably linked to the problem of radical social transformation in every existing society. For this reason alone—it is not the only one—the left has been deeply concerned with the evolution of the Palestinian movements.

The Palestinians have suffered a severe historical injustice in that they have been deprived of a substantial part of their traditional home. I believe that this much, at least, can be conceded by any reasonable person. This injustice is—if we are to be honest—irreversible, except through means that are impossible to execute given the present realities. Even if such means were practical and realistic, they would be intolerable to civilized opinion. The Palestinian groups that have consolidated in the past few years argue that this injustice could be rectified by the establishment of a democratic secular state in all of Palestine. However, they frankly acknowledge—in fact, insist—that this would require elimination of the "political, military, social, syndical, and cultural institutions" of Israel. I am quoting here from the May 6, 1970, program of the Unified Command of the Palestinian Resistance Movement, which included all the Palestinian organizations. The same program enunciates the principle that, since no basic change in Israeli institutions can be achieved by forces within Israel, the elimination of these institutions must be achieved through armed struggle.

I am not concerned here with the abstract justice of this position but rather with its implications. Given the assumptions, the conclusions no doubt follow. Furthermore, acceptance of the conclusions as the basis for action guarantees that the major assumption will remain true—that is, all elements of Israeli society will be unified in opposing the armed struggle against its institutions. Therefore, no basic change in Israeli institutions will be carried out by forces within Israel acting in concert with Palestinians with similar aims. The further consequences are those I have already mentioned. Specifically, the struggle will be a suicidal one for the Palestinians, who have already suffered miserably. Even if, contrary to fact, the means proposed could succeed—I repeat and emphasize, even if, *contrary to fact,* these means could succeed—they would involve the destruction by force of a unified society, its people, and its institutions—a consequence intolerable to civilized opinion on the left or elsewhere. In my opinion, no one who has any concern for the Palestinians would urge such a course upon them.

George Habash has recently described a disagreement in the Palestinian movement as to whether the principle concern should be the struggle over Israel or whether the movement should concentrate first on overthrowing the reactionary Arab governments which have indirectly prevented the liberation of Palestine. It is possible that events may have resolved this disagreement and that the strategy of the left—devotion of more energy to overthrowing the reactionary Arab governments—may predominate. This will be an extremely difficult course; as I noted earlier, one can expect virtually unanimous opposition from the established states of the region, as well as from the great imperialist powers—in particular, the United States and the U.S.S.R. Nevertheless, there are some possibilities of success, perhaps along the Vietnamese model, though one should not push the analogy too far.

Suppose that the first stage of the struggle succeeds, as it may, and a revolutionary government is established in Amman or, perhaps, elsewhere. Consider the implications of the slogan "an Arab Hanoi in Amman." If it suggests that the revolutionary regime of Jordan will be a rear base for a popular resistance in the occupied territories, then the slogan is appropriate in principle, though one may question its realism. But if it suggests that the Arab Hanoi will be a rear base for the liberation of what is now Israel, then the analogy is wholly inappropriate. It would be appropriate only if one accepted the American government's propaganda line that the war in South Viet Nam was exported from the North. For, apart from any judgment of right or wrong, the fact is that the Jewish population of Israel would be unified in opposing this armed struggle. It would therefore in no sense be a war of liberation on the Vietnamese model but rather a war between states that are legitimate in that they receive the overwhelming support of their own populations, as the American government likes to pretend is the situation in Indochina.

I note with interest that a recent statement of the Democratic Front (PDFLP) quotes approvingly the following statement attributed to Lenin: "The victorious proletariat cannot impose any 'happiness' on any foreign people without bringing to an end its own victory." The observation is correct. A society must carry out its own revolution, achieve its own "happiness." Revolutionary struggles cannot be exported. They must be indigenous.

It is widely assumed on all sides that a program of social change implemented by Arabs and Israelis acting in concert is impossible. The statement I quoted from the program of the Palestine Resistance Movement was to that effect. If the assumption is correct, there are only two alternatives. The first is a continuation of the national struggle between Jews and Palestinian Arabs, both sides being locked into the losing strategy that I have already discussed. This will lead either to the physical destruction of the Palestinians or to a much wider—probably nuclear—war, with unpredictable consequences. No serious person will succumb to romantic illusions about these matters. It is difficult and dangerous to speak of inevitability in history, but such an outcome is surely of very high probability. In particular it is erroneous to believe that the situation is in any way analogous to Viet Nam or even to Algeria.

The only other alternative, granted that the assumption is correct, is the establishment of a Palestinian state in the presently occupied areas. Certain groups in Israel and, recently, in the United States government have spoken of such a solution. If such a state were under Israeli military protection (that is, occupation), it would be little other than a kind of Bantustan. I suspect that only extreme pressure from the great powers could lead Israel to accept a truly independent Palestinian state. If this is the end of the matter, the result will be a "Balkanization" of the Levant—an ugly, though conceivably stable, system of small, hostile, suspicious, irredentist societies, very possibly reactionary and repressive as well.

Must we accept the judgment that there is no possibility of a program of social change implemented by indigenous forces in both societies? One can only speculate. However, I think it is premature to accept the counsel of defeat and despair that holds this to be out of the question. What might be the character of such a program, and to whom might it be directed? National states can do very little other than what they are now doing. Such a program could be undertaken only by those in both societies with an interest in some framework other than national conflict. Such groups exist, but they cannot function or gain credibility so long as the fear of "the national enemy" remains paramount.

There may, however, be a different framework. The Jews and the Arabs of the former Palestine claim national rights to the same territory. Each national group demands, with justice, the right of self-government and cultural autonomy. In principle these demands could be reconciled within a federal framework, perhaps in the form of two federated republics with parity, a guarantee of a high degree of autonomy combined with significant economic integration, highly permeable boundaries, and an ending of all legal ties to outside elements (the world Jewish community, and Pan-Arab ties), though of course cultural and social connections could remain. Such a program would involve the abandonment of some degree of independence; one must compare it, however, with the abandonment of independence that is an inevitable consequence of national conflict. It would involve an element of risk—how can we trust our adversary?—but this must be compared with the risks inherent in national conflict. There is, of course, no such thing as a riskless policy.

The primary and most crucial difficulty, however, is the absence of a common program. There is, or should be, a common goal: the creation of a democratic, free, socialist society. For the great mass of the population in the Middle East, as elsewhere, this is the natural and proper goal, much as it may be subordinated in the national conflict. Such a program might, in principle, create a common bond between Arab and Jewish left-wing popular forces. One can only hope that sharp national boundaries will crumble as the struggle for a new society takes precedence on an international scale. But it is certain that no such goal can be achieved, or even imagined, if the means proposed is armed struggle by one society against another. It is certain that if any such goal is to be achieved it will be through the joint efforts of indigenous mass movements in the several societies of the Middle East.

To repeat the phrase attributed to Lenin by the PDFLP: "The victorious proletariat cannot impose any 'happiness' on any foreign people without bringing to an end its own victory."

An editorial statement in the Israeli journal *New Outlook* proposed that "binationalism could . . . be a banner or a long-range program on which Jews and Arabs could unite and which could make them readier to yield the short-range concessions that more immediate agreements will demand." In part, I agree with the statement. I do not agree with the implicit assumption that the "concessions" away from separate and opposing nationalisms are unwelcome, though perhaps necessary. And I think that binationalism alone, without a program of social reconstruction that can bring Jews and Arabs together in a common cause, will not be a meaningful "banner or a long-range program." But the general point is correct. It would be quite important for left-wing groups within each of the warring national societies to formulate a long-range program that would meet the basic demands of the other and would provide a basis for some degree of common effort. I have suggested that this is not impossible. Such a long-range program must, first of all, mitigate the fear that social destruction—destruction of independent institutions—will be a consequence of relaxing the military confrontation. It should also aim to overcome the paralyzing and destructive tendency of people to identify themselves solely, or primarily, as Jews or as Arabs rather than as participants in a common effort—perhaps still remote—to achieve social justice, freedom, and brotherhood—those old-fashioned ideals that are within reach and can be achieved if only the will is there.

For those of us who are removed from the immediate struggle, it is important to try to open channels through which the goals and aspirations of the people of the Middle East can be expressed and to try to respond to these expressions with an attitude that is both sympathetic and critical. There has been far too much hysteria over this issue; although it would be wrong and inhuman to deny the strong emotions it evokes, it is irresponsible to yield to these emotions and to fail to consider consequences, prospects, and costs. Far too much is at stake.

A Palestinian Perspective

Edward W. Said

DESPITE THE INCREASING PACE and complexity of events in the Middle East, the central conflict continues to be the one between Israel and the dispossessed, oppressed, and occupied Palestinian Arabs. Certainly there are many conflicts in the Middle East. There are numerous inter-Arab rivalries, climaxed by the Palestinian organizations' opposition to virtually every one of the Arab states. There is hostility between Israel and the Arab states and, dominating that, the imperial contest between the Soviet Union and the United States. Yet, were it not for the contradiction between Israel and the Palestinians, which began with the development of Zionism in the late nineteenth-century and continued through 1948 and 1967 to the present, none of the other conflicts would be quite the same. It is therefore necessary to find a framework of understanding, based on this central conflict but broad enough to include the complexity of events and rivalries characterizing modern Middle East history. Without such a framework, the situation in the Middle East appears to be one of unmanageable chaos. Only this framework can explain, for example, why, in September, 1970, the Jordanian Arab army massacred Palestinian Arabs as Israel and the United States stood ready to intervene in Jordan to support King Hussein against the Palestinians.

Every non-Arab is entitled to ask whether the Arabs, in refusing to recognize Israel's legitimacy, are victims of a collective mania or delusion. However, this question ought to be preceded by another more important one. One must ask whether the Arab refusal might be, in fact, a collective wish to deny the right of one people wholly to dispossess, victimize, and uproot another. The rise of the Palestinian movement to world attention since the calamitous Arab defeat of 1967 is a sign that this question is the more relevant. In taking up arms—not only military but political and psychological—the Palestinians have affirmed that neither the racist exclusiveness of Israel nor the ossified nationalism of the Arab regimes was adequate to the situation. The Palestinians decided that what was needed was first, political struggle and expression at the popular level; second, political action and organization at the popular level; and third, political foresight at the popular level. In other words, the Palestinians have asserted that liberation from *all* oppression is the right of *all* the people of the Middle East—not just of a few politicians and army officers at the top. Furthermore, they have asserted Arabs and Jews alike are entitled to the liberation of the area from racist ideology, imperialist domination, military forms of life, and colonial remnants. Therefore the goal of the Palestinian movement—a nonsectarian democratic secular state in historic Palestine—is an especially rich one. It takes into account (1) that before 1948 the Arabs always constituted an overwhelming majority of the population in Palestine; (2) that the present population of Israel is made up largely of foreign Jews who are there at the expense of hundreds of thousands of dispossessed Arabs; (3) that, nevertheless, the historical and political existences of both Palestinian Arabs (Christian and Muslim) and Jews are marked by oppression in Palestine and elsewhere; (4) that the existing state structures in the area provide only the minimum possibility for resolving the conflict; and (5) that the future must be fought for as a common goal of the people who have rights to be there.

The Palestinian movement must be understood as a radical and systematic political response to the present conflict in the Middle East, a response that has developed from a radical analysis of the history of the area. Let me just say a few words about the wisdom of taking such a position as the Palestinian one. Modern history is made up of a vast number of events. Unless one is willing to be completely fooled into believing that these events are all disconnected, one must try to identify the relatively small number of forces that explain their logic. Of course the lives of human beings are complex, and human motives are extremely difficult to explain; but it is possible to speak in general terms about the meaning of events within perspectives that make systematic sense of history. The best way, I think, is to identify the major forces which produce a certain kind of event or result and not to be overly concerned with exceptions. A good example of this attitude and its relevance for the politics of the present was found in Bertrand

Russell. According to Stuart Hampshire, who wrote an account of the third volume of Russell's *Autobiography* for the *New York Review of Books,* Russell took the radical position against the liberal one. The radical view recognizes "the unvarying wickedness of governments and of their scientific, commercial and bureaucratic accomplices, and, to a lesser degree, also [fights] against the docility and gullibility of a decent and deceived public." The liberal view perceives such disasters as the Viet Nam War as mistakes—not as the result of the systematic imperialist policy of the United States government.

The Palestinian radical view is to see Israel and Zionism not as an uncomplicated movement of Jewish liberation but as the systematic establishment in Palestine of an alien settler state, existing at the expense of, and as the result of, the dispossession of the Palestinian Arabs. It is as simple as that: Israel cannot be maintained in its present form without *also* systematically excluding Palestinian Arabs. Of course the forces that went into the establishment of Israel in 1948 are complicated—the attachment of Jews to Palestine, the centuries-old oppression and persecution of Jews in the Diaspora, and so on. But, nevertheless, to the Palestinian, Israel is the result of (1) Western imperialism, (2) Western racism and anti-Semitism (against Arabs and Jews together), and (3) colonialism. From its effective origins in the late 1880s, through the establishment of a Zionist congress and the Balfour Declaration, and on to the present, Zionism has had connections with the Western imperialist powers.

The connections between Western imperialism and Zionism have not been accidental but necessary and inevitable. Both of these forces seek to differentiate the privileged from the nonprivileged. Just as in Western society it is less good, economically and politically, to be a black than to be a white, so too in Zionist ideology it is less good, economically and politically, to be a non-Jew than to be a Jew. The alliances between the West and Zionism have always been between capitalist-imperialist powers and those in the Israeli government with similar tendencies. Therefore, the Arab worker and peasant is a class enemy of those powers, and the non-Jew is a racial enemy of the state of Israel. These roles have been thrust on Arabs as a result of Zionism's racial chauvinism.

It will be said that Zionism is the expression of Jewish national identity, of the desire for a national Jewish homeland, and that Zionism includes allowances for the existence of Arabs, and so on. Yes—but how? Arabs are not simply to be separate, but they are to be less privileged as well. The dialectic of Zionism which resulted in Israel—despite the existence of binationalists, men of humanity like Martin Buber and Judah Magnes, and despite the various councils of Arab-Jewish cooperation—inevitably and necessarily included the exclusion of Arabs, their domination and oppression, as well as the principle of acquisition and expansionism.

How does one arrive at such a radical and systematic view, which seems to put aside all the exceptions which ought to be considered? One need only look at the state of Israel and its two basic premises: the Law of Return and the exclusively Jewish institutions. The Law of Return stipulates that any Jew anywhere has the right to citizenship in Israel, and that only Jews have this right. The second defines the state as Jewish. These premises mean that so far as Zionism and Israel are concerned there are two kinds of individuals and that one is more privileged than the other by virtue of race or religion—not by any other criterion. Even if an Arab has lived in Palestine for many years, a Polish or American Jew, by edict, has a greater right than he does to be on the land.

It is interesting and instructive to see how this attitude operates across the Zionist political spectrum. Recently leftist dissenters in Israel have recognized the existence of the Palestinians: this has occurred because, in addition to the several hundred thousand Palestinian Arabs in Israel proper, since 1967 Israel has controlled the lives of over a million conquered Arabs. Shlomo Avineri and Uri Avnery have been critical of the Israeli policy of treating Arabs like nonhumans; they have criticized, for example, British colonial Emergency Defense Regulations, whereby Arabs can be arrested and imprisoned without trial, villages and houses destroyed, land expropriated, and individuals deported or tortured. The Israeli record is a dismal one. Yet neither of these men has said that this policy is not simply a mistake but the necessary result of the Law of Return and of the view that Jews have a greater right to the land than non-Jews. This is also the view of Menachem Begin, a right-wing leader in Israel notorious for his hatred and murder of Arabs. Finally Nahum Goldmann, in an article on the future of Israel that appeared in *Foreign Affairs* in April, 1970, was critical of Israel's militarism and its connections with the West; he generally favored an attempted reapprochement with the Arabs. Yet his entire argument begins with the following passage:

Humanity, having been responsible for hundreds of years of suffering and having failed to do anything radical to save the Jewish people in the Nazi period, owes this people a moral debt which can be discharged only by helping it to secure its survival. Experience has shown that only a country of its own, however small, can serve this purpose. And only Palestine can be this country, in view of the religious, emotional and even mystical attachment of the Jews to "Eretz Israel," the

Land of Israel, in which they made their greatest contribution to human civilization; which in no period of their history they were ready to forget; and for the return to which they prayed and longed for during thousands of years. Only because of this particular attachment of the dispersed people to its country of origin can the Jewish claim to Palestine be justified against the Arab argument that it belongs to them because they lived there as a majority for several centuries. Under normal rules of international life, there is no question that the Arab claim has meaning and substance, and it would be foolish and unfair to deny its justification. Dr. Chaim Weizmann repeatedly declared that the Arab-Jewish conflict with regard to Palestine is a clash between two rights, not between right and wrong, and that is what makes it so complex and difficult. Only if one understands the singularity of the Jewish people (which has nothing to do with any notion of superiority) and its tragic history can one presume that the Jewish claim is morally and historically superior.[1]

Does this not say that Arabs are people but that Jews have higher rights? Is this not another way of saying what David Ben-Gurion and Mrs. Golda Meir have always said—that so far as Israel is concerned the Palestinians do not exist; only Jews do.

What is the political meaning of such an attitude? It is not enough to say that the Israeli view is unjust, for we are not talking about abstract moral problems. We are talking about a concrete historical reality: People are discriminated against by law and are made homeless by law—all because they are not Jews. The political meaning of this is racism, which takes as systematic truth that a state or society can only be maintained by oppressing a different, perhaps less developed, people. This is part of a whole chain of evil; for at the roots of Western society are similar views which assume that it is natural for one group to tyrannize another on the basis of race, power, and economics. Jews have suffered from this in the West, as have blacks; but, because the Jewish movement of liberation was diverted and entered into alliances with the system rather than opposing it, it has perpetrated the system elsewhere. Thus Israel has acted as a surrogate of Western racism. It has not only driven out the Arabs by law but has kept them out by law.

Furthermore, in world politics Israel has allied itself not with oppressed peoples everywhere but with oppressors everywhere: with Britain and France against Egypt in 1956, with the United States in Korea and in Viet

1. Nahum Goldmann, "The Future of Israel," *Foreign Affairs*, XLVIII; no. 3 (April, 1970), pp. 443–59.

Nam, with General Mobutu in the Congo, against mainland China in the
United Nations, with Portugal in Angola, with the French Secret Army
Organization in Algeria, and so on. These positions are not mistakes or the
results of misguided policies that could be corrected. They are the results of
a partnership formed between Zionism and its parent, Western
racism—the white man's way of discriminating politically and economically
against nonwhites in the interest of continued and increased power and
superiority, the white man's way of responding to the demands made on
him by less developed peoples for their human rights.

Frantz Fanon spoke about the chain of racism in *Black Skin, White
Masks:*

> Some ten years ago I was astonished to learn that the North Africans
> despised men of color. It was absolutely impossible for me to make any
> contact with the local population. I left Africa and went back to
> France without having fathomed the reason for this hostility. Mean-
> while, certain facts had made me think. The Frenchman does not like
> the Jew, who does not like the Arab, who does not like the Negro.
> . . . The Arab is told: "If you are poor, it is because the Jew has bled
> you and taken everything from you." The Jew is told: "You are not of
> the same class as the Arab because you are really white and because
> you have Einstein and Bergson." The Negro is told: "You are the best
> soldiers in the French Empire; the Arabs think they are better than
> you, but they are wrong. . . . Unable to stand up to all the demands,
> the white man sloughs off his responsibilities. I have a name for this
> procedure: the racial distribution of guilt.[2]

The implications here are that the black, the Arab, and the Jew are
potential allies because they have suffered the evils of racism. Now the
Third World, or colored peoples, have recognized their bond with the
Arabs, but they cannot count on the Jews as allies because Zionism inter-
venes. This is where the role of the Palestinian movement becomes revolutionary and worth fighting for. It says to the Israeli that the answer to the
Middle East problem is neither $1.3 billion of American military aid nor
Soviet military aid to Syria and Egypt. It recognizes that the imperial interests of both the United States and the U.S.S.R. are not primarily benefiting
the peoples of the Middle East, who, whether for their strategic geopolitical
location or for their vast oil reserves, are being systematically defrauded. It
says to the Jew presently in Israel that a state that in its very essence distinguishes between residents on the basis of race or religion is a flawed politi-

2. Frantz Fanon, *Black Skin, White Masks* (New York: Grove, 1967).

cal institution, so flawed that it can continue to exist—and how ironic and cruel it is for Jewish destiny that the Jew must be in this position—only by remaining in a state of conflict with most of its neighbors.

The Palestinian movement therefore recognizes a continuing political affinity between its enemies today—Zionism and United States and Soviet imperialism—and the early enemies of Arabs and Jews in the Middle East during the past century—the Western imperialist powers, primarily Britain and France, who since the 1880s divided the area up, aborted political independence, and stunted economic, cultural, and social life. If, as it is sometimes argued, Arab nationalism and Zionism are parallel political movements against colonialism and oppression, it must also be said that, whereas Arab nationalism was a direct response to colonialism in the Arab world, Zionism was something quite different. Zionism is a development of Judaism—as Zionists argue—and represents a desire to locate Jewish culture in a land, thereby ending its dispersion throughout the world. Without disputing the fact that all peoples have the right to national self-determination, it can be said that, in translating Jewish culture into a national expression, which is what Zionism is, Jewish culture lost its universalism and became a dispossessing and oppressing nationalism. In implementing its national expression, no matter how pressing and humane the reasons, Jewish culture became guilty of uprooting, oppressing, and depriving another people of their right to national self-determination. So today Arabs are under occupation on the West Bank, severely repressed in Gaza, subject to Emergency Defense Regulations and all kinds of minority discriminations in Israel, and homeless in Jordan, Syria, and Lebanon. That Palestinians have taken up arms in exile is not at all difficult to understand.

The idea of giving Palestinians a piece of land has become fashionable in both the West and Israel. This notion purports to take just account of two national groups, Jews and Arabs, and, according to Shlomo Avineri, to allow their national aspirations to realize and fulfill themselves. *The Quaker Report (Search for Peace in the Middle East)* advocated the same thing. An even more imaginative and daring plan has been put forward by Uri Davis, an Israeli pacifist; in his plan Palestinians would flock unarmed to the borders of Israel and demand entry, thus forcing the Israelis morally to confront the fact of their dispossession of the Arabs. But all of these plans for the existence of two separate entities would perpetuate the extreme nationalist Zionist principle of an exclusively Jewish state, with the Arabs of Palestine confined in a Bantustan to the east.

Palestinians no longer think of themselves as inert refugees or as the passive victims of injustice. They have decided not only that their struggle is a just one but that it is a political one which will not turn the clock back to 1948 but will move into the future. With the true creativity of a genuine popular revolution, the Palestinian answer is to struggle for political and economic equality for Jews and Arabs; the goal is one common state, or perhaps two or four loosely federated structures, in which there would be mutual cooperation of all concerned. The point to be emphasized is that any a priori commitment to a state in which Jews have national privileges over and above Arabs is, according to the progressive Palestinian view, racist and imperialist. No one can deny that there are national communities, a Jewish one and an Arab one. Yet it must be categorically rejected that one community has the national right to put itself above the other, as the Zionist community has done by means of the Law of Return and the exclusively Jewish institutions. Palestinians are by no means obligated to provide land to solve the world-wide Jewish problem.

Neither are Palestinians obligated to fulfill expectations about them held by Western "radical" supporters. Nothing can be more paternalistic and disheartening than to advance sympathy for Palestinians and then to urge upon them realism, which the "radical," in his greater wisdom, finds them wanting. There is nothing politically in such a position that differs from Zionism. In both cases there is a plea for a *status quo* in Israel *and* a patronizing bit of land to the east for the Palestinians. To support the Palestinian movement means support for its progressive, revolutionary thrust and not for some flawed compromise that benefits Israel in both the long and the short run. No reasonable person will advocate an immediate merging of Israelis and the Palestinian Arab masses; neither side in its present condition is far enough along the road of revolutionary transformation to derive profits from the combination. Yet no one can deny that the Palestinians, by virtue of their history, are more ready for the merging and farther along the revolutionary road than any other group, Arab or Israeli. If their published accounts do not correspond with an onlooker's idea of the way things ought to go in revolutions, then the onlooker, not the revolution, has to change; for, after all, a whole people cannot be held to account for what pieces of paper, either by or about them, say. By definition a revolution is in constant change, and this is what, in the Middle East today, only the Palestinians embody.

So let us be clear in understanding that the Palestinians do not advocate driving Jews into the sea and do not practice genocide when they engage in guerrilla warfare. They are determined to avoid their own extermination *and*—more interesting from the point of view of any progressive Israeli—are extending a hand of common revolutionary purpose to Jews in

Israel to participate in a process of dynamic social and political change. It is absolutely wrong to see the Palestinian movement as a politics of blind desperation or to characterize it simply as a spoiling anarchism. Tragedy can be averted only if the Palestinian movement is seen for the true revolution that it potentially is—a revolution of Jews and Arabs alike, a revolution that uniquely offers perspectives for radical social change in an area petrified into xenophobia and chauvinism, a revolution that genuinely offers the wretched of the world a future of decent economic and social equality, a revolution that promises to put production and destiny back into the hands of the people of the area instead of letting these people remain the pawns of the imperialists. It is the role of every progressive and humane person to penetrate to this essence of the impasse in the Middle East of today. Having done so, no progressive can be satisfied with liberal patchwork. He must declare his solidarity with the Palestinian struggle and expect Americans and Israelis to understand the correctness of his analysis.

Discussant's Comments

Eqbal Ahmad

THE PAPERS IN THIS SECTION show a remarkable degree of agreement concerning the risks as well as the opportunities presented by the Arab-Israeli conflict. The contributors agree that a great historical injustice has been done to the Palestinian Arabs through the creation of the state of Israel, and that restoration of justice to the Palestinians must consitute the basis of peace in the Middle East. There is a consensus too that the Jewish community in Israel is not only a religious but also a cultural and political community, and that recognition of its cultural, religious, and political autonomy must form a fundamental basis of a just and lasting settlement. The contributors have implied, although only Professor Rodinson stated it explicitly, that the state of Israel as it is constituted today cannot admit of Palestinian rights. Hence, justice to the Palestinians would inevitably involve the transformation and/or abandonment of some values, practices, and institutions fundamental to political Zionism.

The contributors seem to share a vision of the future in which the Jewish and Arab communities in Palestine would seek their political and cultural expression in a relationship of creative cooperation and mutual respect. All speakers also appear to favor the creation of a socialist, democratic secular state, comprising Jewish and Palestinian communities, as the only viable settlement of the present conflict. However, with the exception of Professor Chomsky, none of the speakers ventured to draw the political and structural outlines of such a state. Because he has been more explicit, I am able to raise some questions regarding his proposal.

Professor Chomsky's present proposal differs substantially from his earlier vision of a binational society in which the autonomy of the two nationalities would be assured through the creation of a socialist state characterized by a high degree of decentralization and constituted by organically linked and interdependent but autonomous and self-managing communities. I find this earlier proposal to be enormously attractive. It responds to my preference for participatory socialism and also appears to be congruent with the community-oriented Islamic and Jewish political cultures. It has been my hope that this alternative would acquire a modicum of ideological and programmatic content and would progressively gain acceptance among the Palestinian as well as the Jewish people.

The problems posed by narrow nationalist and exclusivist attitudes and ideology are enormous, but these are of recent origin among Jews as well as Arabs. Arab nationalism, having grown in an Islamic setting, retains a strong universalistic tendency, which can give it a broadness and flexibility not evinced by Western nationalisms.

Perhaps a more serious obstacle is posed by vested interests. Professor Rodinson's analogy pointing to the inversion of proletarian consciousness in Algeria and Israel lends a certain poignancy to Rosa Luxemberg's warning quoted by Professor Chomsky. The Algerian struggle elicited the remarkable dedication, persistence, and sacrifice from the people because of its positive content. That same element of positiveness also helped to weaken, although it did not succeed in eliminating, the organized hostility of those who had profited from the colonial system. A somewhat analogous, if less clear-cut case is that of the Vietnamese Catholics, to whom the Viet Minh and then the NLF never ceased making special gestures of goodwill and assurance. These are examples which must interest the Palestinian as well as the Israeli left.

With the exception of the Israeli Socialist Organization (Matzpen), no group in Israel has supported the alternative of a binational, socialist society. The present position of the Palestinian liberation groups is undoubtedly an advance over the narrow nationalist pronouncements of their predecessors. The healthy diversity over this and related questions is indicative of the Palestinians' search for new alternatives and their increasing rejection of conventional nationalist ideologies. Nevertheless, differences of orientation have prevented the Palestinians from clearly and unequivocally defining the participants and the programs of a proposed socialist state. The confusion surrounding the Palestinian National Covenant and the clarifications subsequently issued in *Fatah* in November, 1969, and January, 1970, are attributable to the lack of concrete definitions of values and goals. So far only the Democratic Popular Front, a minority faction within the Palestine Liberation Organization, appears to favor this alternative with consistency and has made an effort to define its ideological and institutional content. I realize the difficulties that lie in the advancement and acceptance of this alternative and would regret losing Professor Chomsky's support for it.

I understand Professor Chomsky as favoring a federal state. In the Arab-Israeli situation, the introduction of federalism based on regional division of ethnically definable entities is unlikely to produce the transformation of ethnic and narrow nationalist attitudes, which have provided the bases of popularity and legitimacy for a "suicidal" conflict between a kindred people. Such a system may in fact reinforce these attitudes. Furthermore, federalism is unlikely to disturb the present configuration of power, including imperial power; and, as Professor Rodinson has correctly pointed out, there can be little hope of achieving a settlement, not to mention a lasting settlement, as long as extreme inbalances persist in the distribution of power.

With the current balance of force and with persistent nationalistic values, such a federation could evolve in several unsatisfactory directions. At worst it could result in what Professor Chomsky fears most: the creation of an Arab Bantustan. At best, it could mean a strained, and hence an extremely unstable, collaboration between antagonists of unequal strength. In either case, it might succeed only in freezing two unreconciled nationalisms into a posture of permanent hostility.

Another area of agreement among the contributors, one that may be the most fateful in destroying hopes for a peace based on cooperation between the two peoples, is that the Arab-Israeli problem has been compounded by the concentration of imperialist interests in that region. The role of imperialism in the evolution, continuation, and escalation of this conflict continues to shape the perspectives and the possibilities of peace in the Middle East. Enhancement of imperialist intrusions can only render more intractable the search for a just settlement. A substantial reduction in the controlling role of foreign powers, the United States in particular, is basic to the creation of a climate in which the Jews and the Arabs of the Middle East can approach each other as equals interested in ending their deadly confrontation.

I can only agree with Professor Chomsky that the Middle East has become a theater of imperialist concentration; that in the process of protecting it both Israelis and Arabs might be losing their independence; and that the risk of continued warfare, which may lead to the use of nuclear weapons, is enormously high.

The political and military maneuvers associated with the Middle East cease-fire, the Jordanian civil war, and Nixon's Mediterranean tour have been motivated by America's search for a new strategy to secure its hegemony in the Mediterranean and Indian oceans. There are indications that the United States is in the process of creating a well-armed network of dependable allies—Israel, Greece, Spain, and Portugal—who eventually would supersede NATO in the Mediterranean. If this Mediterranean version of the "southern strategy" succeeds, however precariously, it will produce new risks for the Arabs and will destroy Israel's chances for removing itself from imperialist domination. This plan would lead to greater imbalance of power in the region, intensify the arms race, enhance Israeli intransigence, further arouse the worst apprehensions of Arabs, and deepen their conviction that Israel is only an "outpost of imperialism." One wishes that Israeli liberals, no less than radicals, would begin to question the need for the super-Prussianization of Israel, which has, since 1948, been the strongest military power in the Middle East.

Appendix

Text of Statement and Resolution Released at the End of the Third Annual Convention, November 1, 1970

The Association of Arab-American University Graduates, Inc. (AAUG), an organization dedicated to informing the American people of issues pertaining to the Arab world, at its Third Annual Convention held at Northwestern University, Evanston, Illinois, on October 30, 31, and November, 1, 1970, examined the relationship of the Arab people to various European, American, and Afro-Asian states. In the principal addresses and a series of panel discussions by leading Asian, African, European, and American scholars and active participants in effecting relations between the Arab people and other peoples of the world, the association recognized the growing collaboration between the Arab and Afro-Asian communities to obtain a greater measure of dignity, equality, and justice for all people. Further, the association recognized the growing hostility between the Arab people and Western European and American governments, a hostility resulting from the exploitative practices of the latter and their persistent attempts to deny the developing communities of the world their just demands for a dignified existence. After detailed examination of the relationship between the Arab people and the rest of the world, the Third Annual Convention, in its efforts to bring to the American people an understanding of the feelings and thinking of the Arab people, unanimously adopted the following statement.

Statement

No sooner had the Arab people succeeded in articulating their demand for the establishment of a secular unitary Arab state that would encompass all who share the bond of Arabism and their demand for the full participation of all the citizens of such a state in the conduct of public affairs on a basis of complete equality than European imperialism subjugated the Arab people. The object of imperialism has been to exploit the vast human and material resources of the Arab people by instituting a system of oppression and by frustrating their social, economic, and political aspirations. To effect that exploitation, European imperialism dismembered the Arab world and increased the internal fragmentation of Arab society by encouraging and promoting national, religious, social, and political differences. The national struggle against colonialism was waged in the name of a secular national ideology and the implementation of social justice. The independence of the major part of the Arab homeland was accomplished through the tremendous sacrifices of the Arab people in confronting the enormous power of various imperialist countries.

While the association salutes the Arab people who struggled for freedom, it notes with serious concern that certain parts of the Arab homeland remain under European and colonial subjugation. The association therefore calls upon the Arab people to intensify their struggle against vestiges of European imperialism in the Arabian Gulf areas and calls upon the independent Arab states to render full material and moral support to the valiant struggle of the Arab people in South Arabia.

At the same time, the association notes anew that the just and inalienable rights of the Palestinian people continue to be denied. In this connection, the association reaffirms its statement of September 2, 1970.

The association adheres to the position expressed in its statement of December 7, 1969, namely, that the conflict in the Middle East emanates from the continued denial by the combined forces of Zionism and imperialism of the Palestinian right of self-determination. This right was reaffirmed by the United Nations as recently as December 10, 1969. The Jordanian military attacks on the Palestinians constitute another attempt to deprive the Palestinian people of exercising their legitimate right of self-determination. The association deplores these attacks and calls upon all concerned to bring about their immediate halt. The association deplores all forms of foreign military intervention in the Middle East and believes that such intervention constitutes a flagrant violation of international law and is most detrimental to world peace. The association calls upon all antiwar elements in the United States and throughout the world to mobilize their efforts to frustrate intervention and to render all possible support to the just cause of the Palestinian people and thereby contribute to an enduring peace in the Middle East.

The association salutes the Palestinian people in their just struggle against Zionism and colonialism and assures them of its continued total support. It further calls upon all free people everywhere to rally behind the Palestinian people and to mobilize their efforts to frustrate the attempts of Zionism and colonialism to administer the final solution to the Palestinian people and to frustrate all military and political efforts which seek the capitulation of the Arab people to Israel and its imperialist supporters.

The association notes with alarm that the United States government has been pursuing a policy of duplicity and imperialism in the Middle East and the Third World. The United States government, against the wishes of most of the American people, has pursued a policy of military and economic support to racist settler regimes, to colonial and Fascist regimes throughout the world. The association deplores the military support that the United States has been rendering to Israel which has enabled the latter to conduct a racist war against the Arab people. Similarly, the association deplores the continued support that the United States has been rendering to the colonial regime of Portugal, which is oppressing the gallant fighters of Mozambique and Angola. Also, the association feels that the United States should revise its policies with regard to the settler regimes of South Africa and Rhodesia. The association believes the continued military support which the United States has been rendering to the settler regimes of Israel, Rhodesia, and South Africa and to the colonial regime of Portugal lies at the heart of the continued success of these colonial Fascist systems in thwarting the principles of liberty, dignity, and equality and is an affront to the best ideals of the American people. The association therefore calls upon the American people to pursuade the administration to suspend diplomatic relations with these settler regimes. The failure of the United States to do so and to pursue a policy based on the principles of justice, liberty, and dignity invites definite alienation of free people throughout the world and may become a factor leading to world conflagration.

The association notes that the Arab states have been forced over the past few years to concentrate their efforts and to mobilize their resources to wage successful resistance against colonialism and its agents in the region. While the association welcomes the efforts of the Arab people to defend themselves against colonial aggression, it believes that the successful defense of the Arab people is contingent on the full and scientific mobilization of the human and material resources of the Arab people, on the full political integration of the Arab states, and on liquidation of all manifestations of colonial exploitation and oppression. The association calls upon the progressive forces of the Arab world to eject colonialism in whatever form it expresses itself and to wage a relentless war against reactionary, corrupt, and oppressive domestic systems. Only by doing so will the full weight of the Arab people be brought to bear in the final confrontation with the forces of Zionism and colonialism in the region.

The association believes that with the successful continuation of the Arab revolution, which received a considerable assist from the nationalist revolution in Egypt in 1952, the Arab people will not only be assured of the support of oppressed people throughout the world but will eventually succeed in establishing an Arab society in which the full potential of all citizens will be fulfilled on the basis of justice, equality, and dignity. Not only are the Arab people entitled to the support of all oppressed people, but they in turn have the moral responsibility to render all possible support to the just struggle of all oppressed people in Asia, Africa, Europe, and the Americas.

Resolution

The AAUG recognizes the Palestine Resistance Movement as the only legitimate liberation movement of the Palestinian people and as the vanguard of the Arab revolution. As the association stated in the resolution of the Second Annual Convention, held in Detroit in December, 1969, and further recognizing that recent attempts by Zionism, Jordanian reaction, and Western imperialism to liquidate the Palestine revolution have resulted in the promulgation of the dismembered so-called Palestine entity, it is resolved that:

1. No Arab or Palestinian speaks for or can enter into negotiations on behalf of the Palestinian revolution. The Palestinian revolution, which is the revolution of the Palestinian people, speaks for itself by having gained the complete support of the Palestinian masses. Its aim is the complete liberation of Palestine and not a symbolic part thereof.

2. The Palestinian resistance is part of the Arab revolution, and only within the context of of the Arab revolution will the problem of Israel be solved. The rights of the minorities, including the Jewish minority, are related to the outcome of the Arab revolution. It is therefore the obligation of oppressed people, Jewish and Arab alike, and of progressives everywhere to support the Palestine revolution.